BISON
BOOKS

Virginia Faulkner

A Life in Two Acts

Brad Bigelow

University of Nebraska Press | Lincoln

Publication of this volume was assisted by the Virginia Faulkner Fund, established in memory of Virginia Faulkner, editor in chief of the University of Nebraska Press.

Manufactured in the United States of America

The University of Nebraska Press is part of a land-grant institution with campuses and programs on the past, present, and future homelands of the Pawnee, Ponca, Otoe-Missouria, Omaha, Dakota, Lakota, Kaw, Cheyenne, and Arapaho Peoples, as well as those of the relocated Ho-Chunk, Sac and Fox, and Iowa Peoples.

For customers in the EU with safety/GPSR concerns, contact:
gpsr@mare-nostrum.co.uk
Mare Nostrum Group BV
Mauritskade 21D
1091 GC Amsterdam
The Netherlands

Library of Congress Cataloging-in-Publication Data
Names: Bigelow, Brad (Editor) author
Title: Virginia Faulkner: a life in two acts / Brad Bigelow.
Description: Lincoln: University of Nebraska Press, 2026. | Includes bibliographical references.
Identifiers: LCCN 2025029897
ISBN 9781496230621 hardback
ISBN 9781496245076 epub
ISBN 9781496245083 pdf
Subjects: LCSH: Faulkner, Virginia, 1913–1980 | Women authors, American—20th century—Biography | Women editors—United States—Biography | BISAC: BIOGRAPHY & AUTOBIOGRAPHY / Women | BIOGRAPHY & AUTOBIOGRAPHY / Editors, Journalists, Publishers | LCGFT: Biographies
Classification: LCC PS3511.A858 Z54 2026 | DDC 818/.5209 [B]—dc23/eng/20250725
LC record available at https://lccn.loc.gov/2025029897

Designed and set in Bulmer by A. Shahan.

For Ron Hull, whose last email to me sums up his inimitable spirit: "!!"

Contents

ACT 2. BACK TO LINCOLN

Illustrations

Virginia Faulkner

Prologue

Virginia Faulkner died in mid-September 1980, sitting in her apartment kitty-corner from the state capitol, across the street from the governor's mansion, two blocks from the headquarters of the Woodmen, the insurance company her brother Ed had been running for over forty years, half a mile from the University of Nebraska–Lincoln, the state's largest school, and just two miles from where she'd been born and raised. She was as close to the centers of power in Nebraska as one could get.

Surrounding her on three sides were shelves full of the library she'd been assembling for much of her lifetime. The swashbuckling adventures of Dumas that had inspired her as a tomboy. The snappy humor of Dorothy Parker and Robert Benchley that represented the sophistication of New York City she had longed to escape to as a young woman. The books good and bad she'd prepared treatments of during her frustrating time in Hollywood. Books by Jung and his followers she'd read in search of psychological insights as she grappled with mental illness in the late 1940s—which then served as guideposts when she began looking for hidden meanings in the work of Willa Cather.

There were dozens of books she'd ushered into print after returning to Lincoln and joining the University of Nebraska Press as an editor, including the sturdy paperbacks of the Bison Books series she'd launched with press director Bruce Nicoll. And most prominently, there was a collection of first editions of the works of Willa Cather, the writer she and her partner, Bernice Slote, had been studying for over two decades. Some had required countless letters to rare book dealers to locate: Cather's less popular books had long been out of print when she died in 1947. Others were new editions, collections of Cather's early work that Virginia and Bernice had fought for, labored thousands of hours over, produced with the sometimes-reluctant cooperation of Cather's executors, as well as a small but growing library of Cather criticism she'd helped develop. And there was the copy of *Death Comes for the Archbishop* she'd reviewed as a student at Lincoln High School—also just a few blocks away.

Among the hundreds of books were three now exceptionally rare: her own. The two novels that had established her as a likely successor to Dorothy Parker and the collection of her outrageous Princess Tulip send-ups of the world's rich and glamorous. She'd forgotten them almost as completely as everyone else had. There was also the autobiography she'd substantially written for her friend, the New York madam Polly Adler, a book that didn't bear her name and for which she earned not a cent. Even if she were to add in the magazine stories that made her a household name in the 1930s and 1940s and the play whose spectacular failure had sent her spinning into years of depression and psychological therapy, it was a meager body of work alongside Cather's. Meager in size, but more importantly, meager in weight. It was all frenetic and frivolous and when she left her writing career behind, there were few times when she looked back with regret.

For Virginia Faulkner had put a lie to F. Scott Fitzgerald's adage that there are no second acts in American lives. Her first act had taken her to Washington, New York, Hollywood, and the cover page of America's most popular magazines, but it hadn't taken her to a place where she was able to "give up this smart, know-it-all line for something a little kinder and truer," as she had written her brother Ed before she'd even published her first novel. And to drive that failure home, she had watched the woman she loved first, the songwriter Dana Suesse, leave her behind in a quest to establish herself as a major composer of classical American music and send her spinning into years of institutionalization, wandering, and isolation.

Virginia's second act opened ignominiously. She returned to Lincoln in 1955 on her way to . . . well, even she didn't know. Offered the job of assembling an anthology to celebrate Nebraska, she quickly recognized the potential her work as editor held to recover and advance the legacies of writers she loved and respected: Cather and Mari Sandoz, and later, Wright Morris. Nebraska writers all, which the twenty-year-old Virginia would have considered ironic, given her longing to leave Lincoln and the state and join the smart set in New York. But the forty-something Virginia found in these Nebraskans and others a seriousness of purpose, a toughness of spirit, and a depth of quiet artistry that she came not only to admire but to champion.

She became a ferocious advocate of Cather most of all, working over the course of two decades to eliminate the adjectives she felt inherently limited and diminished Cather's standing as an artist: regionalist, American, feminist, lesbian. Yet as she achieved her greatest success in this effort with the commemorations and works associated with Cather's centenary in 1973, she found these same adjectives being taken up as banners to unite around by a new generation of scholars and critics. Instead of Cather's proponents, she and Bernice came to be seen as reactionaries bent on preserving an austere image of Cather, the artist standing above the mundane matters of feminism and sexual identity.

And as she sat in her chair, a glass of Scotch at her side, watching Monday night football, her second act could not have seemed the unshadowed triumph it might have just a few years before. Forced out of her job as editor, struggling again with depression, finding the mythical Cather she'd created with Bernice and Mildred Bennett being knocked down from her pedestal and embraced as an icon by feminist and queer readers and scholars, the life she'd fought to create in her second act may have seemed on the brink of collapse.

She knew how much of what sat on those bookshelves existed because of what she'd done in Lincoln over the last twenty-five years. A body of scholarship, a body of recovered western American history and literature, a body of Catheriana that staked Nebraska's claim for a place of worth and value in American and world culture. But she also knew that her contribution to these books would likely be forgotten as quickly and completely as her own three books. Such is the fate of those who do foundational work: Their mark gets lost in the subsequent layers of construction and creation.

This book is an attempt to excavate Virginia Faulkner's work and story: her first act as a successful but unfulfilled writer and her second act as an editor of genius, vision, and tenacity. It is, I think, a story well worth telling.

Act 1
To Bohemia

Philistia is usually The Place Where You Live—Eleventh Street in Lincoln, or this side of the footlights. Bohemia is somewhere else—that desert kingdom by the sea, or the Paris of Henri Murger's *Scénes de la vie de Bohéme*.

A note written by Virginia Faulkner, from *The Kingdom of Art: Willa Cather's First Principles and Critical Statements, 1893–1896*, edited by Bernice Slote

1

The Meyers and the Faulkners

Virginia Faulkner's Lincoln roots went deep. When her maternal grandfather Louie Meyer arrived in Lincoln in January 1871, Nebraska had been a state for three years and Lincoln its capital for barely one. The sons of a wealthy Jewish doctor in Karlsbad, Bohemia (now Karlovy Vary in the Czech Republic), Louie and his brother August had decided to try their luck in America, arriving in New York City in 1870. Taking the already-legendary advice of editor Horace Greeley, the brothers immediately headed west.

The Meyer brothers found Lincoln a town with more than its share of aspirations. Thomas Kennard, Nebraska's first secretary of state and the man responsible for laying out the plan for the state's capitol, had gone far beyond the approved scope of his task and platted a town that stretched for miles in all directions. The new Capitol building sat at the highest point in town and to its north, across the central business area, was the campus of the state's first land grant school, the University of Nebraska. In a history of Lincoln published just twenty years after it became the capitol, when it had barely seven miles of paved streets to its credit, A. B. Hayes and Sam Cox claimed that "the growth of Lincoln has been more remarkable than that of any other city in the West," despite the fact that the city had "no fuel, no mines, no water power, no remarkable natural advantages."

Louie Meyer was a perfect fit for a town on the rise: outgoing, charming, and bursting with enthusiasm. He was strong enough to subdue a rampaging drunk, handsome enough to win a prize for his looks at the state fair, confident enough at age twenty to win the backing of the local businessmen when he and August opened their own store in 1874.

Among the homesteaders passing through Lincoln each month were extended families of Bohemian immigrants. They would stop to buy horses, wagons, and goods for the trip out to Saunders, Butler, Webster, and other counties west of the capitol. These were families like the Shimerdas of Willa Cather's *My Ántonia* or the Pavelkas of Cather's own girlhood in Red Cloud, the seat of Webster County. The Bohemians were, on average, more prosperous than most immigrant settlers, but their means sometimes fell short of the cost of settlement. Louie became an informal ambassador on their behalf and often arranged for small loans to help them out.

As Lincoln grew, the Meyer brothers prospered. Their first store burned down in March 1877 and all its inventory was destroyed, but Louie found backers and a new store took its place in a matter of months. Two years later, he married Anna Gunnison in a ceremony officiated by Judge Stephen Pound, father of Louise and Olivia, who would later play influential roles in Virginia's life. When August joined the "Silver Rush" in Leadville, Colorado in 1882, Louie bought his brother's share and expanded the store, taking over a full block along Tenth Street. He threw himself into community affairs, becoming Grand Chieftain of the Pythians fraternal society and chairing the Lincoln community relief committee. The Board of Trade made him treasurer; when he ran for city council, he was elected with a resounding majority. Louie was a local celebrity. "There is probably no business house in Lincoln more widely or more favorably known than that of Mr. Louie Meyer," the *Daily Nebraska State Journal* declared in 1886. By the end of the 1880s, Louie was considered one of Lincoln's "Old Settlers." Hayes and Cox called him "one of the most able financiers and safe businessmen of this city," and ranked him "among Lincoln's foremost citizens in any important public enterprise."

One reason for Louie's popularity was his generosity. His habit of making small loans grew into a reputation as an informal banker. Most of his loans were mortgages on property in Lincoln and farms in the surrounding area. These increased in number over the decade, until by the start of 1893 his liability had grown to tens of thousands of dollars—one creditor claimed it was as much as half a million. As the *Nebraska State Journal* later wrote, "while he was conducting a general merchandise business, he was in reality doing a banking business." He was also speculating, buying land around Lincoln, expecting to cash in on the city's near-explosive growth (from twenty-five hundred in 1870 to over fifty-five thousand in 1890). And in addition to running the store, he was a notary public, agent for several steamship lines, and, in 1891, head of a city delegation sent to Washington DC to lobby for funding for a federal office building.

Unfortunately, in February 1893, Louie's principal financier, the Capital National Bank of Lincoln, closed for insolvency. When other banks around the U.S. began to fail that spring in one of the most severe financial crises in the nation's history, anxious farmers came to Louie demanding their deposits. On Saturday, August 26, 1893, customers arriving at the store were informed that it had been sold to the First National Bank for $8,000. Louie couldn't settle all the claims submitted to the county court and headed east to New York City to try to raise new capital.

There, he appears to have suffered a nervous breakdown. He was examined by Doctor E. C. Spitzka, author of the first American text on mental illness. Spitzka diagnosed his condition as dementia paralytica and ruled him incurable. He argued that Louie was of danger to himself and others if not committed immediately to an asylum. Learning of this, his fellow Pythians collected funds to bring him home. Louie arrived back in Lincoln a broken man. Anna tried to care for him at home while also looking after their children, but she couldn't cope with his manic and violent behavior.

Early in the morning of February 3, 1895, wearing only his nightshirt, Louie shut himself in the basement and began howling wildly. Unable to calm him, Anna called the police for help. Three officers pulled Louie out of the basement and a doctor was called to sign an order of commitment. They then wrestled him into their wagon and drove to the state asylum on the outskirts of Lincoln.

He never returned home. According to staff at the asylum, he was violent, feared suicidal, and put under round-the-clock observation. He cycled between bouts of manic activity and periods of gloominess and despair. Louie died in 1898 at the age of forty-five after becoming catatonic, unable to recognize family members when they visited. In its obituary, the *Lincoln Journal Star* wrote that Louie "was a great hand to tell stories . . . and his laugh could be heard a block when the joke came in." His granddaughter Virginia would inherit the same capacity for hilarity—and struggle with her own mental health issues.

Left at the time of Louie's commitment with five children—Max (thirteen), Pauline (eleven), Leah (eight), Bob (five), and Rit (two)—little money, and a growing cloud of suspicion over Louie's business affairs, Anna Meyer somehow managed to keep the family from falling apart. She rented a house, began taking in boarders, and leaned heavily on her sister Ida, who ran the post office at the university. The children stayed in school, earned awards, and attended parties with the children of the best of Lincoln society. By 1904, Max, Pauline, and Leah, the oldest children, had graduated from Lincoln High School and were enrolled at the university.

Anna wasn't satisfied just keeping her head above water. In 1906 she and Ida left Pauline in charge of the household and boarded a train headed west. Under the Carey Act of 1894, settlers could stake claim to land in Idaho and, after living on it for two years, take legal title. Although intended to encourage the growth of farms in the Snake River valley, the act allowed claimants to sell the property for considerable profit. Anna staked a claim on a section outside Aberdeen, Idaho, and two years later, just days after meeting the requirements for taking ownership, sold the place, returning to Lincoln with a substantial sum.

More remarkable than Anna's ability to restore the family's financial standing, though, was the way she kept the stigma of Louie's failure from affecting them. At the time, bankruptcy, questionable business practices, and insanity would have been black marks that could remain for generations. Instead, the Meyers seem to have moved on without a hint of disgrace. Indeed, the Meyers didn't just survive—they thrived. Pauline was thought the most beautiful girl in Lincoln; Leah was selected for starring roles in high school and college plays; Max was described as a model young man with a promising future ahead of him.

In 1907 Pauline married Thomas Howell, a young man from Lincoln just starting out as a commodities salesman in Chicago. Within five years, Howell would earn a seat on the board of the Chicago Mercantile Exchange; within ten, he would be one of the richest men in the Midwest. Although Leah's star didn't rise quite so high, she reached the pinnacle of Lincoln society when, in 1909, she married Edwin Faulkner, the eldest son of A. O. Faulkner.

Where Louie Meyer was dashing and charismatic, A. O. Faulkner was the essence of stability in a town—and an industry—that valued stability over material success. Born near Fairfield, Iowa, he came from a long line of farmers, but his father wanted better and sent him to Iowa Wesleyan University. After graduating in 1880, A. O. took a job teaching in a one-room schoolhouse in Seward, just west of Lincoln, a place still enough of a frontier settlement that he later told of chasing coyotes out of the schoolyard. One year of teaching was plenty. He decided to try medicine instead and enrolled in the Hahnemann Medical College in Chicago. He then returned to Fairfield, set up a practice, and married a local girl, Jennie Van Doren. Less than a year later, however, the couple headed west to York, Nebraska.

A. O. established himself as an ear, nose, and throat specialist and they took a house on Fourth Street, where their first child, Edwin, was born a few months later. A. O. soon gained a reputation as hard-working, ready to be summoned in the middle of the night, and scrupulously honest. He joined the Modern Woodmen, one of the new fraternal organizations that appealed to Christian charity and civic boosterism, and became interested in discussions about schemes for mutual aid among the Modern Woodmen's members. He'd seen farmers go bust after something as simple as a broken leg. And in a time when farm structures were built from wood, lit with oil lamps, and heated by wood stoves, fires were common and devastating.

In 1890, he enlisted the support of leading Woodmen and started an organization with the purpose of providing financial protection if subscribers became disabled or lost property due to accident. Nebraska's first insurance cooperative, the Modern Woodmen Accident Association was, at first, intended only for members of the Modern Woodmen. Policy holders paid three dollars to join and annual dues of two dollars. The association offered limited coverage at cost and, initially, neither A. O. nor the other officers took a salary. Within a year, however, it became clear that insurance was more than a sideline. A. O. moved his family to Lincoln, set up offices, and began to take a monthly salary. He recognized it would be to the association's advantage to have easy access to state government offices and the legislature. Demand grew rapidly. A. O. turned the association into the Woodmen Accident Company, and it began offering other types of insurance. The Woodmen (operating today as Assurity Inc.) remains a thriving business and one of Lincoln's largest employers.

Insurance is a notoriously conservative business and A. O. was well suited to it by temperament. He may not have had Louie Meyer's charm, but he was a man universally trusted. When a tornado hit St. Louis and claims ate up the company's available cash, A. O. cut his salary and those of his directors to compensate. He served on the board of the two biggest banks in Lincoln, the City National and the First National; was president of the deacons of the First Presbyterian Church; and helped organize Lincoln's city tram company. Whether by his will or his example, A. O.'s sons—Edwin, Albert (born in 1890), and Richard (born in 1894)—not only followed their father into the Woodmen Accident Company but carried on his work as community leaders.

As A. O.'s status ascended, the Faulkners outgrew their home near the Capitol. In 1899, A. O. bought Park Hill, a mansion situated on a small estate just south of Lincoln's city limits. The house was approached by a long driveway that let out onto South Street, then one of the few streets in the area south of the city center. From here, the three boys and their sister Cora (born in 1886) traveled to Lincoln High School and later the university, and Park Hill regularly hosted their dinners and parties.

When Edwin Faulkner entered the university in the fall of 1900, he was sixteen but already knew where he wanted to go. He took business courses, then entered law school, intending to join the Woodmen upon graduation. In the 1904 yearbook, he declared that his aim was "to make a million dollars" by the time he was thirty. He began courting Leah Meyer, who was two years behind him at the university, but she had goals as well. Intending to become a teacher, she majored in English and education, and took classes in psychology, still a relatively new subject.

For one of these classes, Leah wrote an essay now preserved among Virginia's papers. Titled "Fixed Ideas," it deals with what we would today call obsessive compulsive disorder, but it's difficult not to think of her father when reading it. "At the point of departure from the normal states of mind is to be caught the genesis of mental disorders," she writes. She admits that she suffers from a mild form of the disorder herself. "If I forget to enter the campus gate with my right foot," she confesses, "I have a vague sense of discomfort." But she goes on to describe pathological forms of fixed ideas that can incapacitate an individual completely. She mentions, as an example, a patient in a mental asylum who, in a manic state just days before his death, kept repeating, "Saw off my leg. Saw off my leg." Was this someone she observed at the state asylum, perhaps even her father?

Fig. 1. A. O. Faulkner and his family, around 1918. Virginia is the girl sticking her tongue out. Courtesy of E. J. Faulkner, Professional Papers, Archives and Special Collections, University of Nebraska-Lincoln Libraries.

During her senior year at the university, Leah, Cora Faulkner, and a dozen other young women established a chapter of the Alpha Phi sorority, one of the first in Nebraska and a sign of how colleges were beginning to incubate social networks that would reach beyond graduation. With her degree, Leah took a job teaching in the high school in Lyons, a town about ninety miles north of Lincoln, and after a year she moved to nearby West Point, where she became assistant principal of the town's high school and continued to teach English.

Leah's absence must have helped Edwin make up his mind and propose. In the spring of 1909, their engagement was announced, and the couple were married the week after her return to Lincoln. When they returned from their honeymoon, Leah and Edwin moved into a two-story house that A. O. had built for them on a plot of land behind Park Hill. There, a son, Edwin Jr., was born in 1911 and a daughter, Virginia, in March 1913. Lincoln was no longer a town on the edge of the frontier and the Faulkners no longer new arrivals but mainstays of the city's power and society. Both town and family would serve as anchor points and constraints in Virginia's life.

Ginny and Eddie

The snapshot shows two kids dressed up like doughboys outside their home. Ginny is eight, Eddie ten. She wears a service cap, Eddie a floppy hat, and their arms are around each other. Both wear proud, goofy grins. "Dear Dad," one of them has written on the back. One can read too much into a photograph, but it's clear that these were two kids who enjoyed each other's company. And through ups and downs—more hers than his—they continued to be companions until the day Virginia died. Ginny and Eddie were barely out of each other's sight for the first two decades of their lives. Though Eddie was twenty months older than his sister, she was his main playmate in their early years—and would become his classmate as well.

On the first day of class in September 1919, Eddie was sitting in the third-grade classroom at Prescott Elementary School when the principal entered, followed by his mother and Ginny. Having taught her daughter to read from the time she could hold a book, Leah knew Ginny was too advanced for kindergarten. She insisted on speaking to the principal, who offered Ginny several different books to read from, moving year by year through the school's standard texts. After she handled the sixth-grade reader without difficulty, he decided to advance her directly to third grade. For Eddie, it was humiliating. From that point on, he would be saddled with the shame of going through school in the same class as his little sister.

In the snapshot with Eddie, taken around 1920, Ginny is a tomboy. She's abandoned dolls and frilly dresses in favor of the same rough-and-tumble outfits as Eddie. When she was twelve, she asked for a pair of football pants for her birthday, and she was known as a bruising defender. Her cousin Sarah Louise Meyer, who had a column in the *Daily Nebraskan* in the mid-

Fig. 2. Ginny and Eddie, around 1915. Courtesy of E. J. Faulkner, Professional Papers, Archives and Special Collections, University of Nebraska-Lincoln Libraries.

1930s, wrote several recollections of Virginia—"just Ginny then." Ginny was "chubby, energetic, athletic, and very movie-struck." "Unhappily for me," Sarah recalled, Ginny "did not fancy the wearing of trains and the playing of helpless femininity. She must be the cavalier, the swordsman, the gallant." In choosing her role models, Virginia would have agreed with Willa Cather, who had written a few decades before, "The fact that I was a girl never damaged my ambitions to be a pope or an emperor."

By then, Edwin Sr. had begun to build a large two-story house across the street from A. O.'s estate. Decades later, Virginia would tell the novelist Wright Morris that she and Eddie felt that they lived on edge of civilization, the place where South Street turned into a country road. But there was little that was rural about the Faulkners' lives by the time Ginny became a teenager. Edwin, his brother Bert, and several other businessmen joined together to establish the Lincoln Country Club, the city's first private golf club, located on farmland south of Park Hill. The Country Club was where Ginny and Eddie learned to swim, where they played tennis, hosted dinners, and attended dances. Edwin Sr. served on the club board, as did Bert,

Richard, and Eddie, in turn, and the club would remain a focal point of the Faulkners' social life until Eddie's death in 1992.

The larger house allowed Edwin Sr. and Leah to host social events as well. A. O. looked increasingly to his eldest son to handle the social side of the business, as it was becoming essential that business be carried on outside the office, that senior members of management and visiting executives be entertained for dinners. The house had a large kitchen, dining room, and living room to accommodate guests, as well as an expansive patio in the rear where outdoor parties could be held in summer. To deal with the work of taking care of these needs, Edwin built servants' apartments above the large garage and storeroom set off from the main house.

Edwin and his brothers also turned away from prevailing conventions in their embrace of alcohol as a social lubricant. A. O. was a temperate man, but his sons were of the generation that took drinking out of the saloons and into homes and private clubs, replacing beer and rotgut with wine and labeled whiskies. Even after the sale of liquor was banned by Prohibition in 1920, Edwin, Bert, and Dick kept their cellars stocked and continued to serve cocktails at parties.

By the repeal of Prohibition in 1933, alcohol was not only accepted in Lincoln society but celebrated. The Faulkners also considered it acceptable for women to drink, something that would remain controversial in much of the United States. The change from saloon to salon and the equal rights of women to drink didn't eliminate the problem of alcoholism, however. Despite the challenges imposed by Prohibition, Virginia's uncles Bert and Dick earned reputations as heavy drinkers, and Virginia would too.

Edwin's status meant that Leah had to take on leadership roles as well. Already active in running the Mortar Board, the university's honor society, she helped organize the Lincoln chapter of the Junior League in 1922. Established in New York City in 1901, the League involved its members, mostly affluent women, in charitable and educational efforts at a time when many businesses refused to employ married women. Lincoln's chapter was one of the first thirty established and Leah was selected to report on its activities in the League's national magazine. Her summary of the chapter's initiatives in its first year mentions efforts from sewing layettes for the county Detention Home to monitoring cases in juvenile court. Junior

League members often had a not-so-secret agenda of providing a positive way to channel their daughters' energies.

Leah was no exception. She helped Ginny establish a Junior Civic League chapter for Prescott Elementary and saw that her daughter served as its first president. And as much as Virginia chafed at Lincoln's conventions, she dutifully joined the Junior League, remained a member for decades, and sponsored numerous applicants. Even during her wildest years in Hollywood and New York, she took care not to upset sensibilities back in Lincoln. She might be oblivious to her own reputation, but she was never willing to risk damaging her family's, particularly if it might reflect on the Woodmen's as well.

Edwin and Leah passed other duties of community leaders to their children. As early as 1925, when Ginny was just twelve, she and Eddie were hosting a cotillion for fifty teenagers at the South Street house. The occasion was a visit by their cousin Helen Howell, Thomas and Pauline's daughter. Just a year older than Ginny, Helen often spent time in Lincoln, and the two cousins became close. Through Helen, Ginny could feel the pull of Chicago's glamour even as a teenager. A photo from the *Star* society section in 1926 shows Ginny and Helen dressed up with cloche hats, fur-trimmed overcoats, and legs exposed from just below the knees. For Ginny, though, the outfit was just an experiment.

Ginny and Eddie entered Lincoln High School in the fall of 1926. Though both excelled academically, Eddie was much more in his element socially. He took a leading role in every activity he joined. Except for the Writers' Club and the school yearbook, the *Links*, however, Ginny avoided these groups. A photo of the *Links* staff taken in the spring of 1927 suggests one reason. The age difference between Ginny and her classmates is striking. The other young women are wearing dresses and necklaces. Ginny, on the other hand, is in a childish smock, baby fat still lingering in her cheeks. As intellectually advanced as she might be, she was still several years younger than her classmates and under her mother's protective umbrella.

It was at Lincoln High that Ginny met women who not only encouraged her to write but established her first connections with Willa Cather. Cather's younger sister Elsie taught in the English department and advised the Writers' Club. Olivia Pound, whose sister Louise had been Cather's classmate and intimate at the university, was vice principal and adviser for the school's girls. The Pound sisters provided Ginny with remarkable role models. Louise was an exceptional scholar with a doctorate from the University of Heidelberg, the first female member of the English faculty at UNL. Outside her high school duties, Olivia published on subjects ranging from "The Social Life of High-School Girls" to Swinburne's dramas. Olivia twice served as president of the National Association of University Women; Louise was president of the American Folklore Society at the time Ginny started high school. They lived together in a house on L Street where Ginny attended some of the Sunday teas they hosted for promising young women in Lincoln. The Pound sisters were also accomplished athletes who fought for the rights of women to participate in sports. Louise had earned varsity letters in both basketball (the first year it was played at UNL) and tennis and competed in tennis at the national level. Olivia was instrumental in the introduction of girls' sports in Lincoln schools in 1919, and by the time Ginny was a freshman, girls could compete in six sports.

To her family, Ginny's interest in sports was considered a passing phase, but the Pound sisters took it seriously. Ginny was an avid swimmer and played on Lincoln High's girls' tennis team. When Lincoln's first private tennis club was opened in 1928, she made sure that Edwin joined, and she competed in its first tournament. She still loved to roughhouse with Eddie and his friends, though, and managed to break his leg during a football scrimmage not long after they entered high school. Her classmates poked fun in that year's edition of the *Links*, crediting her with writing a book titled *How to Play Football.*

In early 1927 not long after Ginny and Eddie had been moved forward into the junior class, A. O. Faulkner died after a brief illness. The news was splashed across the front page of the Lincoln papers. As the eldest brother and the most knowledgeable from his role as general counsel, Edwin was the logical choice to succeed his father as the president of the Woodmen Accident Company. Edwin's promotion was soon overshadowed by another tragedy, however.

During the family's summer vacation on Madeline Island in Lake Superior the year before, Edwin had become concerned about Leah's health. On the way back to Lincoln, they stopped in Rochester, Minnesota, for a consultation at the Mayo Clinic. Leah was examined by Dr. Claude Dixon and his findings were reviewed and endorsed by Dr. Charles Mayo.

While the specific diagnosis is unknown, Edwin was later to write Dr. Mayo saying, "I know something of the scourge of cancer" and asking him to recommend where he could donate to research on "a cure for this terrible disease."

For a while, Leah seemed to recover. In the summer of 1927, the family returned to the island. Thomas Howell now had a mansion there, and they attended receptions for General John J. Pershing and Vice President Charles G. Dawes during their stay. When the Faulkners arrived back in Lincoln in late August, however, Leah's condition rapidly deteriorated. Her bedroom was turned into a sick room and round-the-clock nursing care arranged.

With their mother now seriously ill, Eddie and Ginny returned to school as seniors. Eddie was now one of the big men on campus: president of his class, managing editor of the *Links* yearbook, and star debater. Ginny was elected president of the Writer's Club, though she much preferred to write than lead. Ironically, her first accomplishment as a writer that year was an enthusiastic review of Willa Cather's latest novel, *Death Comes for the Archbishop*, in the Lincoln High newspaper. After noting that critics considered Cather past her prime as an artist, she argued that *Death* represented a significant advance in both subject and approach. She did not recommend the book "promiscuously," though. "For those who wish to have gory murders, races with death, and maudlin romance with their after-dinner caramels, this is hardly a wise selection." Instead, in a preview of how Virginia would come to defend Cather decades later, she wrote that it was intended for those "who like a book for what it is, who care for artistry of style, and nicety of word, and who appreciate a well-turned phrase and subtle plot finesse."

By early October, Leah's cancer had spread, and her prognosis was grim. Edwin informed the family to stand by for the worst. Thomas Howell prevailed on his friend L. B. Lyman, general superintendent of the Burlington Railroad, to make his private rail car and a dedicated engine available. When told on the 15th that Leah appeared to be close to death, Lyman ordered the train to be given exclusive right of way along the route. Carrying Pauline Howell and her brothers Bob and Rit Meyer, it made the run from Chicago to Lincoln in record time, enabling them to speak with their sister one last time.

The news of Leah's death on October 18, 1927, was announced on the front page of the Lincoln newspapers. At fourteen, Ginny, who already resisted being molded to conform with conventional notions of young

Fig. 3. Eddie and Virginia, from *Links*, the 1928 Lincoln High School yearbook. Courtesy of E. J. Faulkner, Professional Papers, Archives and Special Collections, University of Nebraska-Lincoln Libraries.

women of society, was left without a strong female influence. Her grandmother Jenny was still mourning A. O.'s death and her aunts Cora and Pauline were too busy with their own lives to intercede. Bert's wife Eugenia showed some interest, but Ginny had a lifelong dislike of her aunt. So, she was left largely on her own to cope with the emotional toll of losing her mother at such a young age. Depression and isolation are common reactions of teenagers to the death of a parent, and Ginny may have begun at this point to struggle with the tendency toward periods of dark moods that punctuated her entire adult life. She seemed to understand that her adult life was beginning. Now, to everyone but Eddie, she left Ginny behind and became Virginia.

School provided little relief. She couldn't tolerate the slow pace and busywork. Though she and Eddie continued to rank among the best students in their class, where Eddie sought the approval of his teachers and classmates, Virginia saw school as a necessary but tedious burden. And socially, she was two years younger than her classmates, awkward, accepted

Fig. 4. Virginia jumping with Shannon, 1929. Courtesy of Richard Faulkner.

more as Eddie's sister than as an equal. If anything, Leah's death made her seek Eddie's support and reassurance even more.

Writing, however, challenged her creatively and intellectually. The school's newspaper gave her an outlet for publishing reviews and the *Links* published her poems and comic pieces. And school events gave her opportunities to write sketches and short plays, opportunities she seized with relish. The *Links* joked that she had written nine plays for Joy Night, the annual talent show.

The other outlet for her energy was horse riding. Her Uncle Dick was bringing equestrianism to Lincoln. At the time, using a horse for something other than transportation, farm work, or racing was a novelty, but horse shows began to spread through the Midwest, and in 1926 Omaha hosted Nebraska's first horse show. For men flush with cash, show horses were prestige purchases and equestrianism was a rare sport open equally to those men and women able to afford it. In 1927 Bert and Dick bought a dairy farm just east of A. O. and Edwin's places and converted its barn into stables, constructing an equestrian course on part of the old pasture. Edwin joined in and he, Eddie, and Virginia started taking riding lessons. It gave Edwin a chance to spend time with his children away from the house, and the three started taking long rides together as a Sunday morning ritual.

Uncle Dick organized Lincoln's first horse show in May 1928, just weeks before Virginia and Eddie graduated. Virginia took first prize in the jumping competition, riding Shannon, the stallion her father had bought her, and Edwin won first in walking/trotting. The show was a relatively small affair, held on the paddock of the university's agriculture school, but it gave Dick the appetite for bigger things, and the following year's show was held at the Nebraska State Fair grounds. Bert's wife Eugenia won first place in two categories and Virginia took the jumping competition again.

Virginia and Eddie entered UNL as freshmen in September 1928. The differences in their experiences were even more pronounced in college than they had been in high school. Eddie dove into college. He checked all the boxes short of making a varsity team. He signed onto the staff of the *Daily Nebraskan* and rose from sales manager to contributing editor. He also joined in the preparation of the annual student directory. To most students, this seemed the most forgettable of all the student publications, but it was also the most profitable, as many of its pages were filled with paid advertisements. Eddie recognized the opportunity it gave him to get to know local businessmen and he ultimately became the directory's editor. He also became active in student government, and through his willingness to take on thankless duties, worked his way up to election as president of the student council by his senior year. Eddie pledged with the Phi Kappa Psi fraternity, or Phi Psi, as most students called it. Although he wasn't a boarding member, his loyalty was absolute. He continued to attend Phi Psi events into his seventies, often sponsoring Rush Week dinners at the Lincoln Country Club and favoring Phi Psi brothers in hiring and promotions when he became president of the Woodmen.

As if all these activities, on top of a full course load, weren't enough, Eddie also joined a unique UNL tradition, the Kosmet Klub. The Kosmet Klub began in 1911 as a group of male students interested in organizing musical and dramatic shows. Eddie's reasons for auditioning had less to do with a love of performing than a recognition that the Klub was the most powerful student group on campus. Although its character changed in later years, at the time it operated like a secret society—more like the Skull and Bones at Yale. There was no clearer demonstration that Eddie intended to become a leader in Lincoln's establishment than his decision to audition for the Kosmet Klub.

In contrast, Virginia avoided rather than embraced the college experience. She confined her studies to three subjects: French, English literature, and philosophy, which leads one to wonder if she ever seriously intended to get a degree. Her transcript certainly doesn't list the kind of prerequisites that fill a typical undergraduate's schedule. She found college both duller and more liberating than high school. Duller in part because she was still rarely challenged by her coursework. Her attitude toward assignments was blithely irreverent. Professor Lowry Wimberly later told how Virginia would sit in the front row of his class, staring at her notebook as she doodled away, as if deliberately ignoring his lecture, until she would suddenly awaken and try to argue with him over some point he'd made. Duller as well because, unlike Eddie, none of the school's many extracurricular groups held the slightest interest for her. Out of respect for her mother, she pledged the Alpha Phi sorority, but avoided its events. Otherwise, Virginia couldn't see how college was taking her anywhere she wanted to go.

On the other hand, her mother's death and her father's commitments left Virginia free from much of the parental oversight she'd grown up with. Edwin had given both Virginia and Eddie their own cars, and for Virginia, her roadster was an escape outlet. She would race around the streets of Lincoln, steering with one hand while waving around a cigarette in the other, paying little attention to where she was going and picking up more than a few speeding tickets.

Virginia was growing up in the age of the flapper. The term first became popular through Frances Marion's 1920 movie *The Flapper*, in which a sixteen-year-old girl wears makeup, flirts with boys, sneaks out to parties, and dresses up in stolen gowns and jewelry. The flapper came to symbolize the generation of young women then coming of age: slim, sophisticated, free-thinking. They flouted conventions and morals, "necked" with boys in the backseats of cars, danced the Charleston, and most of all, smoked.

Virginia took to smoking after her mother died and spent many of her waking hours with a cigarette in her hand. She also left her girlish smocks behind and adopted the flapper's slim dresses and shorter hairstyles—indeed, she stuck to a cut known as the Eton crop the rest of her adult life. But most importantly, she found the flapper's independent, slightly defiant manner truer to her nature than any other role models she'd seen so far.

When Edwin decided to remarry in June 1930, just after the end of Virginia and Eddie's sophomore year, her rebelliousness escalated. Edwin's fiancée, Betty Thornton, was just two years older than Virginia and just a year out of UNL. Virginia saw the marriage as an insult to her mother's memory and knew her father would be even less attentive to her needs. She humored Edwin by hosting the bridal shower and putting on a bright face at the wedding, but privately Virginia despised the new Mrs. Edwin J. Faulkner, calling her "the Itch-Bay" behind her back. Fortunately, an escape route out of Lincoln soon opened.

During a trip to Europe in early 1930, Grandmother Faulkner had visited a finishing school in Rome run by Paulina Moxley, a middle-aged woman originally from Kentucky. She had a letter of introduction from General Pershing that described her as "an acquaintance and friend of my of many years' standing." She was impressed by the school's sophistication, tiny enrollment (just eight girls), and Miss Moxley's firm control over her students. She returned to Lincoln with the aim to send Virginia for a year.

Edwin welcomed the idea. "Frankly, I am in a quandary as to what to do in regard to Virginia's schooling," he confessed in a letter to Paulina Moxley. "Her life here has been one of almost unrestricted freedom—born and reared in a suburban home with ample grounds, close access to country clubs, her own riding horses, car, etc.," he admitted. Although Virginia at sixteen was younger than her classmates, he wrote, "She finds her work very easy—in fact, too easy to interest her as much as it should." The problem, as he saw it, was that the lack of an intellectual challenge left her too much time and energy. He considered her "mentally advanced to far beyond her years," even "worldly wise and sophisticated"—but not so sophisticated that she should be "allowed to go unrestricted and unchaperoned in any European city." He knew what Virginia got up to on her own in Lincoln and was uncomfortable with the idea of her roaming a foreign city by herself.

Edwin clearly hoped that Miss Moxley would replace the parental oversight missing since Leah's death. Miss Moxley forbade her girls to smoke, for example. "I am glad of this enforced vacation from the habit," he wrote—but added hesitantly, "while I will not attempt to prohibit her taking it up again when she leaves school, I very much prefer that she would not." He didn't mention the fact that with her mother's death, his own busy schedule, and

LINCOLN STATE JOURNAL, SUNDAY, SEPTEMBER 7, 1930

Society

Miss Virginia Faulkner . Mrs. James Sine w Nancy

Miss Virginia Faulkner leaves soon for Italy, where she will attend school in Rome during the coming season.

Mrs. James Sine with her daubter, Nancy of Los Angeles, is in the city for about two months as the house guest of her parents, Mr. and Mrs. Lewis Trester.

Fig. 5. Virginia about to depart for Rome, 1930. *Lincoln State Journal*, September 7, 1930, p. 31.

an unwelcome stepmother at home, handing Virginia over to Miss Moxley meant one less headache for him.

Everyone in Lincoln soon learned of Edwin's decision. As Virginia's departure neared, the society pages reported on all the farewell parties given in her honor. Edwin organized a "riding breakfast," where she took a last ride with twenty-four other young equestrians. The *Lincoln State Journal* published a photo of seventeen-year-old Virginia in trench coat and bobbed hair, looking confident and ready to travel. After a final party at Grandmother Meyer's, Edwin, Betty, and Virginia boarded the train to New York City, where he handed her over to Miss Moxley aboard the SS *Augustus* on September 26, 1930. It was the last time Virginia would see her father.

3

Rome

Virginia arrived in Rome with Miss Moxley and seven other girls in early October 1930. While Lincoln's lawns were covered with autumn leaves, Rome was still enjoying the lingering heat of its long summer.

At $2,000 a year—over $32,000 today—Miss Moxley's School was one of the cheaper European finishing schools. For this price, the school offered exclusive arrangements. It was housed in the Villa Hélène, a beautiful neoclassical structure on the Via Stanislao Mancini built about ten years earlier by the son of the writer Hans Christian Andersen. Rome, Moxley promised Edwin, offered more "pageantry and Old-World splendor" than any other city in Europe, "with the royal court, the Vatican, and Mussolini and the Fascists." "The girls adore it," she assured him.

In an early letter home, Virginia admitted that she found the school much different than she had expected. "In the first place, we don't have to do anything for ourselves—we are treated like house-guests, even to having our pajamas laid out—no beds to make, no menial tasks to perform. 'Except, of course, our sewing,' she said with a ghastly chortle." She never did take to any kind of domestic work.

Her chief complaint was that "I have so much less time to myself"—which Edwin would have been pleased to read. On a typical day, the girls rose at 7:00 a.m., dressed, then ate a continental breakfast: "Tan shoe-polish called cafe au lait and hard rolls with jam and marmalade—no ge-dunking allowed," Virginia explained. After breakfast, they met in twos and threes for instruction in art history, Italian, and French until 1:00 p.m. Lunch was followed by an hour spent in the villa's salon in polite conversation—or, as Virginia referred to it, "chumming with Paulina." Miss Moxley emphasized the finish in finishing school. Although she tried to enrich the girls' knowledge and appreciation of art and other aspects of culture, her goal was to train them to be helpmates to upper-class husbands as sophisticated society hostesses. Though the school closed in 1940, for decades afterward, wives of CEOs and Cabinet secretaries would proudly declare themselves as graduates of the Moxley School.

After conversation, the girls were either taken to visit a church or museum or instructed in sports. Virginia usually played tennis and boasted that she could beat all her classmates. Finishing took precedence again in the late afternoon, with tea at the villa or in the Borghese gardens. The girls then bathed, studied, and met again for dinner. If she was lucky, Virginia reported, she might get a half hour to herself. Miss Moxley tolerated no dissent. "I often tell the girls that they can always have their own way if their way is my way," she told parents.

On Saturdays, the girls would be taken on trips to sites around Rome, and classical music concerts were a staple of Sunday afternoons. Miss Moxley said that the girls loved to go to concerts as much for the audience as for the music. "Strange faces soon become thrillingly familiar," she would say, "and they look forward to seeing their friends with unbounded enthusiasm." Virginia's enthusiasm, however, was always moderated by her skepticism and sense of the comic. "Four of us went for a long ride in some fiacres and stopped at the Spanish Steps for flowers," she reported in her first letter home. "That ought to raise a howl," she joked: "imagine daughter Virginia getting a bang out of buying posies."

Miss Moxley often took the girls to restaurants for the evening meal. Knowing how to order, which fork to use for which course, and how to be a charming dinner companion were all part of being an accomplished society woman. Virginia joked that Italy had forced her to reconsider her attitude toward food. "You know how I used to be finicky about my food?" she asked Eddie. "If I thought a human hair was involved in a viand I was consuming, I would very nearly be sick at the table." Now, however, after getting used to Italian standards of hygiene, she boasted, "If I found a partially decomposed horse in the vermicelli, I would only make a slight moué of distaste and eat around it."

Of the school's staff, Evelyn Merriman was by far Virginia's favorite. She had taught music at private girls' schools in the U.S. before joining

Miss Moxley in the late 1920s. Virginia found her "a grand person" and "a marvelous musician." Miss Moxley, however, was someone to be feared but not necessarily respected. "Her French is rotten," she sniffed to Eddie.

As the girls became accustomed to the two languages, instruction and conversation tended to flow from one to another in a single sentence. Asked if she wanted to go to the cinema, Virginia wrote her family that she would likely respond, "Si, j'irai avec vous, ma non e possible per me passer trop de temps in the damn place parce que la signorina Moxley desidero que je sois ici alia cinque." Eight switches in thirty words—Virginia had already learned the comic effect of exaggeration.

When asked to pick a book to translate into Italian, Virginia chose Ursula Parrott's *Ex-Wife*, a bestselling novel of divorce, drinking, adultery, and abortion set in Manhattan. It was hardly likely to meet with Miss Moxley's approval and might have been in her mind when she wrote Edwin in December that there were problems "with Virginia's advanced ideas." But she felt Virginia was "really trying to adapt herself to a more conventional state of existence than she has been accustomed to," a bit of a dig at how little Edwin had tried to rein in his daughter in Lincoln.

In addition to Italian and classical culture and the manners of international society, Virginia was getting exposed to different models of how a woman might live. Though Miss Moxley didn't approve of *Ex-Wife*, she would have agreed with Ursula Parrott that matrimony wasn't the only possible end for a woman. "There are women about whom it is more significant to know that they work at this or that," one of Parrott's characters asserts, "than to know that they were once married to someone or other." Both Paulina Moxley and Evelyn Merriman had managed to live independently and hold respected places without the need for a Mrs. in their names.

The other girls, Virginia confided to Eddie, were "much nicer than I could have hoped." She was the youngest of the eight, but just by a few months. When one looks at the tiny snapshots from school outings in her papers, however, the differences between Virginia and her classmates again become apparent. The other girls are slim, wear stockings, high-heeled shoes, cloche hats, and sleek flapper-style dresses. Virginia, in contrast, wears oxford shoes, boxy skirts, and large, loose blouses. They are young women eager to blend in with the adult world; she is still a teenager, for all her intellectual sophistication. Though her fashions were adolescent, Virginia had other decidedly adult tastes. Out of Miss Moxley's sight, she still stole an occasional cigarette, and she knew how to get her hands on hard liquor. Years later, she told of smuggling a pint of bourbon into the school at Christmas when they were all feeling "thoroughly homesick."

In January, Miss Moxley took the girls on a trip to Sicily and Tunisia, where they visited Greek, Roman, and Carthaginian ruins. The trip inspired Virginia's first serious work of fiction. "A Room with a Bath," published the following year in *Prairie Schooner*, is written in an uncommon—but for much of Virginia's magazine fiction, characteristic—voice: the second-person plural or the royal "we." "We chose the room with the bath instead of the room with the view," it opens.

The story tells of a visit to Syracuse in Sicily. The narrator abhors the earnest Englishwomen found in every hotel. Of one she writes: "She is well hung with devices, some ornamental and studded with garnet and cat's-eye, others utilitarian and suggesting an imminent departure to remote unexplored regions." Virginia already had a knack for turning her spotlight on her characters' most glaring flaws.

Yet what makes the story exceptional among Virginia's fiction is that the narrator also acknowledges the suffering the city has witnessed through the centuries. "Here seven thousand captive Athenians were starved to death. . . . Perhaps the bodies of the ignobly dead have enriched the once sterile soil and find an unsatisfactory reincarnation in this restless, omnivorous plant-life," she writes. Rather than brood on this history, however, the narrator opts "to postpone reflections until we have managed a tub in the handsome bathroom." This sort of dismissal of the world and celebration of selfishness would become a common feature in Virginia's fiction. The story's recognition of the grim past shadowing the present would not. Its blend of comic and tragic rarely reappears in her later commercial stories.

When the group returned to Rome, there was a letter from Virginia's father waiting for Miss Moxley. He'd come to trust her judgment, wanted her help, and asked if she would be coming back with the girls to New York at the end of the school year. "I would particularly like to have a visit with you," he wrote, "to get your ideas firsthand as to future plans for Virginia." He assured her that "anything you may say along this line in the way of recommendations will be greatly appreciated." Edwin understood that the usual path for a young woman of her social class, the one followed by her mother, his sister Cora, and his new wife, Betty—university degree, a bit of work, marriage to a man of suitable standing—the path Miss Moxley was preparing her girls for—was not the one for Virginia.

Still, some of Miss Moxley's attempts to smooth some of Virginia's rough edges had succeeded. She took advantage of lower prices in Italy to have some more fashionable dresses made. She also sought out the advice of Italian hairdressers and was pleased to report that they all said her hair was "much better short, and much smarter."

More than anything, though, the school taught her about Rome. "I could find my way around this town blindfold," she boasted at the end of March. "I know the name of every fountain, park, and public building. I can tell you the life story of every statue, martyr, or mosaic." "What is more," she added, "I know places for tea, where to shop, the night clubs, restaurants, and theatres. I know it better than I know Lincoln." How much of this knowledge was due to Miss Moxley's influence and how much a result of Virginia's keen powers of observation, one cannot judge. But she would put it to use in her first novel, *Friends and Romans*.

In May, Edwin sent his last payment and wrote, "We have missed the young lady very much and I am looking forward with a great deal of pleasure to meeting her in New York." He also sent Virginia a letter saying that he had a busy month ahead, with a trip to Washington DC and the Lincoln Horse Show. He also wrote that Betty was expecting. This last was not good news for Virginia. Her father would only be pulled more strongly to his new family.

The year at Miss Moxley's culminated in a tour to Florence, Milan, the Riviera, and Paris before returning to the States from Le Havre. Though they spent just a week in Paris, Virginia managed to tuck away a stock of impressions that she later incorporated into her second novel, *The Barbarians*.

Edwin had planned to meet Virginia in New York when she arrived on the *Ile de France*. On June 3, 1931, the night before boarding his train back east, however, he complained of chest pains while having dinner at his mother's house. He was taken to his home across the street, but within an hour, he was dead of a heart attack. He was just forty-six years old.

"Can't help repeating the old admonition to be careful of what you eat, drink and do on your travels," Edwin has cautioned Virginia in his last letter. "I want to welcome my girl home all in one healthy chunk." Instead, there was no one at the dock to greet her. Evelyn Merriman escorted Virginia to Penn Station and put her on a train bound west. She was now an orphan.

4

Limbo

When Virginia stepped off the train in Lincoln, the whole Faulkner family was there to greet her. Even her stepmother, Betty—a reminder that she was returning to a home that was now Betty's domain. Virginia's room, with her beloved desk and books, would no longer be a sanctuary. The room down the hall—the room where her mother died—had been turned into a nursery. Just two months after Virginia returned, Betty gave birth to Edward, her new stepbrother.

Although Uncle Bert took on the role of guardian to Eddie and Virginia, both still under legal age, he preferred to focus on his fiduciary responsibilities. Edwin had updated his will after Leah's death in 1927. In it, he left nearly everything to Eddie and Virginia. In addition to the house on South Street and other pieces of property in Lincoln, the largest share of his estate came from the proceeds from his life insurance policies, amounting to over $200,000. Edwin had not revised his will after marrying Betty, but by law she was entitled to one-fourth of his estate. In Virginia's case, Bert considered his duties consisted primarily in controlling her monthly allowance. For everything else, he was more comfortable dealing with Eddie. It was Eddie he trusted; it was Eddie he could relate to.

Although the Faulkners were among the elite of Lincoln's society, they were not rich in the way rich people assess wealth. A. O. and his sons had grown the Woodmen into one of the largest insurance companies in the Midwest, but they only ran the company; they did not own it. As a cooperative, the value of the company was held jointly by its policyholders. A. O. took a relatively modest salary as president, a practice that Edwin, Bert, and, eventually, Eddie continued: enough to buy large houses and a bit of property and to do a modest amount of investing in the stock market, but not enough to indulge in lavish spending.

Lacking experience in investment, Uncle Bert reached across the family tree to Leah's brothers Bob and Rit Meyer, who had followed Thomas Howell to Chicago and were brokers in the Mercantile Exchange. "I think they are in a position to help advise us," he explained in a letter to Eddie. "In these times advice is of great value." Bob and Rit recommended putting Virginia and Eddie's legacy into a mix of government bonds and blue-chip stocks. Bert wrote Eddie in advance of every trade and always sought his approval before acting. But he relied on Eddie to keep his sister within the limits of Lincoln's proprieties.

Like all the tasks Eddie undertook, he carried it out conscientiously. He was no surer than his father what the future should hold for Virginia, but he seems to have recognized that she had the potential to become something other than another Lincoln hostess. She was no longer a tomboy, but she had no interest in becoming anyone's obliging—and deferential—wife. Virginia didn't see herself as someone to be controlled by Eddie or any other man. Although the *Daily Nebraskan* announced in September 1931 that she was returning to the university, she never even bothered to register.

So, how did Virginia spend her time? Out of respect for her mother's legacy, she helped out at Junior League events. She and Eddie were no longer free to host parties at the house where Betty was busy with her new baby, but she lent a hand at several organized by old schoolmates. The highlight of her summer was serving as bridesmaid for her cousin Helen Howell's wedding to John Barnes, a Chicago banker, in early September.

For the most part, though, she ran wild. Once again, she raced through the streets in her roadster, picking up more tickets. She took up smoking again. She developed a taste for bootleg liquor and turned up at gatherings where Lincoln's few bohemians drank and talked and she could hold forth as a woman of the world, becoming, as she later put it, "a star recruit of Lincoln's leper colony." She simmered with the same frustration that George Eliot had expressed in her novel *Daniel Deronda*—"to have a man's force of genius in you, and yet to suffer the slavery of being a girl"—without a way to break free. But she was determined to find that way—somehow.

To the self-determination of the flapper she'd mastered before going to Rome, Virginia had added an Italian ingredient: *sprezzatura*. In his *Book of the Courtier*, Castiglione held that of all the attributes a civilized gentleman should display; the most essential was to affect in everything "a certain casualness" (English translators struggled to find an equivalent term for *sprezzatura*) "which conceals art and creates the impression that what is done and said is accomplished without effort and even without its being thought about." Virginia would have seen Italian men attempting the same nonchalance in their approaches to Miss Moxley's girls: earnest and ardent—but not too. She would later give this same manner to Ricardo dei Retti, the Italian nobleman and romantic interest in her novel *Friends and Romans*.

It became part of her public persona: never too eager, never too serious, always just slightly bored. On the outside, it gave the impression of tremendous self-assurance. But it also served as a shield. "You could not insinuate yourself into her life," recalled Richard Giannone, who came to know Virginia in the 1960s. It allowed her to mask doubts and misgivings that she was willing to share with only a few—Eddie at first, and later her partners.

Her chief diversions were frequent visits with Helen in Chicago. Helen wasn't just the cousin Virginia felt closest to; she was also an inspiration. Her marriage to John Barnes didn't slow down Helen's pace (nor did her three subsequent marriages). Like Virginia, she was an avid rider. She loved the spotlight and enjoyed having her photo taken with visiting movie stars. She and Virginia made the front page of the *Chicago Daily Times* striding arm in arm along a downtown sidewalk. Another *Daily Times* photo from July 1932 shows Helen and Virginia at the racetrack, with Virginia nonchalantly wearing a monocle.

When Virginia did sit down at her desk at the house on South Street, however, she put her time to good use. If she had anything to show for the year after returning from Rome, it was the start of her career as a published writer—even if the journals involved were neither prestigious nor well-paying. Starting in early 1932, she placed six articles in the *Junior League Magazine*. Several were book reviews, including one of Wyndham Lewis's novel *The Apes of God*. She thought the book would amuse and irritate anyone interested in London's Bohemia but found herself "weary after a third of the six hundred twenty-five pages of verbal cannonading," evoking the title and tone of Lewis's Vorticist magazine *Blast*. Reviewers of her own work would later criticize similarly relentless barrages of quips and witticisms.

Fig. 6. Helen Barnes and Virginia. *Chicago Sunday Tribune*, July 31, 1932, p. 53.

Whether Virginia had yet begun to focus on Willa Cather, she recognized one fact when she considered other such examples of successful women authors from Nebraska: They were *from*, not *in*, Nebraska. Rome had only been a temporary solution. She understood that there were only three ways out that Uncle Bert would accept: marriage, school, or a job. Marriage was out: Even if she hadn't yet begun to identify herself as lesbian, she viewed the whole business of romance and matrimony as absurd. And a handful of stories and articles in nonpaying publications wasn't enough to generate a job offer.

So, it had to be school. Not UNL, which would have sentenced her to two more years in Lincoln. One possibility, which she had dismissed when it first presented itself, was Radcliffe College in Massachusetts. Back when Virginia was still at Lincoln High School, Olivia Pound had nominated her for one of fifteen scholarships offered each year by Radcliffe. Though Virginia declined the grant at the time, feeling the need to stay close to home after her mother's death, she now contacted the school and confirmed that it was still available, along with admission as a sophomore.

Radcliffe had not yet integrated with Harvard, but the two schools coordinated closely on courses and curricula and Radcliffe was recognized as one of the finest women's colleges in the country. Its prestige helped in gaining Uncle Bert's approval, but what convinced him was when Eddie announced he was heading east for school too.

Approaching graduation in the spring of 1932, Eddie was concerned about his own future. At UNL, he was one of the big men on campus. If he took the next logical step, he would join the Woodmen as an ordinary clerk, with Uncle Bert looking over his shoulder. Eddie had bigger plans—for himself and for the company. He thought the Woodmen had the potential to become one of the Midwest's leading insurance providers. If he were to lead the firm (eventually), he wanted to study at the country's leading business school: the Wharton School of Finance in Philadelphia. He and his classmate Russel Mousel both applied and were accepted. In Bert's mind Philadelphia was close enough for Eddie to keep tabs on his sister. And Virginia's scholarship, while not sufficient to cover all expenses, reduced the need to draw upon her capital. Bert agreed but put them both on monthly allowances: sixty dollars for Virginia and eighty dollars for Eddie.

The emotional atmosphere in Lincoln improved a little that summer when stepmother Betty transferred the house on South Street to the estate in return for a cash settlement. Soon after, she took young Teddy and moved to Omaha, where, within about a year, she remarried and cut her ties with the Faulkner family for good. Uncle Dick and his new wife Milly agreed to rent the house while Eddie and Virginia were back east in school.

In late June 1932, the Lincoln papers announced that Eddie and Virginia would be driving east in September, along with Russell Mousel. Before then, however, she headed to Chicago again to spend time with Helen, riding, going to the racetrack, and attending parties. Getting ready for academics at Radcliffe was not one of her concerns.

5

Radcliffe

In early September, Virginia, Eddie, and Russell Mousel piled into Eddie's Model A Ford and headed east. Arriving safely in Philadelphia a week later, Eddie put Virginia on the train to Boston. One of the oldest women's colleges in the U.S., Radcliffe was unique in its proximity and close ties to Harvard University. Indeed, as one Radcliffe president put it, "a Radcliffe degree is a Harvard degree. Radcliffe exists to give women a Harvard education."

Virginia took a room on campus in Briggs Hall, the school's largest dormitory. Uncle Bert paid her tuition and board—$183 a term—and began sending the monthly check for her allowance. The pace of her daily routines was a bit of a shock after her year of idling. "I have lost 7 pounds," she wrote in November. "My clothes won't stay up. Damned embarrassing." The dormitory food didn't help. "Two bits says we'll have gangrenous calves' liver and rotten apple floating in mucilage," she joked about a typical lunch. "This is the kind of life which results in books like *All Quiet on the Western Front*."

From the start, Virginia found classes at Radcliffe a big step up from UNL. Writing Eddie in early October, she reported that her Italian class "has already covered more ground than a half semester would at home" and confessed, "If I don't keep working all the time I'd literally be swamped." A few days later, she wrote that she'd never been so busy in her life. "I don't have many classes—9 or 10 a week—but there's so much outside reading and notetaking, and then my tutor assigns me books outside too." Her Radcliffe curriculum mirrored that of Miss Moxley's school to an extent—Italian, French, European history, and Renaissance art, with English literature added—but with considerably tougher academic standards. Facing her first exams in early November, she asked anxiously, "You won't mind if I flunk, will you?"

Among her papers are pages from a three-ringed notebook with her lecture and reading notes. For the most part, these are typical undergraduate cribs, if more detailed than the average student's. But every so often, Virginia slips into a mocking editorial tone. Of the painter Fra Angelico, for example, she wrote, "In fresco a notorious little cheat—he worked mostly *a secco* or *tempora* and his works will not last like real frescoes." To which she added, "I'm glad to know he was a cheat. I detest the bird."

Virginia wrote to Eddie each week, sometimes more often. Her letters were an outlet for her frustrations, fears, and comic inspirations. Early in her first semester, she lamented, "By God, I'd like to know when I have time to pour out my heart into the typewriter." She regretted not having had a batch of form letters printed up:

> Dear Edwin:
> I did/did not get your letter which I enjoyed/bored me to tears.
> I am (_) well, (_) unwell, (_) lousy, (_) making it ok.
> The weather here is (_) hot, (_) dry, (_) wet, (_) snowy, (_) as usual.
> I hope you are (_) well, (_) sick, (_) suffering from alcohol poisoning.
> I am studying (_) hard, (_) occasionally, (_) very little, (_) not at all.
> There is (_) no news, (_) not much happening, (_) hardly anything doing.
> Write me (_) soon, (_) next week, (_) when you have a stamp.
> I remain (_) as ever, (_) as never before, (_) anyway.
>
> Your loving sister/devoted admirer/severest critic,
> Virginia

Despite her anxiety about keeping up, Virginia rated her classmates a cut below her intellectually: "The fems around here are just as dumb as they are most places," she confided to Eddie. As worried as she was over her own exam results, she boasted, "I've averaged in the 80s in the quiz sections, while the other kids have been getting in the 50s and 60s."

Virginia began emerging from her routine of school and dorm after returning to Radcliffe from a quick Christmas trip back to Lincoln. She and a classmate went out with a couple of Harvard Law students ("who are alike the world over") in early February and ended up walking home when the car ran out of gas. She made the dean's list for the first semester, and she was able to relax a bit. She started keeping lecture notes for English 32 (English Literature of the 16th Century, Exclusive of Drama), but these soon degenerated into a comic interior monologue: "Don't you just love sea stories? I'm awfully fond of Mr. Conrad, but he comes later, and he was a Pole or something." English 32 was taught by Professor John Livingston Lowes, a formidable scholar of Samuel Taylor Coleridge. Virginia, however, was neither impressed nor intimidated by Lowes. "He's a bit smaller than a midget," she wrote Eddie, "wears a toupee and thinks we Radcliffe girls is louses." Lowes, in turn, didn't appreciate Virginia's humor in her answer to a question about George Peele's play *The Old Wives' Tale*: "One can only conjecture the reason for anyone's having a name like Huanebango—is it possible that his mother was a harelip?"

One classmate managed to earn Virginia's respect: Florence Meyer. Virginia wasn't quite sure of Florence's background when she first mentioned her to Eddie, writing that her "pa is in the govt. somewhere and quite a big shot I gather." Florence's father was, in fact, Eugene Meyer, a New York financier then serving as chairman of the Federal Reserve Board. Although Florence was a senior, she and Virginia found they had much in common. Both played an aggressive if not skillful game of tennis and they started playing several times a week. Like Virginia, Florence had a restless spirit and was searching for an endeavor worth sinking her energies into. And she adored Virginia's rapid-fire repartee and wanted to share with her father, who loved lively conversation.

Though insulated from the Depression gripping America, Virginia was occasionally confronted by its effects. In early March, she found it almost impossible to cash her allowance check when it arrived on the first day of the national bank holiday declared by President Roosevelt to prevent financial collapse. With all the banks closed, her only recourse was the post office. "I forewent my nine o'clock to beetle down to the local P.O.," she recounted to Eddie. "They said they didn't have any money but had borrowed $1,000 from Boston which would be there at noon and to come back then." When she returned at noon, the clerk told her the cash wouldn't arrive until 1:00 p.m.

"And at one I came back," she wrote, "and a mob was storming the place with cops 'n' all and so it seemed the $1000 had come and been dispersed. So I sat down to think and watch the fun. And what should I see but a guy beckoning me from behind a door and I thought, 'Hell I might be able to pick up 10 bucks that way.' But lo! It was me old buddy the postal clerk and he said, 'Lissen, sister, I saved out your $75 for you.' Chiskey-wisky, I could have kissed the gink."

Fearing the country might be on the brink of a revolution, she advised Eddie, "You better keep the car filled with oil and gas so if worse comes to worst we could head back to the prairie country." Ironically, Eddie and Russell had taken the train down to Washington to witness FDR's inauguration, an act that would have seemed anathema to his uncles. The elder Faulkners were rigidly Republican and certain that Roosevelt would lead the country to ruin. Eddie himself would soon adopt their views, eventually becoming a stubborn, almost reactionary, Republican.

Everywhere she looked, people were worried about money. She knew that Bert and Dick confided in Eddie about the Woodmen, so she broke out of her usual flippant tone to ask, in a letter in late March, "How are things at home—financially?" The answer was: uncertain. Within days of Virginia's letter, Eddie received another from Bert filled with concerns about cash flow and the company's survival. "This banking holiday has been considerable of a jolt to us as you appreciate," he wrote. The company had thousands of dollars in checks, but with many banks still not reopened or only operating on a limited basis, he confided, "There will be lots of this money that we will never be able to recover." Though he assured Eddie that "everyone here in the office is working in splendid harmony," Bert closed the letter with a confession that revealed just how insecure he felt at the helm of the Woodmen: "I have certainly needed you during these stormy times and have almost been on the verge, or at least tempted, to ask you to come home."

Soon after, Virginia wrote Eddie a letter begging to abandon her own studies. "Your account of your scholastic successes is gall and wormwood to this poor creature trapped and helplessly shuttled back and forth between books, professors, libraries, reading notes, and other units of education. Oh, MON FRERE, why did you let me do it?" She was clearly uneasy about the cost of another year at Radcliffe: "Who knows from where the next dollar will come—who, indeed, knows what a dollar *is*?"

Virginia was pleased to have received a request from the editor of the *Junior League Magazine* for a photo that would appear in the July issue. She assured Eddie that Bachrach's studio in New York, then the East Coast's premier portrait photography studio, would give her the photo for free "since it's for a tony mag." She also knew that it would raise her visibility as a writer among the wealthy and influential women who read the magazine.

The photograph shows us how far Virginia had traveled in her development since arriving in Rome almost three years before. Her babyfat cheeks are gone. Her expression is not just serious but intent. She knows she is going somewhere. But even more apparent is the fact that Virginia had chosen a model who wasn't like conventional notions of what a young woman should look like.

Anyone familiar with the literary world in 1933 would have recognized in an instant who she was emulating: Radclyffe Hall. Hall was an English novelist who lived openly as a lesbian. In 1929 her novel *The Well of Loneliness* had been branded obscene for its depiction of a lesbian romance. In the publicity surrounding the controversy, photographs of Hall appeared in U.S. newspapers. In them, Hall wears a man's suit, dress shirt, and tie. Her hair is short, parted and neatly combed, like a man's. In the words of biographer Diana Souhami, to those who disapproved she was "clearly lesbian, a decadent apostle of hideous and most loathsome vices, a moral derelict and a poisoner of souls." Like Hall, Virginia wears a mannish suit jacket, dress shirt, and tie. Her hair is short, parted, combed to the side. She looks androgynous, not feminine.

She knew she was making a statement. The other nine women on the two-page spread wear dresses, jewelry, bobbed hair. Anyone would find their eyes drawn directly to Virginia's photo, out of place in a magazine intended for women of education and social status. Anyone coming across that photo would remember Virginia Faulkner.

Virginia spent the spring unsettled. She was anxious about exams, but she was also unsure what her own next step should be. She'd registered for another year at Radcliffe but hadn't reserved a dorm room. She and Florence Meyer were now playing tennis every morning. Florence's graduation was one of the reasons Virginia dreaded the idea of returning to Radcliffe: She would have to make friends again from scratch, and given her opinion of her classmates, the prospect for that seemed grim.

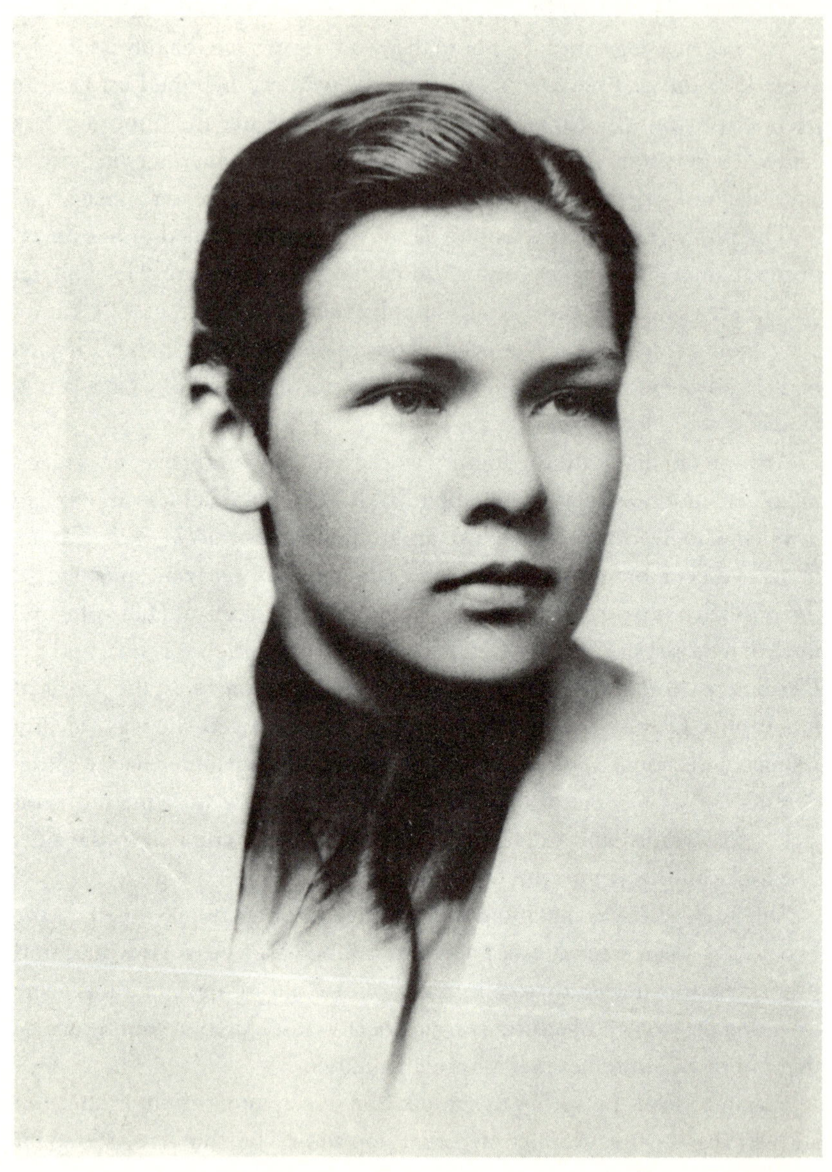

Fig. 7. Virginia's Bachrach portrait, 1933. Courtesy of Bachrach Photography.

She had several alternatives to consider. She thought of working for the National Municipal League or for the Institute of Public Administration. Both were run by men with daughters in her class. Evelyn Merriman had invited her on a trip to England, but Virginia feared England would be too much like Boston. What she really wanted to do was "get back to Wopland [Italy]," and though she understood that was impractical, she cautioned that "you know when I'm not happy what a strain it is on us all"—which suggests Eddie had already seen Virginia in her black moods. And she had a small but growing stack of manuscripts. "I have been doing no little creative work," she had told Eddie in March, and since then she had finished thirty pages of a novel set in Rome.

A week later, she'd made up her mind: "I don't think I'm going to come back to Ratcliffe [*sic*] next week." If Eddie insisted she stay in school until she was twenty-one (March 1934), then she proposed to go to Nebraska Wesleyan in Lincoln. To make her feelings clear, she scribbled across the bottom on the letter, "FIRE ESCAPE: THIS WAY OUT!"

The problem was: out to where? "My feet are mates but not yet pointed in a single direction," Virginia confided to Eddie. Radcliffe had given her "a chance to look around, get about, and begin to figure some things out that slipped by in the rush of earlier days." But she desperately wanted to have time to talk over her options with him. They both had ambitions, they both felt they had the potential to do great things. But first, she wrote, "We've got first to arrive in our respective lines."

Yet another option arose when she joined Florence on a visit to her family's country home in Mount Kisco, New York. Eugene Meyer had decided to buy the *Washington Post*. He had made a secret offer of $5 million to its then-owner Edward "Ned" McLean in 1929, but McLean refused it. Now, due to McLean's profligate spending and alcoholism, the paper was being put up for sale at a bankruptcy auction on June 4, 1933. Meyer was intent on placing the winning bid.

Years of losses and staff cuts had devastated the *Post*'s reputation. Meyer knew he would have to bring in talent to regain lost subscribers and revive ad revenues, and when he sat down with Florence and Virginia on the terrace at Mount Kisco, he quickly saw the potential of turning Virginia's stream of quips into material for the paper's lighter sections—society, culture, the Sunday magazine. Before the young women left, Meyer offered

Virginia a job as a reporter—if he got the *Post*. When she wrote to Eddie about the opportunity, she said it was the best bet "in the long run": "It's just beginning and is located in the city that should be the journalistic hub of the country."

Once her exams were out of the way, Virginia planned to travel to Philadelphia and then ride back to Lincoln with Eddie and Russell. "Thank God I won't have so much to pack as most of my clothes are rotting on my back and can be given to the flames," she informed him. A few days before she checked out of her dorm, Virginia learned that Eugene Meyer had bought the *Post*. She had a way out now and put little effort into her Radcliffe farewells. Her last message to Eddie was a telegram sent on June 7: "ARRIVE TOMORROW SIX FIFTEEN PM. EXPECT A CORPSE."

Washington

Virginia's first task upon arriving in Lincoln was to help with Eddie's wedding. Eddie and Jean Rathburn had decided to get married back in 1930 when Virginia was still in Rome, but in keeping with his habit of careful planning, Eddie had postponed making the engagement formal until he was sure he was going to finish Wharton and come back to join the Woodmen. Eddie couldn't have found a better match. Jean Rathburn was beautiful, stylish, sophisticated. Her father, Merle, was a respected banker, her mother, Jessie, a leading society hostess. Jean was also smart, a better student than Eddie, in fact, and for many years after their graduation ran the Mortar Board academic society chapter for UNL.

Virginia hosted a lavish luncheon for Jean and fifty friends and relatives and stood as one of Jean's bridesmaids. Russell Mousel was Eddie's best man. Eddie and Jean took a meandering honeymoon journey through Chicago, Montreal, Boston, and New York City, arriving in Philadelphia just in time for his final year at Wharton.

When she wasn't busy helping with the wedding, Virginia was writing. She turned the thirty pages she'd brought back from Radcliffe into a full-length novel she referred to—jokingly?—as *Written to Sell.* In August, she sent the manuscript to publisher Alfred A. Knopf and received an encouraging reply from editor Louis Kronenberger a few weeks later. Virginia felt it imperative that she push Knopf for a firm answer, so she arranged a meeting in New York after the wedding. At the same time, she contacted Eugene Meyer about the *Post* job he'd offered back in May.

As she wrote Eddie on her way back from New York, the trip was "a bang-up, rip-snorting, gosh-danged enormous success." She'd had a good talk with Kronenberger, whom she described as "youthful, attractive, and not noticeably Yid." (Virginia sometimes referred to Jews as "Yids" even though her grandfather Louis Meyer had been Jewish.) She said that Kronenberger thought the book was "absolutely cock-eyed" and had encouraged her to make it more so in her revision.

Eugene Meyer was even more enthusiastic, apologizing, in fact, for not contacting her sooner. "He kept up a positive monologue for well-nigh an hour, going into the entire newspaper siteration [*sic*]." Meyer didn't say what her job or salary would be, however, explaining that it was up to Eugene MacLean, the paper's general manager. All Virginia needed to do was notify MacLean a week or so before she planned to arrive.

Virginia told Eddie that she would leave for DC after she'd revised the novel based on Kronenberger's feedback. Once back in Lincoln, she made quick work of her revision, and in early November she was off to Washington. She did not go alone. Uncle Bert had insisted that she take along someone to help (and possibly report back to him): Linda Schroeder, who'd been working as a housekeeper for Bert and Eugenia for several years. Linda was ten years older than Virginia and would help check her wilder inclinations. Linda agreed to work for expenses only—"until I hear that my book has been taken or am getting a decent salary," Virginia informed Eddie.

The two women arrived in Washington DC to find a city undergoing its biggest change since the end of the Civil War. The status quo solidified through the unbroken string of Republican administrations since 1921—Harding, Coolidge, and Hoover—was being overturned by the Democrat Franklin Roosevelt's New Deal. Roosevelt had inherited a nation in its greatest economic crisis. Within the first hundred days of Roosevelt's taking office, thirteen major new laws were enacted, establishing an alphabet soup of agencies designed to stem the wave of bankruptcies, foreclosures, and unemployment that had begun with the stock market crash of 1929. Ripples of the changes being made by Roosevelt were even being felt in the bedrock of Washington society: the long-term residents whose antediluvian attitudes had earned them the nickname of "cave dwellers," who regarded elected representatives (including the president) and federal officials as little more than transients.

Virginia would later mock the cave dwellers in a comic piece published in the *Post* in March 1934. In "The Social Revolution," she imagines a time when society dames have taken over the presidency and Cabinet, Congress been replaced by the Junior League, and the two political parties turned into the White-Ties and the Black-Ties. A messenger arrives at the White House to announce that a revolution has broken out. "The public be damned," President Hope Hopkins Chace replies. She—Virginia was one of the first to put a woman in the White House—offers to let the people have their "silly old country" if they leave Newport, Palm Beach, and Southampton as fortified cities, remarking that, in the end, "the Riviera is the only possible America."

But Virginia's sensibilities were closer to those of the cave dwellers than those of Roosevelt's reformers. She was not one of FDR's supporters. "There's always the hope somebody will wipe out Franklin Delano before the fourth of March," she wrote Eddie after his election in November 1932. She wasn't inclined to forgo her pleasures—equestrian riding, fine food, and sophisticated conversation—to start marching in the streets. While she recognized the shift that was underway, she wasn't convinced it was all for the better.

The paper Virginia was joining was also undergoing a shift. Eugene Meyer had put a new management team in place and some were skeptical whether he could make a go of it. Rival publisher Gardner Cowles warned that Washington was an afternoon paper town, catering to government workers who were able to head home as early as four thirty. As a morning paper, the *Post* didn't stand a chance. But Meyer wanted to establish the *Post* as a nonpartisan, independent voice. Ready to pay decent wages and offer job security, he was bringing in new talent—of whom Virginia was just one. And he had the benefit of coming in at the paper's lowest point. As his daughter Katharine later recalled, at the time he bought the paper, Meyer considered the *Post* "mentally, morally, physically and in every other way bankrupt."

Editor Eugene MacLean gave Virginia a hearty welcome when she arrived in mid-November and introduced her to the staff, "all of whom seemed way above average," she wrote Eddie. MacLean initially assigned her to work under Frederic Pitts, who was responsible for the *Post*'s Sunday magazine and related sections—clubs, fraternal organizations, society—and assured her she had the job for at least six months "even if I turn out as sour as a garlic pickle." "It takes that long to find out whether or not you're lousy," she explained.

Washington DC has long been notorious for its housing problems, with Congress's biannual turnover of temporary residents, "an influx of at least 5,000 to be house, clothed, fed and amused from January until adjournment," as Don Bloch wrote in the *Post* not long after her arrival. Virginia was competing with them for a place to live. Luckily, she soon found a suitable flat at the Woodley Park Towers, although the sleeping arrangements were less than ideal. Virginia slept on a foldaway bed and her maid Linda slept on a sofa bed.

Finances, on the other hand, were harder to sort out. "I'm pretty baffled about bank accounts," she wrote Eddie. "I wish you'd write pronto what to do." She had gone to open an account at the Riggs National Bank and been flummoxed: "Ye Gods! such hocus-pocus. All talk about signature cards and minimum deposits," she wrote in exasperation. While Virginia never had much appetite for business, she resented the tendency of men to exclude women from discussions of money matters. But at least she had enough money to worry about managing it. While she was deciding whether to take the taxi or the tram to work, hundreds of young women in Washington were coping with "run-down heels, stockings with gaping holes, pitiful ragged frocks . . . and the terrifying specter of starvation," according to an article published in the *Post* around this time.

Virginia threw herself into her work at the *Post*. Her first bylined pieces appeared just two weeks after she started: a review of Helen Waddell's historical novel *Peter Abelard* and a brief profile of a fellow Nebraskan Dorothy Thomas, whose first novel *Ma Jeeter's Girls* had been published that spring. But her big debut came in early December, when her story "The Last Day Before Prohibition" was splashed across the front page of the Sunday Magazine section. As she later told Eddie, she'd spent days "tramping the streets of our capitol getting dope for the story" and "encountered many birds such as the chief of police, hotel managers, and barkeeps"—not to mention "some old dodoes who are famous for doing naught but reminiscing about the old days."

Virginia's sense of humor was on display from the start. "Like good Americans," she wrote, on the last day before Prohibition took effect in 1919, "the inhabitants of Washington took things standing up—anyway they did at the beginning of the evening." Having weeks to prepare, "thoughtful individuals had begun to buy liquor in large quantities" and could be seen "wobbling homewards laden with arms, baskets, boxes, automobiles and hand carts full of bottles." Those who could not afford to be so far-sighted "had to get in their best licks during the 17 legal hours on that last legal day." Through the combined efforts of the city police and responsible federal agencies, Washington became, in the words of Stanley Walker, Prohibition's first historian, "the worst city in the country in which to obtain a drink of good liquor."

The article was linked to the imminent repeal of the Eighteenth Amendment to the Constitution, which had established Prohibition as a nationwide law. When Utah became the thirty-sixth state to ratify the repeal in December 1933, the fourteen-year "noble experiment" ended. Virginia wondered what effect the end of Prohibition would have on drinking habits. "The pre-dinner cocktail made for congeniality and patience," she wrote, and noted that wine and other forms of liquor had long been considered part of "the fine art of enjoying a meal." For her part, Virginia was more often to side not with congenial, patient consumers but serious two-fisted drinkers.

Her first social engagement in Washington, in fact, was a cocktail party. She'd been invited by Mrs. George Holmes, an acquaintance of her Aunt Pauline Howell and wife of the head of the Capital Press Bureau, which meant that Virginia got to "meet other news klucks." Her social calendar quickly filled up. She went with Agnes Meyer, Eugene's wife, and her daughter Katharine to a concert by violinist Jascha Heifetz. She saw Katherine Hepburn perform in *The Lake* at the National Theater. "The play, I may say, was loo-zey," she wrote Eddie: "A mess." She missed the biggest social event of the season for Washington journalists, however: the annual Gridiron Club dinner, where the press corps roasted the new president with a series of comic skits, was strictly a stag affair.

She did attend the National Press Club dinner a few months later, if only as Agnes Meyer's guest. "Everyone was there from Mrs. Roosevelt to Fanny Hurst . . . practically every female celebrity in America," she later wrote Eddie. Virginia was seated at a table with Agnes and Katharine Meyer, the aviatrix Amelia Earhart, and Alice Longworth—"just a bunch of the goils." After the dinner, Longworth invited the women at the table to her house where, according to Virginia, "the inimitable (alleged) Alice gave us a private view of her imitations of Mrs. Roosevelt describing her travels and a tableau called the Blue Eagle." According to one biographer, Longworth needed little encouragement to roll out her impersonation of Eleanor: "She contorted her mouth to mimic ER's prominent teeth, and copied Eleanor's high voice, ending her exclamations in a screech." Virginia took careful observation, then stored her memories away for future use. Years later, she would employ them in a withering parody of Longworth in a piece for *Town & Country*. Already developing a taste for drinking, Virginia reported the best part of the evening to Eddie: "The likker was prime."

The highlight of her first month in Washington, however, was a chance meeting with Lincoln Schuster, cofounder of the publishing firm Simon & Schuster. Schuster had dropped by to see friends on the *Post* staff and book editor Theodore Hall introduced him to Virginia, saying she'd written a novel that was about to be published by Knopf. In fact, her deal with Knopf had just fallen through. Knopf had returned her revision with a brief note stating they were no longer interested. Virginia told Schuster she was still looking for a publisher, which piqued his attention. Simon & Schuster wanted to promote young writers and were looking for books with musical themes, he explained, and asked her to send the manuscript to his office in New York. He promised to personally take charge of its consideration for publication.

The day after meeting Schuster, however, Virginia received a letter from Louis Kronenberger at Knopf saying they'd changed their minds and wanted the book again. Furious, she called Lincoln Schuster and asked for help. Schuster promised to call Kronenberger and make it clear that Virginia had taken their rejection at face value and submitted the manuscript to Simon & Schuster in good faith. "Of course, I'm off Knopf," she confided in Eddie. "You would think the bastards could make up their mind; I'd rather Schuster would publish it, but Jeez, the main thing is for one of 'em to."

Within a week, she received Simon & Schuster's feedback. "At our editorial meeting today, we gave special priority to a spirited and highly affirmative discussion of *Written to Sell*," Lincoln Schuster wrote. Christopher Fadiman, Simon & Schuster's editor in chief, followed up with a detailed set of comments. "As it stands now, it is only a semi-success," he wrote. "It begins beautifully and ends badly." The firm's readers spotted what would remain Virginia's greatest strength—and her greatest weakness: "The characters of course are just mediums for the author's astonishing wit. They all talk alike, all talk brilliantly, wittily, fancifully, sophisticatedly."

But only its main character, the pianist Marie Manfred, was anything more than a mouthpiece for Virginia.

Fadiman was optimistic about Virginia's prospects as a writer, however. "I definitely think that you are a writer, and providing *Written to Sell* is not autobiographical, there should be many more good books from your pen." Virginia took Fadiman's criticism in its most positive light. "So hot-cha!" she wrote Eddie. She figured she could make short work of the next revision—three or four days at most.

Of course, the book wasn't autobiographical. As worldly wise as Virginia might present herself, she was still a twenty-year-old whose eight months in Rome had been spent under near-continuous supervision. Her narrator and heroine, Marie Manfred, on the other hand, is a thirty-six-year-old woman considered the world's greatest classical pianist and notorious for her many romantic involvements. "It was true that any life of me without my love-affairs would make a slim volume," she admits.

The book opens as Marie, exhausted from a relentless performance schedule, rents a villa in the Alban Hills south of Rome, hoping to relax. Soon, she meets Ricardo dei Retti, a handsome nobleman with an unspecified role in Italian politics—"one of Mussolini's many left hands." Their brief, intense affair is not the stuff of first loves. Marie is mature, sophisticated, financially and emotionally independent. "I had had a good life; I liked it all," she reflects. "Gay moments and great moments, honor and wealth and friends and lovers; good things to eat and stirring things to do, yes, many things to remember, people and possessions to treasure." This is not a list a typical twenty-year-old would draw up. Ricardo, too, is a man of experiences and commitments. "I am one of those poor devils who must always be running back and forth between Piazza Venezia [where Mussolini kept his office] and the Senate House."

Retitled *Friends and Romans* at Fadiman's suggestion, the novel depicts Mussolini's rule as Virginia would have witnessed it during her time at Miss Moxley's. About a month after her arrival, Mussolini celebrated the eighth anniversary of the march on Rome by which he seized control of the government with the help of thirty thousand of his black-shirted followers. Yet signs of dissent could still be seen throughout the country. Trials of anti-Fascist conspirators were a regular event: a group backed by

Yugoslavia one month; an assassination plot against Mussolini by retired military officers the next.

That unsettled nature of Italian politics is reflected in Ricardo's activities. More reactionary than revolutionary, his true master is not Mussolini but Machiavelli, his ambition "animated not so much by a love of his country as by a passion to make himself a power in Italy." Ricardo's intrigues subject him to a variety of threats. Driving his limousine one evening, Marie is stopped by a group of men hoping to give him a beating. While Ricardo is relaxing at Marie's villa, a member of her staff attempts—unsuccessfully—to assassinate him.

Though she'd collected her impressions under the watchful eye of Miss Moxley and other chaperones, Virginia manages to reproduce Italy in a convincing manner throughout the novel, incorporating all her sensory memories. The constant clangor of church bells on Sundays—"enough to club the most recalcitrant conscience into dumb, brute submission." The roads around Rome, where the trees let through such "a strange light—it is damp and green, like an enchanted wood." The scent of Italian shrubbery: "a bitter odor after the sun goes down, and at high noon when things are extremely still and not resisting the heat, everything smells wanton." The cool of marble inside a church and the wall of heat one hits when stepping out into a summer afternoon.

More remarkable, however, was how Virginia deals with a subject she would always say was "a holy mystery to me": music. Marie Manfred is a classical pianist, a woman whose decades of practice and performance has made music intrinsic to her being. She performs dozens of pieces in the book, demonstrating that Virginia's own listening was broad and eclectic. Not just Debussy, Mozart, and Chopin, but Liszt's *Années de pèlerinage* and Brahms's *Ballades*, which "makes you think of shining trumpet notes and the arched necks of cavalry chargers." She imbues Marie's approach to performance with the same *sprezzatura* she took as armament herself. Critics praise Marie, in fact, for possessing "none of that almost naïve reverence for the great musical prophets which is noticeable about other virtuosi."

Ricardo, however, is utterly uninterested in music. He dismisses her achievements: "You may have learned to play the piano very well, Marie, but you have not yet learned to be a woman." As much as she feels attracted to Ricardo, Marie at first rejects the idea that she might give up her career for him. "How do women who are not concert pianists occupy themselves?" she wonders. "Sew? Well, perhaps. Read?" "I'm neither maid, nor wife, nor widow, nor *donna mantenuta* [kept woman]!" she informs Ricardo.

Unfortunately, the last is, in fact, his intent. "I should love to marry you," he tells Marie, "but it's impossible. . . . A public man may not have a public wife." In any case, it's also impossible because she's not Italian. "*Moglie e buoi ai paese suoi*"—"Women and cattle from your own country"—is his principle. So, all she can be is a mistress: "I shall honor you and take care of you, Marie. I shall install you in a house . . ." "I am not," Marie replies, "A modern convenience."

Throughout *Friends and Romans*, Virginia plants seeds for what would become her second novel, *The Barbarians*. She gives Marie Manfred an extensive backstory, focusing her time spent studying piano in Paris in the early 1920s. There Marie lived as part of a loose band of artists and musicians who referred to themselves as the Barbarians. Although she never refers to the Barbarians in anything but a passing manner, we meet most of its main characters: Sarkesso, a painter; Jill Johnson, a sculptress; Tavo von Keinelohe, an exiled German nobleman; and Reagan Nicholl, a writer. Virginia may have been enticing the reader's curiosity about the Barbarians in a deliberate attempt to stimulate demand for a second novel. If so, she succeeded, as Simon & Schuster was to publish *The Barbarians* just nine months after *Friends and Romans*.

Virginia's work at the *Post* kept her in Washington through the Christmas 1933 holidays, but she was relishing her exposure to the newspaper business. Early on she wrote Eddie, "I am getting along swell on my job, and while I was never one to snap-judge I think it is the best business in the world." Eugene MacLean decided to make her assignment to the magazine permanent. The magazine didn't offer much room for innovation—of its usual sixteen pages, half were devoted to regular features: art, books, bridge, the crossword puzzle, and a full page of cartoons.

Still, Virginia convinced Pitts to include a new column, "Stroller's Luck," odd bits of observation inspired by the "Talk of the Town" section of the *New Yorker* magazine: a sketch of a scissors grinder; a report on the disappearance of cigar store Indian statues; an anecdote about a streetcar conductor. Though its title changed to "Footsteps and Footnotes" the following week and later to "Odyssey" ("This modern Ulysses, wandering over and through the highways and byways of the District of Columbia"), the column was a hit with the *Post*'s owner. "Pa Meyer stopped to tell me how much he loved all my stuff—and both he and MacLean told Pitts it was the best magazine the *Post* had ever put out," she told Eddie. Virginia wasn't shy to claim credit: "You saw how much of it had sparkled off my typewriter—so surely you have the wit to draw your own conclusions." She was less pleased, however, with MacLean's suggestion that she write a serial for the paper "in my spare moments." "The great lousy bastard," she remarked to Eddie.

The idea stayed with her, though. In the first issue of 1934, the *Post*'s Sunday magazine included a piece written by Virginia titled "Our Own Washington Letter." It took the form of a chatty letter from a fictional feather-brained society woman named Penelope to her friend Coralie in New York. An amusing bit of fluff, it gave Virginia an opportunity to poke fun at Washington's politics and pretenses. Ever since hearing the story of George Washington chopping down the cherry tree, Penelope explained, "I have been dying to come here, because I have always heard that ever since then practically everybody in Washington has had the axe out for somebody."

"Our Own Washington Letter" became a regular feature of the magazine, appearing for the next seventeen weeks—longer, in fact, than Virginia was to remain in DC. The letters allowed Virginia to refine a talent for one-liners that would later make her quotes popular with columnists. Recounting a costume party she attended, Penelope wrote of one particularly scanty outfit, "I mean it was one of those costumes that leave nothing in doubt except a young lady's character." She clearly loved to explore the comic possibilities of Penelope's malapropisms (confusing Philistines and Philippines, for example) and attempts at profundity, concocting such cliché sandwiches as "I think we ought to take a blank slate and start from scratch at the very beginning all over again."

Virginia considered herself just as adept at straight reporting as she was at comic invention. After finishing an overview of the history of the French royalty that would appear on the front page of the magazine in February, she boasted to Eddie, "The enclosed yellow blank is for your memory book—it is my assignment for the royalty story. The rest of the material I had to get for myself. This ought to demonstrate my ingenuity." Aside from a clever line or two, however, the story is no more memorable than an undergraduate essay. She relied entirely on secondary sources, offered no original analysis, provided no compelling narrative. Although she published a few more such pieces while at the *Post*, reporting was not her forte, and she never attempted it again.

MacLean wanted more of her satirical work, but in succeeding pieces we can feel Virginia's strain in reaching for jokes. The pressure to be funny on demand began to wear on her. By April, she'd decided she'd had enough of the newspaper business. She explained her rationale in a letter to Eddie. "I doubt if I can ever make it clear to you or anyone but this is the layout: all I have been doing is high-class wisecracking in the literary world, and while it happens the world loves that now—and may for some time—still I have gone as far as I can, being a smarty." As she saw it, her work at the *Post* marked "the end of one line of development." If it were simply a matter of survival—"supporting an invalid sister, etc."—she could resign herself to continuing. But she was tired of simply "being a smarty" and sick of keeping up the pretense.

In her letter, Virginia reasons, pleads, reassures, both confiding to Eddie and arguing her case:

> I have tried to intimate since you were down in March that all was not well with me, but brothers always think that if you have a job, are fed, clothed, and free from scandal everything is oke. Well, that ain't so. And (though this isn't the main thing) I've felt so lousy for the last three weeks that I decided I wouldn't stick it any longer because I would just be doing it on acct. I was afraid of what you and the family would say. All I'm getting down here is 35 dollars a week and the jitters, and the former is not high enough for the latter—even a raise wouldn't make it high enough.

She pointed out that staying in DC without her *Post* salary was not an option. "I would have to send Linda home anyway; I can't afford either her or this expensive an apartment." And she tried to placate him. "Before you begin to rage and despair," she wrote, "I can have it [the *Post* job] back with more pay and privileges whenever I want it—IF I ever do."

Agnes Meyer had assured Virginia on this last point. Mrs. Meyer had been forewarned by her daughter Florence, who was pursuing a career as a dancer and more receptive to putting artistic freedom ahead of financial security.

Virginia informed MacLean and Pitts of her decision and they relayed the message to Eugene Meyer. Both he and Agnes wanted to hold onto Virginia, if possible. Agnes met with Virginia, praised her work on the magazine, and asked if she wanted to try working in a different part of the paper. But Virginia was adamant. "Finally she saw what I was driving at," she wrote Eddie, "and agreed with me, but said for God's sake to come back when I was in the mood, and in the meanwhile to count on her like an abacus."

For a twenty-one-year-old woman with less than six months' experience as a reporter, Virginia demonstrated remarkable maturity and self-confidence with her decision. The path of least resistance would have been to continue at the *Post*. It offered her the foundation of a paper rapidly regaining its reputation and the possibility of expanding to a national market if her work was picked up for syndication. She was turning her back on these for the uncertain prospects of an as-yet unpublished novel and a few words of encouragement from editors in New York. But she knew she had to take the risk. "If I'm ever really going to be any good," she wrote Eddie, "I'll have to give up this smart, know-it-all line for something a little kinder and truer."

Virginia also knew she would go forward without a chaperone. At first, she had enjoyed the luxury of having Linda as a maid, but by now the glow had worn off. "I will be glad to get rid of Linda," Virginia confided to Eddie. The tension between the two reached a breaking point when Linda began to share Virginia's taste in liquor. "I invested four dollars in a bottle of Scotch (for medicinal purposes) and was treating it like liquid gold—but Linda didn't." Her annoyance bubbling over, Virginia put Linda on the train back to Lincoln, then followed a few days later.

Virginia had no intention of staying long—just enough to start on *The Barbarians* and decide what she was going to do in New York. Lincoln, she wrote Eddie, was nothing more than "a pleasant vacuum." If she had any doubts about moving on, her uncles quickly erased them. "I was scarcely off the train before I was pounced on by Dick and Bert," she reported. They were upset with her for quitting the *Post*, upset with Eddie for spending too much money in Philadelphia, upset about Eddie's plans for the house on South Street. Dick complained that the place was too expensive to heat and they both thought Eddie was nuts for proposing to pay off the remaining mortgage so that he and Jean could live there once he graduated from Wharton.

Virginia's first letter to Eddie from Lincoln echoes the one she wrote as her time at Radcliffe was coming to an end. Then, she had reflected on their respective ambitions and quoted his remark about having to compete in the world: "There seem to be so damn many people as good as we are." "Want to talk it all over with you this summer," she'd written. Now, however, she was more insistent, "I wish I could talk to you straight sometime when sober, so you would pay a little attention to what I say."

Having not just survived but succeeded in her first attempt to make it on her own, she was ready to stand her ground. "I know that you will always think of me as a brainless wonder who gets the breaks, but that's not your fault—it's simply the result of being my elder brother and taking things seriously." She took some pleasure in seeing Eddie bear the brunt of the family's criticism for a change: "You know now a little bit, maybe, how I have felt these 21 years with all of you." And she faulted Eddie for being one of her most vocal critics: "picking at me, pointing out the error of my ways, and generally making it impossible for me to share any of my enthusiasms."

Yet in the end she wanted to assure him of her loyalty. As she had ever since their father's death, Virginia considered Eddie her one true ally: "Whatever is mine is thine and always will be, and as I am just about one jump from being in the money these aren't empty words." Whatever disagreements the two might have, she knew she had in Eddie someone she could count on as a bedrock of support. She would need it years later as she found herself struggling with alcoholism, depression, and increasing disappointment in her life as a writer.

Bert and Dick's concerns about Eddie calmed down when he graduated with honors from the Wharton School and headed back to Lincoln with Jean. Virginia wrote that everyone was "putting up pickles and dressing oxen and stuffing chickens and twisting crepe paper and dying bunting so that you shall not want at the feast." She was more concerned to prepare Eddie for the shock of seeing Nebraska suffering the effects of the first of the three droughts that devastated the ecology and economy of midwestern America, creating the Dust Bowl. "You wouldn't know the breadbasket of America," she warned him. "Unless there is rain in the next three days there is not a chance of crops in the Midwest." Even on the streets of Lincoln, "dirt in some places is drifted like snow as high as the fences." Worse, there was talk—"and more than talk"—about the possibility of famine.

From Virginia, however, the news was all good. "My affairs are simply booming," she wrote. She'd received a letter from *Vanity Fair* asking for short stories and sending a check to pay for her to fly to New York. *Town & Country* wanted her to join its staff. *The Barbarians* was progressing. "I work at it night and day," she told Eddie. Lincoln Schuster had written saying that *Friends and Romans* was in final preparation before printing and asking when she might have the new book ready. Her prospects of making a go of it in New York seemed sure and she planned to leave before the middle of July. She was ready to take the next step in her career: writer.

Time for a reunion and talk with Eddie was brief. He and Jean arrived back in Lincoln at the end of May; barely a month later, they were hosting Virginia's farewell party. The first copies of *Friends and Romans* reached Lincoln stores on July 12, 1934; the next day, she wrote to Eddie from New York in triumph: "Well, I have arrived!"

Before leaving Lincoln, Virginia did one last job for the *Post*. At Fred Pitts's suggestion, she wrote a review of *Friends and Romans* for the Sunday magazine. She assured her readers that, "confronted with the opportunity—which seems vaguely indecent—of reviewing my own novel, I have decided that starkest honesty is not only the best but the most practicable policy." She acknowledged that "whatever nice things I say about the book will be taken with a grain of salt as large as Lot's wife after she looked back."

As she had learned to do, she presented herself as relaxed, confident, and slightly self-mocking. "*Friends and Romans* isn't one of those books you flaunt on parlor tables (although you can if you want to) when entertaining the mightier minds," she admitted. But she was still proud of her work. "Quite a few exciting things happen—for example, an attempted assassination and a successful seduction." The seduction, she thought, was "handled so as to offend no one and yet be explicit enough so that no one will be in doubt as to what actually took place." In the end, it was all just a bit of fun—"and you can't beat fun," she concluded. It would take her years to figure out that fun alone wasn't enough to satisfy her own ambitions as a writer.

New York City

If publicity was a factor in Virginia's planning her arrival in New York City, she couldn't have timed it better. *Friends and Romans* arrived in all the bookstores by the middle of July and reviews had begun to pop up in book sections. And she arrived in style, riding with Pauline and Thomas Howell in their chauffeured limousine from Chicago and spending her first nights at the Ritz.

One of the first reviews was that of syndicated critic Hershell Brickell. His remarks set the template for many that followed. Virginia had sprinkled epigrams "with a lavish hand," but he found it "genuinely amusing." She couldn't have asked for a better closing line: "The novel is for sophisticated tastes: of its kind there has been nothing more enjoyable this year." Another syndicated reviewer, Theodore Hart, was slightly tougher, chiding Virginia for her "enthusiasm for puns and a regrettable weakness for the indefinite second person pronoun." But he expressed his fear that having started at such a high level of sophistication, "it is difficult to say what characteristics Miss Faulkner will develop when with advancing years comes naïveté." The *Omaha World Herald* called Virginia a "high-browed Colette." The *ne plus ultra* of compliments for the worldliness of Virginia's writing came from the brief notice in that benchmark of urbanity, the *New Yorker*, which saluted the book's "*je-m'en-fichisme* [the French equivalent of sprezzatura]" "Brother, I'm eating it up!" she confided to Eddie.

The press loved the novelty of Virginia publishing a book at the age of twenty-one. The *Literary Digest* gave her lead billing in a feature titled "They Stand Out from the Crowd" that appeared not long after *Friends and Romans*. "Seldom has a first novel been written with higher good humor or a more disarming wit," wrote *Time* magazine's reviewer. "If you were choosing an author to write about a few weeks in the life of the world's most famous pianist, aged 37, a woman who took her lovers in her stride," asked another, "would you select a girl of 21, educated in Lincoln and the state university of Nebraska?"

The *Lincoln Star* celebrated its hometown's newest author's success with a feature in late July that sampled the most positive reviews. "Virginia Faulkner's Saucy First Novel Wins Acclaim of Critics" read the prominent headline. Earlier, the *Omaha World Herald*'s reviewer had asked: "One wonders what the people of Lincoln . . . will think of this book. Will they claim Miss Faulkner among their great ones, as they have the impeccable General Pershing? Or will they groan in their misery . . . ?" If the columns of Lincoln's newspapers accurately represent the feelings of most Lincolnites, Virginia shot straight to the status of favorite daughter. In the months after *Friends and Romans* came out, every accomplishment great and small was worth a mention. Her photo in *Town & Country* alongside other young women with acclaimed first novels; her photo in the Junior League's magazine. By October, the *Lincoln Star*'s anonymous society columnist had to apologize, "We hope you're not tired of hearing about Virginia Faulkner," when reporting that *Friends and Romans* was among the top ten lending library rentals in the country. To Eddie, however, she joked that the chief complaint of Lincoln's intellectuals was that the book had no pictures.

H. Bond Bliss, in the *Miami Herald*, was one of the few reviewers whose complaint was not with the relentlessness of Virginia's wisecracking but with her failure to realize her artistic potential. He called upon her to stop "dishing out such intellectual dessert and . . . start serving the substantial fare." It was as if he had read that soul-searching letter to Eddie: "If I'm ever really going to be any good, I'll have to give up this smart, know-it-all line for something a little kinder and truer." The problem, as she soon learned, was that the world couldn't get enough of her smart, know-it-all line and was willing to pay well for it.

Editors H. J. Whigham of *Town & Country* and Harry Payne Burton of *Cosmopolitan* both invited Virginia for interviews in hopes she would agree to provide stories for their magazines. Lacking an agent, she looked to Clifton Fadiman for advice. Fadiman was now dividing his time between Simon & Schuster and the *New Yorker*, where he was the new book editor and in a position to know everyone in the publishing business. He cautioned her to focus on finishing the second novel and avoid becoming a one-hit wonder. And he passed his informal client along to the agent he trusted most: his brother Bill, then working for Leland Hayward's agency.

In September, Max Schuster took Virginia and Florence Meyer out for "dinner, drinks, theater, and all the trimmings." Schuster had taken Virginia on as his unofficial ward and was arranging dinners where he could show off his newest author's incisive repartee. Virginia provided something New York's literati was dying for: fresh quips. As one columnist put it, "Talk about a mental cocktail in a dry and thirsty land—Faulkner can furnish them in deliriously fast succession, and never repeat herself."

Schuster introduced Virginia to another Simon & Schuster author whose first book, *The Unpossessed*, he'd published earlier that year. Tess Slesinger was a New York native who'd been active in leftist political and literary circles. Her marriage to Herbert Solow, an activist, had ended in divorce and Slesinger had satirized Solow and his fellow intellectuals in her novel. Slesinger took Virginia to Greenwich Village to show her how New York's bohemians lived. Virginia was not impressed. She said they visited "poets and such lice" and she later reported to Eddie that the Village was "just like a large privy."

Yet Virginia's New York debut was not without shadows. Among the letters in Eddie's papers are four on Hotel Bedford letterhead written by Evelyn Merriman, Virginia's teacher and chaperone from Miss Moxley's school in Rome. She had come down to New York for a visit in early August and found Virginia upset, so distraught, in fact, that she wired Eddie to raise an alarm and beg him to call his sister. The first letter asks Eddie to apologize for the telegram: "We had a stormy night and I was alarmed at her state of mind." Not having placed any stories yet and with the advance for *Friends and Romans* running out, Virginia was afraid her plan to launch her career as a writer was failing before it started. "Waiting for regular work is getting on her nerves," Merriman wrote.

This letter is followed by another, written later the same day. "I fear that neither my note of this morning nor my answer to your telegram may be perfectly clear." Virginia had come to Merriman at three o'clock that morning in "a desperate state of mind." She had decided that the only way to solve her money worries and convince Eddie that she would be able to settle in New York was to marry Russell Mousel—and she had just sent Eddie a telegram to that effect.

The flurry of messages got Eddie's attention. "By the time you telephoned," Evelyn Merriman wrote the next day, "Virginia was awake and thinking more clearly and it gave her the greatest relief and pleasure to talk to you." As she interpreted the situation, Virginia was finding it difficult to keep up her usual blasé, self-assured front. "She says you think she is happy. I hope I am not making a mistake in telling you something about her real state of mind."

She diagnosed the source of Virginia's anxieties: "For a girl of her temperament, the loss of her parents is tragic in a special and intense way." Merriman had, after all, been with Virginia when she learned that her father had died, had put her on the train back to Lincoln, had been the one adult Virginia could look to for comfort and support at that time. "She talks of her parents so often and is feeling now that she belongs nowhere." In a statement that would prove prescient twenty years later, she wrote, "If she could be contented in Lincoln, she would rather be there than anywhere."

When Virginia next wrote Eddie, she had regained her confidence and brushed off the incident as a trifle: "About the Russ episode: please, not so much sound and fury. It was a mere fit of whimsy—just my sole effort to solve the New York housing problem." In fact, she shifted some of the blame to him: "I thought you were so nuts for me to get hitched." She neglected to mention she'd promised Evelyn Merriman that she would stop drinking for three months.

Soon after, Russell sent Eddie a letter that attempted even more strenuously to minimize the matter. Again, it was chocked up to a housing problem. "The situation had become so difficult for us at that stage of the game," he explained, "that the old logic that two can live as cheaply as one—you know the 'two by two' style inaugurated by Noah and carried on by you [by marrying Jean]—over-influenced us." So, like Virginia, Russell suggested that it was really Eddie's fault. "We neither had a notion of doing it until your consent arrived." In fact, Russell tried to argue, "Virginia and I were both thinking of you"—although he acknowledged that "the drinks may have been a bit strong." If all this weren't enough to strain Eddie's goodwill, Russell closed by asking for a credit reference to a Manhattan haberdashery where he had run up a considerable bill. Whether their friendship survived this episode is unclear: This is the last letter from Russell Mousel in Eddie's papers.

Word soon made the rounds that this new arrival from the cultural wasteland of the Midwest could hold her own over a cocktail as ably as any veteran of the Algonquin roundtable. Though the Depression and Prohibition reduced the roar of New York nightlife from its peak in the 1920s, there was no shortage of customers at the more exclusive restaurants—Henri's, 21, Jack Dempsey's—or the Harlem nightclubs to which people headed after midnight. And though leading figures of café society like Robert Benchley and Dorothy Parker had begun to slow their pace, a younger generation was carrying on their tradition of hard drinking, club hopping, and nonstop talk.

One was the elegant young Virginian, Joseph Bryan III. From a family of peerless Bluegrass pedigree, he'd graduated from Princeton and, after a few years as a reporter in Richmond, Virginia, had come to New York to work for *Town & Country* as an assistant editor. Bryan would have been happy to encourage Virginia's drinking: While in Richmond, he had organized a group calling itself the Crusaders that campaigned for the end of Prohibition. Bryan, who was tapped to take over as editor, was in a perfect position to advance both Virginia's social life and professional career. At *Town & Country* and later at the *Saturday Evening Post*, he supplied Virginia with regular commissions for yet another comic short story or satirical piece.

Bryan knew everyone one worth knowing. Through him, Virginia was introduced to some of New York's most indulgent debauchées: Libby Holman, a singer who'd had her start as one of Polly Adler's call girls; Lucius Beebe, a gossip columnist, closeted homosexual, and public snob; and Woolworth heir Jimmy Donahue, a gay man who protected himself by posing as the city's most eligible bachelor. Most notorious was actress Tallulah Bankhead, whose appetite for drinking, smoking, and sexual affairs made her the worst person for Virginia to set her pace by. Tallulah—no one ever referred to her by her last name—was openly promiscuous, frank about her attraction to both women and men, and may have led Virginia to consider seriously where her own desires lay.

Despite her hectic social life, Virginia put her best effort into finishing her novel, now called *The Barbarians*, writing over a hundred pages in the space of three weeks. She was aided, she later joked, by a typewriter with no backspace key. By early November, she was able to send a manuscript to Clifton Fadiman and turn her attention to the stories for *Cosmopolitan* and the *Herald Tribune*. Fadiman's feedback was prompt and brief. The *Saturday Evening Post* was interested in serializing it; but first, she needed to "de-gag it a little."

The succinct correspondence between Simon & Schuster and Virginia about *The Barbarians* illustrates the constant tension between artistic values and commercial interests that is the reality of life in the publishing industry. Had Virginia followed Fadiman's advice and cut back on the gags, she would have struggled to know when to stop. Once again, wisecracking dialogue represented at least 90 percent of the book. Unlike *Friends and Romans*, however, there was scarcely the skeleton of a plot upon which the smart talk could hang. Fadiman knew it was a weak book. But second novels are often weak compared to glittering debuts, and the sales of *Friends and Romans* showed there was a ready market for Virginia's brand of humor. So, they took the book.

But the truth is, *The Barbarians* is not so much a novel as the pencil shavings from *Friends and Romans*. Instead of a protagonist—Marie Manfred—there was a cast of supporting players—the Barbarians, a loosely knit gang of artists, writers, performers, and groupies, many of them making return appearances from *Friends and Romans*. Instead of a plot, there was a series of episodes even more loosely knit than the cast.

The Barbarians takes place in 1922 and opens in the Left Bank apartment of Sakesso, a painter of "slatternly nudes whose thick thighs and popping bosoms were heavily daubed with green highlights." We proceed to be introduced to the rest of the Barbarians, so-called merely because "We don't have such awfully good manners"—which suggests that Virginia had not yet been exposed to the sins that bohemians could actually commit. The blond German count, Tavo von Keinelohe, is vacuuming the floor in a top hat and a pair of pants. Jill, a pretty American sculptress, crashes onto the scene and immediately pops out with a classic Virginia quip (or an attempt at one): "Gracious—*mon Dieu*! You look like a youth movement trying to grow up."

After bringing the rest of the Barbarians onto the stage—and if anything, the novel is closer to a play in construction, with scenes full of dialogue linked with stage instructions and scene changes—the band sets off for the Riviera. Once arrived on the Côte d'Azur (having traveled in a rented

Rolls Royce), they are caught up in another set of capers, all with the aim of wedding Andreas Vauban, one of their ilk, to Lise, a beautiful heiress.

Virginia may not have seen any of the infidelity comedies of Georges Feydeau (*The Flea in Her Ear*, etc.), but she managed a good imitation of one, with people sneaking in and out of hotel rooms, hiding under beds, scrambling over balconies, and fooling the unwary with the slimmest of pretenses. In the end, Lise runs off to Paris with Andreas, followed by the rest of the Barbarians and her parents in pursuit. Or rather, near the end. For, having brought her cast back to Paris, Virginia realized that to simply to marry Lise and Andreas wasn't antic enough. And so, in the last twenty-some pages of the book, Virginia has Lise kidnapped and taken off to Tunisia as a sex slave. If nothing else, it allowed her to work in local color recalled from her visit with Miss Moxley. Several heroic Barbarians set off, track down, and rescue Lise in the space of a couple of pages. Now, the two lovers can wed. A page later, the story ends.

Simon & Schuster's cover blurb promised that "there are enough epigrams here for seven books." Which was precisely the problem. Not only was the book overstuffed with wisecracks, but many of them weren't very good. Early on, starving as stereotypical artists do, the Barbarians brainstorm ways to make some quick cash: "'We might start a new religion,' said Phip moodily. 'People are always giving money to swamis and amateur messiahs who have a new god in mind.' 'That's a good idea, Phip,' said Jill eagerly. 'I know a girl down on the rue Jacob who has a Chinese studio, and she has two gongs we could borrow.' 'Two gongs don't make a rite,' said Manfred." Virginia is more concerned with getting in a punchline than with developing character or advancing plot through dialogue. In a short story, it can be amusing. In a book of over three hundred pages, it's exhausting, as reviewers were to remark.

While waiting for Simon & Schuster to release *The Barbarians*, Virginia polished off her first commercial story, "The Hate Match," for *This Week*, a syndicated magazine included in newspaper Sunday editions around the country. "The Hate Match" is a dry run for the sort of story Virginia would specialize in. Eugene Gaston is a brilliant pianist invited as guest of honor to a party at the Boston mansion of Mrs. Pell, a generous patron ("first in the arts of her countrymen"). As the guests arrive, he strikes up a conversation with a bored young woman lounging on one of the sofas, only to discover she is Drake Pell, a writer and Mrs. Pell's daughter: "He had no respect for the printed word, while she made little distinction between music and noise."

And so, learning each other's identity, they proceed to dismiss each other's art: "Pooh! You don't even know your A B Cs." "You don't even know your tra-la-las." This high-class form of playing the dozens continues through the party and into the following months when both return to New York. Drake wires Eugene that her party got up and left as soon as he came on stage at his first town hall recital. He writes her publisher to complain that her bestseller *No Quarter for Women* is immoral and should be banned. When they find themselves at the same nightclub, he asks her to marry him, purely in the spirit of a challenge. She accepts in the same spirit.

Drake moves into Eugene's apartment and proximity fans the flames of their mutual contempt. He cannot practice while she is typing. She gets angry when he ignores her attempts to entice him. They end up in an argument, each threatening divorce. Instead of trying to quell the dispute, two visiting friends encourage the split. Suddenly, the adversaries unite to defend their marriage. The friends depart and the curtain descends on the now-amicable newlyweds.

"The Hate Match" has the elements of dozens of stories that followed. Romance as conversational contest. Wealth and all its trappings—New York apartments, cocktail parties, celebrity, men in tuxedos and women in designer gowns. Comic complications. An ending that is closer to armistice than happiness. And oh-so much clever banter.

It was not, however, what *This Week* was looking for. "We are determined to enlist you as one of the regular authors," wrote the magazine's fiction editor in late November, "but we need to get together a little bit more on the question of what we can and can't get away with in a magazine which will have a circulation of nearly five million." Whether that get-together ever happened, *This Week* decided it couldn't get away with "The Hate Match." Bill Fadiman managed to sell the story directly to a few papers, most notably, for the folks in Lincoln, the *Omaha World Herald*.

By then, she had landed another deal. "SOLD STORY TO COSMOPOLITAN FOR FOUR HUNDRED LET US REJOICE" she wired Eddie on November 19. The story, "The Sitting-Room Safari," was her true debut in national magazine fiction—a field that at the time still represented the most lucrative form of employment for writers in America outside of Hollywood.

With this second effort, she hit upon a formula that she would go on to use in most of her magazine stories: the eternal triangle. Into the lives of Connie and Jukes Laurence—young, sophisticated, cocktail-tippling, and wealthy (but not gaudily)—descends an "other," the famed English explorer Drusilla Evans. They expect her to be mature, weathered, stout. Instead, she is young, petite, stylish. Jukes is immediately attracted and plays the host with an eagerness that Connie resents. On top of the strain of a potential rival is added the chaos of Drusilla's menagerie, which includes a rambunctious Russian wolfhound.

Patience wears thin, tempers flare, animals crash in and out of doors, but matrimony proves stronger than infidelity, particularly after Drusilla Evans is revealed to be a great fake, a world traveler who's barely set foot outside Mayfair. It's a madcap comedy of errors, in other words, balanced on the thinnest thread of plausibility, a story to be read, chuckled at, and quickly forgotten: a description that could be applied to almost every story Virginia ever sold.

Virginia came to magazine fiction when it presented authors with an irresistible combination: big money and big audiences. Weekly magazines such as the *Saturday Evening Post*, *Collier's*, and *Vanity Fair* sold hundreds of thousands of copies nationwide, and in their relentless demand for material offered now-astonishing fees to writers who could produce clever, quick-moving stories with novel plot twists or lively repartee. And it was a business in which women writers could not only compete with men but were actively sought by editors, since most of their readers were women. *Vanity Fair* editor Frank Crowninshield declared himself a "determined bigoted feminist," arguing that women "are contributing what is most original, stimulating, and highly magnetized to the literature of our day." At the same time, however, Crowninshield and his counterparts also preferred contributions that reinforced the message that wars between the sexes would always end with man and matrimony triumphant.

In Lincoln's eyes, Virginia was now a celebrity: a bestselling book, stories coming out in national magazines, dinners with writers and actresses. The *Nebraska State Journal* wrote in late November asking her for a note on what she had been doing recently, part of a special holiday feature surveying the activities of famous Nebraskan expats. "I'll bet they would!" she retorted on the letter, forwarding it to Eddie for his amusement. Though she wrote "NUTS!" and drew a heart around it, she did provide the letter as requested.

She apologized that "I have nothing gaudy to report": She was too busy writing. More magazine stories were in the works. *The Barbarians* would be coming out soon. Her plans, she wrote, were vague. "I suppose I will start on another book soon" or "go to Europe in the spring." She closed with a salutation that managed to dismiss the paper, Lincolnites, and herself at a stroke: "Deprive none of your readers of my holiday greetings if you think they are at all anxious for them."

Despite the sprezzatura of her note, Virginia was still struggling to establish herself. Frank Miles, a Broadway producer, had bought the rights to adapt *Friends and Romans* for the theater, but wouldn't commit to bringing Virginia on as playwright. (Miles never managed to stage a production, despite repeated attempts over the next two decades.) There were reports that Tallulah Bankhead had asked Virginia to write a comedy as a star vehicle, but this never got past the cocktail napkin stage.

Chances are this was merely Tallulah's excuse to draw Virginia into her cortege as she careened on her regular rounds of Manhattan nightclubs in search of a laugh and a thrill. Virginia was a strong contender for a spot on Tallulah's wrecking crew. Her talk was fast, funny, and full of gossip—and she had already demonstrated a capacity to keep up with Tallulah's relentless drinking pace. And it would not have been past Tallulah to seduce another young thing fresh on the New York scene. Whether Tallulah played a role in the transformation or not, the coming months would show that Virginia had grown comfortable with both heavy drinking and the idea that she was not looking for a heterosexual relationship.

After a brief visit to Lincoln, in February 1935 she set off on a twelve-day cruise to the Caribbean. Her traveling companion was her fellow Simon & Schuster author Tess Slesinger. Slesinger's collection of short stories, *Time: The Present*, was queued up with *The Barbarians* for publication that spring. Virginia took to Tess. Slesinger had a sophistication and wit that was more than a front, and she'd had experiences—social activism, divorce, abortion—that Virginia had no equivalent to. Virginia refers to Slesinger as Tess in letters to Eddie and implies that the two were confidantes. There is no evidence, however, that Slesinger felt the same way. She was only the first in a series of celebrities who never seemed to remember Virginia quite as well as she remembered them.

When their ship docked in New York on March 1—Virginia's twenty-second birthday—boxes of *The Barbarian* were on their way to bookshops around the country. She expected her next mention in the news would be reviews of *The Barbarians*. Instead, she was about to be featured in papers across the country as an object of ridicule.

Though the story would be reprinted hundreds of times, the details remain sketchy. On Saturday, March 16, two weeks after her return from the cruise, Virginia was entertaining friends, including Everett Weil, the son of a New York real estate magnate, in her apartment at the Hotel La Salle. The group then decided to go for dinner to Tony's, an Italian restaurant on West Fifty-Second Street popular with the *New Yorker* crowd. Tony's was also a favorite starting point for Tallulah's club crawls. Tallulah appeared and began to cheer everyone on to round after round of drinks. Sometime around midnight, by Weil's account, he and Virginia left and headed to Harrison, a town in Westchester County about twenty-five miles north of Midtown Manhattan. They were going to get married.

Weil managed to roust the town clerk, who prepared the license and woke the Justice of the Peace, who came down to the town hall and conducted the ceremony at around 3:00 a.m. Weil then packed Virginia in the car and headed for his apartment. Virginia passed out on his bed and woke a few hours later when Weil appeared with a plate of scrambled eggs for breakfast. Hungover but conscious, she told Weil she was leaving—immediately. Downstairs, she hailed a cab and asked to be taken to a friend's, intending to get some advice on what to do next.

It might well have been to Tess Slesinger's apartment on Sheridan Square. Slesinger was one person she knew in New York who'd been through a divorce. She also called Thomas Howell in Chicago for the name of a New York attorney. Her request for annulment was filed with the state court on Monday, March 18. By then, however, the story had been passed to the Associated Press by the Harrison town clerk, who realized after the ceremony why Virginia's name seemed familiar. "Virginia Faulkner Wed" read the front-page story in the *Lincoln Journal Star*. Everett Weil was identified as a "cotton converter" based on the license application, though his primary occupation was spending his father's money. Most bizarrely, Weil was quoted as saying that "it is a marriage of intellectuals"—a statement Virginia would only have let pass if she had been, as she later testified, blind drunk.

Several reporters went in search of Virginia and located her at the Hotel La Salle. "I have nothing to say," she told them. With little else to go on, the United Press sent out a seventy-word story with that quote and an opening line about her "very unhoneymoonlike behavior." Over the next week, the story ricocheted its way across the country as a column-filler, repeating the same few facts in a hundred words or less. Morgues were mined for facts about Virginia. Someone at the *Chicago Tribune* invented two things that would have particularly irritated her: a quote describing herself as "the Shirley Temple of literature" and a mention of Gertrude Stein and Ernest Hemingway as literary influences. It would be hard to imagine two writers she would care less to be compared to.

How did Virginia feel about being held up as a national object of amusement? "I have nothing to say" is all that remains in the record. If she wrote to Eddie to explain, excuse, or complain, those letters are gone now. After months of regular appearances in the news and gossip columns, she lay low and waited.

Reviews of *The Barbarians* soon began to replace items about the wee-hours wedding. John Selby, whose column "The Literary Guidepost" was syndicated throughout the country, was delighted, calling it a book "calculated to wrench a smile from the sourest face." Virginia, he said, "writes about quite improbable people, manipulates them in a quite unreal Paris, and makes you like it." The *St. Louis Star*'s reviewer found it "excellent entertainment . . . provided simply through a great deal of brightly sophisticated chatter and stimulating situations." Margaret Wallace in the *New York Times* thought *The Barbarians* "even funnier" than *Friends and Romans*, even though its plot was "nonsense" and Virginia worked too hard at "industriously studding her pages with laughs."

As more reviews rolled in over the next weeks, critical consensus emerged. The quality of humor, most critics found, is not strained. The *Pittsburgh Post* found it "just a shade too self-conscious, the brilliant epigrams a trifle too forced." In the *New York Herald Tribune*, David Tilden wrote that the wit that shone in *Friends and Romans* "suffers the embarrassment of being all dressed with no very important place to go." Of all the reviewers, only

William Soskin in the *San Franscisco Examiner* considered what this tendency might mean for Virginia's future work. "Miss Faulkner, I understand, is now at work on a long, serious novel. . . . If she gives her epigrammatic talent a little rest, it may be all to the good."

Mentions of a third novel were to appear from time to time in the next few years. Whether it was long and serious or short and comic, we will never know. Everything she published in the coming years would either be short stories like "The Hate Match" or sketches like the Penelope features in the *Washington Post*. And those, too, would be consistently overcrowded with wisecracks. The smart, know-it-all line was already Virginia's public persona; and now it was becoming her trademark as a writer.

The New York Supreme Court granted Virginia's annulment application in mid-May, enabling newspapers to revive the story, the filing supplying more details. According to Virginia's statement, she had drunk at least fifteen Scotch highballs before getting into the car with Weil. Of the ceremony with the justice of the peace, her application states, "I was wholly unable to understand the nature of it by reason of my complete intoxication." Her only memory was of being awoken by Weil in his apartment and fleeing moments later.

"Writer Blames Drink for Marriage" was the headline supplied by the United Press with its wire story, but the *New York Daily News* reveled in the comic potential, splashing their story with a photo of Virgina and the headline "HIGHBALL ELOPEMENT SCOTCHED BY BRIDE." Others were less clever and blunter: "Drunk at Wedding, Annulment Granted"; "ELOPES IN FOG, WEDS IN HASTE; NOW IS SINGLE." The final insult was to come months later from the Library of Congress, which attributed the copyrights to *Friends and Romans* and *The Barbarians* to "Mrs. Everett V. Weil."

Virginia's brief marriage may have embarrassed her family back in Lincoln, but among her sophisticated friends in New York, she could wear it as a badge of honor: she had managed to remain erect in front of a justice of the peace while blackout drunk. Sterling North and Carl Kroch, who were putting together a collection of cocktail recipes from well-known writers, *So Red the Nose, or Breath in the Afternoon*, asked Virginia to contribute a drink. She proposed "The Barbarians": three parts bourbon, one part "white mint" (clear crème de menthe), and ice. "Pour into cocktail shaker and shake as though you were a terrier with a dead rat." In the brief write-up about her

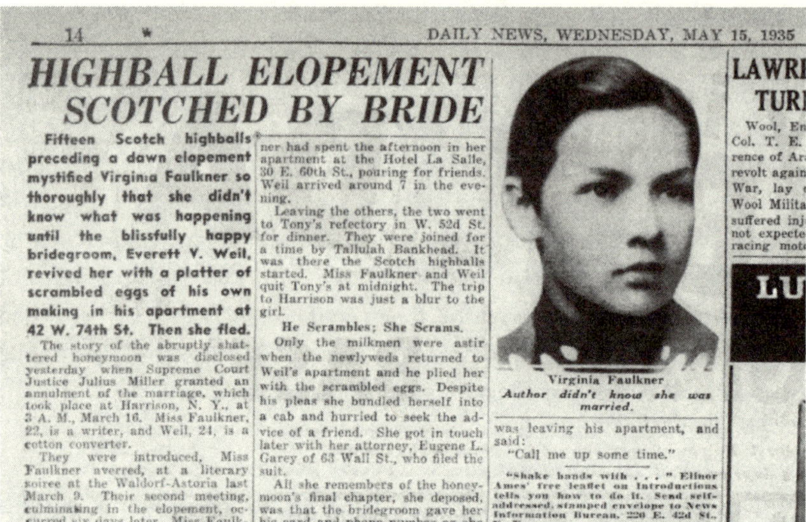

14 DAILY NEWS, WEDNESDAY, MAY 15, 1935

HIGHBALL ELOPEMENT SCOTCHED BY BRIDE

Fifteen Scotch highballs preceding a dawn elopement mystified Virginia Faulkner so thoroughly that she didn't know what was happening until the blissfully happy bridegroom, Everett V. Weil, revived her with a platter of scrambled eggs of his own making in his apartment at 42 W. 74th St. Then she fled.

The story of the abruptly shattered honeymoon was disclosed yesterday when Supreme Court Justice Julius Miller granted an annulment of the marriage, which took place at Harrison, N. Y., at 3 A. M., March 16. Miss Faulkner, 22, is a writer, and Weil, 24, is a cotton converter.

They were introduced, Miss Faulkner averred, at a literary soiree at the Waldorf-Astoria last March 9. Their second meeting, culminating in the elopement, occurred six days later. Miss Faulkner had spent the afternoon in her apartment at the Hotel La Salle, 30 E. 60th St., pouring for friends. Weil arrived around 7 in the evening.

Leaving the others, the two went to Tony's refectory in W. 52d St. for dinner. They were joined for a time by Tallulah Bankhead. It was there the Scotch highballs started. Miss Faulkner and Weil quit Tony's at midnight. The trip to Harrison was just a blur to the girl.

He Scrambles; She Scrams.

Only the milkmen were astir when the newlyweds returned to Weil's apartment and he plied her with the scrambled eggs. Despite his pleas she bundled herself into a cab and hurried to seek the advice of a friend. She got in touch later with her attorney, Eugene L. Garey of 63 Wall St., who filed the suit.

All she remembers of the honeymoon's final chapter, she deposed, was that the bridegroom gave her his card and phone number as she was leaving his apartment, and said:

"Call me up some time."

Virginia Faulkner
Author didn't know she was married.

"Shake hands with . . ." Elinor Ames' free leaflet on Introductions tells you how to do it. Send self-addressed, stamped envelope to News Information Bureau, 220 E. 42d St., N. Y.

Fig. 8. "Highball Elopement." *New York Daily News*, May 15, 1935, p. 14.

drink, Virginia wrote that "her only eccentricities are (a) making money, (b) spending it, and (c) talking about what she would do if she were you."

Inclusion in *So Red the Nose* (the title was a play on Stark Young's recent bestseller *So Red the Rose*) was, in a way, the most convincing demonstration that Virginia had successfully established herself in New York. The first cocktail in the book was offered by Ernest Hemingway ("Death in the Afternoon"—all the drinks took their names from the authors' recent books). Virginia's recipe was accompanied by a cartoon showing her in a slinky gown leaning on a table with a large punch bowl and four tuxedo-clad suitors approaching to lay siege. It was as much fiction as the notion that Virginia would waste her time drinking anything but Scotch. The most honest thing on her page was the last statement. Her favorite pastime, she said, was "sitting in a chair."

Joe Bryan III convinced his bosses at *Town & Country* to bring Virginia on board as a staff writer in June. Despite publishing two novels since leaving the *Post*, Virginia's first contributions to *Town & Country* demonstrated little progress in terms of style or imagination. No progress, in fact: After a year on hiatus, her bubble-headed friend Penelope had simply returned with a new name, Lucinda. "With This Ring," which ran in the June 1935 issue, is nothing more than a conversation between the narrator and Lucinda, a conversation that's just a frame upon which to hang a succession of quips: "'I went to school with Vicky Pomery, who was from Dorset, and she always vowed she would never marry until she was asked by a man named Livingstone.' 'What an adorable little mania!' I said. 'Had a bee or two set up light-housekeeping in her chapeau?' 'Stupid! Let me finish. She wanted to marry a man by that name so that when she awoke in the nuptial couch she could say to him, "Ah, Mr. Livingstone, I presume?"'"

The piece opened with a quip that would often be quoted in subsequent years as evidence of Virginia's wit: "I always hate to be alone in Lucinda's sitting-room. A decorator named Henry Mosely has been not so much period as exclamation point."

Other set-pieces starring Lucinda appeared monthly after that, but from the very beginning Virginia knew that *Town & Country* was a stopgap. In late June, she wrote Eddie that her agent had wired with an offer to work for the movie studios. "I am asking $500 a week for a short-term contract"—which was a fortune compared to most working women's salaries in 1935 but not exceptional by film studio standards. Meanwhile, she was busy with other writing jobs in addition to *Town & Country*. She had written a synopsis of a play for Broadway producer Jed Harris and was waiting for his decision. *Cosmopolitan* was willing to pay $8,000 for a novelette, and King Features Syndicate was offering her ten cents a word for fancied-up advice articles: "How to get a husband, etc." She admitted it was "Stupid reading but I cannot sneer at the dough."

Virginia had little time to think about these opportunities. After weeks of back-and-forth, she received an offer from MGM for a six-month contract at $500 a week. It was exactly what she wanted. Or so she thought.

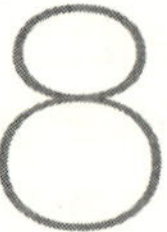

Hollywood

The Hollywood Reporter announced Virginia's arrival on September 30, 1935. Gossip columnist O. O. McIntyre reported the news, proclaiming that "Virginia Faulkner is being hailed as another Dorothy Parker." Virginia dove headfirst into Hollywood, moving into a cottage at the famous Garden of Allah, a complex of cottages and apartments in a hybrid of Spanish mission and Sahara oasis styles that was notorious for its wild parties and something of a refuge for expats, gays, lesbians, and outcasts in general. She was so busy getting settled it took her weeks to answer a letter from Eddie full of questions and cautions about her finances and living arrangements. After itemizing her income and expenses, she promised to consult him on "what to do with the dough I save."

She also wrote that things were slow in getting started at MGM, mostly because the great German theater impresario Max Reinhardt had arrived for the opening of *A Midsummer Night's Dream*, the Warner Brothers film based on his stage production. Reinhardt was the father of Gottfried Reinhardt, the production assistant with whom Virginia had been paired. With Gottfried busy escorting his father around town, she was lucky to see him for "20 minutes at a time." It was not an auspicious start to a partnership that, in the end, produced no auspicious results.

Gottfried provided Virginia with entry to the salon of expatriate Europeans hosted by Salka Viertel at her house in Santa Monica. An Austrian actress, Salka, her husband, German film director Berthold Viertel, and their sons Peter, Hans, and Thomas had first come to Hollywood in 1928. They decided to stay after Hitler came to power and it became clear that as Jews, they would not be welcomed back in Germany. Gottfried had been introduced to the Viertels shortly after arriving in Hollywood in 1933 and soon began an affair with Salka that lasted over a decade, despite the twenty-two-year difference in their ages.

Salka reigned as queen of the growing population of German and Austrian intellectuals who had found a haven from Nazi persecution in sunny California: writers such as Thomas Mann, Bertold Brecht, and Lion Feuchtwanger; composers such as Erich Korngold and Bronislaw Kaper; and countless film directors, screenwriters, designers, and actors and actresses. On Sunday afternoons, she opened her house and welcomed in an impressive and ever-changing array of talents.

Years later, in a rare moment of nostalgia, Virginia recalled a typical gathering in a letter to the playwright S. N. Behrman:

> The fight for the piano—like the fight-for-the-gun scene in westerns: George Gershwin and Oscar [Levant] and Edouard Steuerman and Dimmi [Dmitri] Tiomkin and Erich Korngold and Bronik [Bronislaw] Kaper and George Antheil all but shoving each other off the piano bench; and there is a ping-pong game going on just outside the French doors; and [Ruben] Mamoulian and Miriam Hopkins on the sofa before the fire; and a large white dog whose tail is knocking over glasses; and Gottfried arguing with someone in the dining room; and Tommy Viertel in the window seat rendering "Jiggs and Maggie" and "Orphan Annie" into German for the edification of a covey of little Korngolds.

For Virginia, the Viertels had an added attraction: They belonged to a stable. Just two weeks after arriving, she went riding in the foothills above Santa Monica with Gottfried and Hans Viertel. At one point, Hans had ridden up too close behind Virginia and her horse had "hauled off and delivered him a terrific kick in the leg," which she hoped would teach him a lesson.

She soon found herself bored with studio work. "For every one hour you work you warm your can for twelve," she complained. The studio assigned her and Gottfried to work for producer Bernie Hyman, and Hyman put them to work on developmental projects. They read books, plays, and magazine stories, prepared story proposals, and occasionally contributed bits of dialogue to other films. Although Virginia claimed she and Gottfried came up with material for "at least three movies" in their first week of working together, almost nothing they touched ever made it to the screen. Like most writers on the MGM lot at the time, Virginia was asked to help with *Conquest*, a film about Napoleon's romance with the Countess Marie Walewska, a film whose tortuous production nearly brought an end to Greta Garbo's career. As she later told Behrman, who ultimately rescued the film's script, no one wanted to use the one line she contributed: "Want to come up and see my collection of cannonballs?"

She tried to progress on the novel she'd started before leaving New York, but found she didn't have the energy. "I find myself so sleepy most of the time that I'm nearly going nuts. About 10—or even earlier—I feel ready for my dear bed." And she hated the climate. But when MGM exercised its first option in December 1935 and extended Virginia's contract for a year, she went along. She and Gottfried were now working on a project titled *Ladies Are Useful* that was intended as a comic vehicle for the German actress Luise Rainer. Virginia joked that she preferred to call it *It Happened Twice One Night in the Salzkammergut*.

Gottfried introduced her to the Russian-born film composer Dimitri Tiomkin, who mounted a campaign to entice her into his bed—a campaign that ended when his wife, a professional dancer, returned home from a tour. Tiomkin's pursuit was doomed to fail for other reasons though. Coming to Hollywood helped Virginia realize something about her own desires. In early 1936, after pleading that the demands of work wouldn't allow her to come back to Lincoln for Christmas, she was stopped and fined ten dollars for reckless driving—even though she was the passenger. The driver was a woman named Tone Price, who owned an exclusive antiquarian bookstore on Sunset Boulevard. A Texas native, Price had come to Los Angeles for a holiday in 1929 and ended up staying. She got a job working for Jake Zeitlin, a book dealer with a shop in Westwood and discovered that she had a knack for selling rare books—particularly to Hollywood celebrities with cash to spare. Zeitlin later recalled Price as "a peculiar kind of a woman, given to attract members of her own sex," and descriptions of Price from the time note her short haircut and preference for "mannish dress." After four years with Zeitlin, she and Gladys Barbieri opened the store at 9045 Sunset and soon became known as booksellers to the stars.

Virginia had been introduced to Price by Leonard Spigelgass, a playwright and songwriter who had become another of Irving Thalberg's protégés.

Costume designer Miles White recalled that Spigelgass "was very well connected, very influential and very respected—and everyone knew he was gay." He was also at the intersection of three communities that Virginia saw herself part of: the studio writers; Hollywood's literati—or rather, literati who found themselves in Hollywood; and the discreet network of gay and lesbian talents in and around the movie business. When Spigelgass hosted a dinner for the visiting British novelist G. B. Stern, Virginia was in attendance, along with Jake Zeitlin and Tone Price. The dinner led Virginia to say, in a remark soon after quoted by columnist Sidney Skolsky, that she was forming the "Hollywood Sex and Culture Club."

Price and Barbieri's store was on a stretch of Sunset Boulevard that fell outside the jurisdiction of the Los Angeles Police Department and thus was not subject to the frequent vice squad raids on homosexual gatherings that the department was notorious for. Just two blocks down the street was a tiny nightclub known as the Club Bali, popular with both Hollywood's gay community and straights who wanted to wander over to the wild side. In April 1936, Virginia moved into a bungalow on Roxbury Drive in Beverly Hills, just a little west of the Club Bali, and her name began appearing regularly in connection with the club in gossip columns. The fact that Virginia was often seen there is less relevant than with whom she was seen. Actress Ona Munson, who went on to have an affair with dancer Mercedes de Acosta, one of Greta Garbo's lovers. "Baron" Nickie de Gunzberg and his partner, the actor Erik Rhodes. Helen Ainsworth, a heavy-set actress who was often cast in "butch" roles.

In this circle of sexual outsiders, Virginia found a place where she didn't feel like the queen of the leper colony. She was not only accepted by this community but received the greatest social compliment Hollywood could offer at the time: Greta Garbo came out of her legendary seclusion to attend a party that Virginia hosted in 1937. Not only did Garbo show up, but as newspapers around the country reported over the following weeks, she came wearing slacks, something then still considered scandalous due to the suggestion that the wearer was lesbian. Virginia later confided to her cousin Sarah Meyer that Garbo was "as magnetic in the flesh as on the screen" and "not too very reserved."

The only direct evidence for believing that Virginia found in Hollywood the freedom to explore her attraction to other women is the testimony of the photographer Ruth Bernhard. Decades after the fact, Bernhard told her biographer Margaretta Mitchell: "She was brilliant and adventurous, a boyish, roly-poly girl who would arrive and scoop me up in a blanket and we would go in her sports car, driving through the Hollywood Hills to see the moon rise. We never even kissed, though she wanted me to be her lover and would give me anything. She thought that I should have a shop to show my work, and she offered to get it for me. She admired me and I her, but I did not wish to be more than a friend." Bernhard had met Virginia through Zeitlin, who hosted her first U.S. exhibition at his bookstore. Bernhard had recently begun photographing women in the nude, encouraged by Edward Weston, and Virginia was intrigued by Bernhard's ability to see women both sexually and aesthetically. Talent and intellectual sophistication, more than beauty, however, were what attracted her most.

It would be interesting to know how much Virginia shared with Eddie about this side of her time in Hollywood. Unfortunately, we never will. If we have any of Virginia's personal letters, it is because Eddie was meticulous in his record-keeping. His papers in the UNL archives amount to over a hundred boxes of personal and professional papers, including such minutiae as the bill from his honeymoon stay at the Blackhawk Hotel in Chicago. But there is a gap in Eddie's papers, a complete absence of records of any type that starts in early 1936 and continues to the early 1950s. Sometime in the mid-1970s, there was a water leak in the basement of the house on South Avenue where Eddie kept his papers. Dozens of boxes were saturated and disposed of, including twenty years' worth of Virginia's letters—an irreplaceable loss.

Though little of her studio work reached the screen, Virginia's quips were regularly quoted by Hollywood columnists. Louella Parsons gleefully reprinted Virginia's description of Katherine Hepburn's style of acting as "a cross between Sarah Bernhardt and Huckleberry Finn." Sidney Skolsky quoted her in his column over thirty times in two years. Unlike in the Hepburn remark, however, the targets of most of Virginia's barbs were unnamed. Some of her quips were aimed at the studio production process rather than individuals. "The trouble with motion pictures is that when you least expect it, nothing happens," Skolsky quoted her in April 1937. Moviemaking, she argued, would be more efficient "and they'd get things done faster if they'd shoot the retakes first." She joked that a certain producer "calls in his advisors when he wants to make an indecision."

A few of Virginia's witticisms hinted at the more liberal sexual mores she was encountering in Hollywood. She said that the sign of a good Hollywood party was that "there weren't enough sexes to go around." Of a popular resort, she reported that "there are ten women to every man and that man wants another man." But she was also willing to make herself the brunt of her jokes. Asked to comment on an incident at a celebrity's party, she remarked, "There have been conflicting stories—all mine."

Virginia often attended parties in the company of the English writer John Davenport. A young Cambridge-educated poet, Davenport had been brought to Hollywood in early 1936 to help adapt A. E. W. Mason's novel *Clementina* for RKO, but his time as a screenwriter produced even fewer results than Virginia's. Davenport's genius was for the spoken word, not the written. His talk, wrote a friend, was "witty, informed, at once blithely Rabelaisian and slanderously uninhibited." No wonder it appealed to Virginia. Already known for her sharp tongue, Virginia found that time in Davenport's company tested her own skills. Nora Sayre, who came to know Davenport in the 1950s, recalled, "Being exposed to that dazzling vocabulary was truly an education for the ear: his speech intensified one's sensitivity to language and bestowed a heightened awareness of its possibilities." The effect of a conversation with Davenport, she said, was to make one "immediately want to go home and write."

It must have had that effect on Virginia. After a visit in July 1937, her aunt Cora told the *Omaha Evening Bee-News* that Virginia was getting her third novel ready for Simon & Schuster, had written a one-act play, and had signed contracts for more magazine work. If Davenport inspired Virginia, he also depended upon her to help him navigate a system that mystified him. Years later, he wrote that she always "seemed to have the hang of the place." But he also admitted that part of his problem had been alcohol. "I was drunk all the time," while "you, darling Virginia, were only drunk half the time. Unfair, really."

In early February 1938, Virginia decided to leave. She boarded a boat bound for New York via the Panama Canal, traveling with John Davenport and his wife, Clemency. Her plan was to spend time with the Davenports in England, and then to tour Europe. If she had gained nothing else from working for MGM, she had saved enough money to travel in style.

Virginia later gave herself an opportunity to reflect on her experience of Hollywood in one of the earliest stories featuring her garish creation

Princess Tulip Murphy. Published in the June 1938 issue *Town & Country*, "Princess Tulip Comes Out in Hollywood" referred to a debutante's entry into society rather than a disclosure of sexual preferences, but it's easy to read today's usage into the piece given how Hollywood freed Virginia to see herself as lesbian. The piece certainly reveals her mixed feelings about coming to Hollywood in its opening line: "I never thought I would really go to Hollywood, because I have always thought I would and I never do what I think."

Like Virginia, Princess Tulip appreciates Hollywood's flexible dress code: "The only place pajamas are not *de rigeur* in Hollywood is, amusingly enough, in bed." She mocks the unique landscape of urban Southern California: "Below stretched a bewildering vista of patios, swimming pools, barbecue pits, badminton courts, scenic railways, and even a wee emergency hospital tucked away in the crotch of a giant redwood." Hollywood, she observes, "is laid out in the shape of a dollar sign, and is divided into quarters, nickels, and dimes." She also took aim at the proliferation of titles among Hollywood's expats ("the nobility not mentioned in the *Almanach de Gotha*") and of gossipmongers among the crowd at any gathering ("Columnists outnumbered the paying guests about 2 to 1"). What Princess Tulip never once mentions is the film industry. The movie business had made about as much of an impression on Virginia as she had made on it.

Virginia's sole screen credit didn't appear until almost two years after she left Hollywood. The project that began in 1936 as *Ladies Are Useful*, with Luise Rainer as its intended star, had a history as complicated as *Conquest*, with multiple changes in cast, directors, titles, and screenwriters. Robert Montgomery, Robert Taylor, and the French actor Fernand Gravey were announced as the lead at various times. Luise Rainer quit MGM in early 1938, and after a survey of its stable of European stars, MGM settled on the French actress Annabella. Finally filmed in early 1939 as *Maiden Voyage*, with Robert Young as the male lead, the film's title was changed to *Bridal Suite* just before release to take advantage of Annabella's recent wedding to Tyrone Power.

The lightweight tale about the romance between a charming but aimless American heir and a bright and hard-working young Austrian woman, the daughter of an innkeeper, was not worth the wait. The synopsis of the film in *Harrison's Reports*, an industry magazine aimed at theater owners, is damning in its accuracy: "A silly romantic comedy, with a trite plot. The action is slow and tiresome; as a matter of fact the story is developed mostly by dialog. In addition, the characters, particularly the hero, are unappealing. This is due not to the fault of the performers, but to the inanity of the material."

Snappy dialogue was not just a hallmark of 1930s comedies but also Virginia's stock in trade. Yet *Bridal Suite* is proof that there is more to a good comedy film than just clever dialogue. Robert Young is an amiable but lightweight lead and pales beside Annabella, who is strenuously charming. Samuel Hoffenstein earned the ultimate credit for the screenplay, so it's impossible to determine how much of Virginia's work survives in the final product.

The contrast between Virginia's credits and those of her former Simon & Schuster colleague Tess Slesinger offers a harsh verdict on how little she accomplished in her time in Hollywood. Virginia managed to coauthor the story for one forgettable film released over a year after her departure. In the same two years, Slesinger won an Oscar with her first screenplay for *The Good Earth* and scripted two other films. Virginia left Hollywood by choice—but she left a failure.

All in Fun

By leaving, Virginia broke her contract with MGM. That fact came out later and suggests she was deceiving when she told reporters that she was planning to return to Hollywood. She never had anything good to say about the place in later years. But in choosing to quit for a trip with a vaguely defined itinerary, one gets the sense that this was more of a running away than a running toward.

On the other hand, the moment presented her best opportunity. She had been talking of returning to Europe for years. And there were people she could see: Florence Meyer was in France with Max Reinhardt, preparing a tour of his biblical epic *The Eternal Road*. John and Clemency Davenport were returning to England. A handful of acquaintances from New York—James Thurber and his wife, John O'Hara, the actress Tamara Geva—happened to be in London. She would be a visitor, then, not just a tourist.

She parted from the Davenports upon arrival in Southampton and headed for the Italian Alps, where Florence was skiing, taking a break before rehearsals. Virginia declined to try skiing. "Anything requiring balance does not appeal to me," she explained. She returned to Paris with Florence after ten days, but did not linger. It was the Easter holiday and much of Paris society was down on the Riviera. Still, she had the honor of being invited to a dinner at the Brazilian embassy along with other celebrities who happened to be in town.

When she arrived in London, however, Virginia was ushered into the heart of London's intellectual and artistic circles. Clemency Davenport's mother, Beatrice Forbes-Robertson, had impeccable credentials in both. She had performed on stage in London and New York at the turn of the century before marrying a wealthy American. After they divorced in 1920, she returned with her three daughters to London and became an advocate for social reforms. An old American acquaintance, Roosevelt's secretary of labor, Frances Perkins, paid a visit while Virginia was staying at Forbes-Robertson's house in Pimlico. Virginia strode into the parlor, not realizing there was a special guest, and was startled to see Secretary Perkins having tea. "She scared me," Virginia later recalled. "I curtsied and slunk out of the room." Forbes-Robertson also arranged an invitation to a reception held by the new American ambassador, Joseph P. Kennedy. London's social whirlwind eventually wore on Virginia, though, and she headed to the countryside in Wiltshire, where she took a room at the Prince of Wales Hotel in Ludgershall and visited with the Davenports, who'd taken a house outside the town.

It was there she finished the last pages of her third novel, started months before in Hollywood, and dispatched it to Simon & Schuster. A new editor, Maria Leiper, shepherded the work through its in-house review and her report arrived from New York just days before Virginia was to board the ship taking her back to the U.S. It was not good.

"The general opinion is that, in its present form, the confusion of your story and characters overbalances the brilliance and undoubted entertainment value of the book." There followed two pages of specific criticisms, all of which pointed to problems that had been evident in both *Friends and Romans* and *The Barbarians*. There were too many characters and "most of your people sound like you talking, that they're all witty and facile and flip, without much differentiation." The plot was too insubstantial to provide "enough solid framework under all the frothy talk." There were no central figures: "For a long while we shifted in a dizzying way from one person to another." The one novelty Virginia had introduced—a murder mystery—was a complete failure. "Suggestion: why not cut it entirely?" And there was the now-familiar request: "What about sifting some of the wisecracks, too? They're all good, Virginia, amazingly good; but when there are so many to every page they lose their effectiveness." Leiper's letter is the last evidence of Virginia's third novel, which she appears to have abandoned.

The frantic pace at which she sowed wisecracks across her fiction mirrored the intensity with which Virginia sought to be the liveliest and funniest person in any conversation—and she was often competing with world-class talkers. But it was more than just sprezzatura, part of her "smart, know-it-all line." Relentlessly funny people often use humor as a shield, a defense—against others and their own reflections.

In the summer of 1938, Virginia was still just twenty-five. The success of *Friends and Romans* and, to a lesser extent, *The Barbarians*, and the appetite of magazine editors for her comic stories and sketches did not change the fact that she hadn't yet managed to achieve "something a little kinder and truer" in her work. If, three years before in New York, as Evelyn Merriman had written Eddie, she was "feeling . . . that she belongs nowhere," there is no reason to think that feeling had changed. Her ship was sailing to New York, but where was she going to live? There? Hollywood? Lincoln? Did she even know? And after her time in Hollywood, she must have known that her attraction to women was both more than a passing phase and something not accepted outside select clubs and social circles. As much as she trusted and confided in Eddie, these were things that wouldn't have been easy to discuss.

When Virginia arrived back in Lincoln in early August, she found that Eddie had become an extremely busy man. Uncle Bert's health had been declining rapidly and Eddie was taking on more of the responsibility for running the Woodmen. Hospitalized in July, Bert had been released but could only manage to work a few hours each day. By mid-August he was unable to leave his bed, and on the 27th he died at home. His doctor told the *Lincoln Journal Star* that the cause was cirrhosis of the liver. Bert had stopped drinking too late to reverse the damage of years. The next day, Eddie was named president of the Woodmen Accident Company. He had just turned twenty-seven. He would run the company for almost forty years.

Virginia left Lincoln soon after Bert's funeral, headed for New York City. She had abandoned any plans for returning to Hollywood. Maria Leiper had loaned the manuscript of her novel to Joe Bryan III, now working at the *Saturday Evening Post*, as a possibility for syndication, but he recognized there wasn't enough of a plot to keep readers going from issue to issue. What it did demonstrate, though, was that Virginia was still adept at turning out the same quip-packed prose that he and readers of his old magazine, *Town & Country*, loved. Harry Bull, the magazine's editor, extended an offer to rejoin the staff, working on uncredited assignments as well as contributing pieces under her own name.

Bull wanted Virginia to carry on with the adventures of Princess Tulip Murphy. "Divorced many times, friend of kings, knaves, and human flies, authoress, huntress of all sizes of game, always to be found with the mode hot at her heels," Princess Tulip had debuted in *Town & Country* in September 1937 with "My Place in the Midnight Sun." Like all subsequent stories, it was "as told to Virginia Faulkner." In it, Princess Tulip recounted a trip she'd taken to the Arctic with a band of vagabonds aboard a Norwegian tramp steamer. She steps on stage—or rather, deck—in the first of the many hodge-podge costumes she would model: "I was wearing a ten-piece pebble-knit sport suit, an airplane fabric tam with matching muff and leggings, and carried a bamboo-and-serge duffel bag cleverly made in the shape of an elephant gun." The article was accompanied by a series of illustrations by the designer Erik Nitsche showing the homely and heavily made-up Tulip in her outrageous outfits.

There is really no story to this story. From the tramp steamer, she caroms through Scandinavia, meeting real and fictional celebrities (the Finnish track star Paavo Nurmi, actor Walter Huston, "the Peer Gynts"), attending gala events of all shapes and sizes, and improvising ever-more ridiculous dress ("a scarlet play-suit [with drop seat for parachute] and sickle-shaped pelisse of genuine *droshky*") before striding off into the next adventure: Russia.

"My Soviet Adventure," which appeared the following month, was a parody of the reports of westerners who allowed themselves to be persuaded that collectivization and other aspects of Stalin's rule were overwhelmingly beneficial. "No matter what you hear about Russia," Princess Tulip declares, "their beauty parlors are most economical. You can get a shampoo, wave, massage, facial, manicure, and abortion all for about seven rubles ha'penny." What little Virginia knew of Soviet Russia she had heard from Florence Meyer, who had spent a few months in Moscow studying ballet. Not that she was concerned with realism. The only mention of Russian ballet, in fact, is as an aside in a joke: "I also went to see a good many puppet shows—puppet shows have supplemented the ballet in the favor of the people—and was amazed to see how many strings you have to pull to get the simplest things done."

After Russia came Hollywood. From then on, Princess Tulip ventured out three or four times a year. Unconstrained by reality, she could go wherever Virginia felt needed a good skewering: India, Mexico, Switzerland—even

Hell, in a two-parter published in 1944. Still, there were times when Princess Tulip's travels managed to coincide with Virginia's: to Washington, where she visited Eddie while he was assigned to the Pentagon during the war; to New Orleans; to Santa Fe.

Princess Tulip was Virginia's most memorable creation. She was also her most sustained piece of work. Between 1937 and 1949, nearly two dozen Princess Tulip stories would appear in *Town & Country*. It's difficult to fully appreciate the Princess Tulip stories outside the context of the magazine. Individually amusing, at times laugh-out-loud funny, what they lose is their deeply subversive impact.

What Princess Tulip satirized was *Town & Country* and its world. The magazine's pages were a parade of privilege. Its "Calendar" section listed engagements and weddings of the scions of America's elite, in places like Oyster Bay, Philadelphia, and Newport, Rhode Island. Each year, there was an issue focusing on the premier kennel club shows, another on the upcoming yachting season. Its real estate ads offered real estates: "Lattingtown: 20 acres of North Shore Long Island"; a "charming home secluded in 300 acres of beautifully landscaped gardens" in Duchess Country, New York. Interspersed through each issue were photos with captions like "Mrs. Reginald Norman, who winters in Capri and summers in Newport, with Thane, her Scottish deerhound that she has just brought all the way from Macbeth's Glamis Castle."

Unlike Mrs. Reginald Norman, Princess Tulip's family was more redlight than blue blood. In her introduction to *My Hey-Day*, a collection of the first ten stories published in 1940, Princess Tulip bristled at the very idea of having to trace her family tree. "Introductions are so much bourgeois nonsense, because if you don't already know who someone is, why on earth would you want to meet him?" She was proud to point out, however, that her grandmother was the first woman called "Madam" west of Rock Island, Illinois. Her mother being an actress with traveling troupes, Tulip was left in care of this grandmother, who kept an open house full of friendly young women year-round, and whom she credited with teaching the art of being a hostess. Coming from a line of commoners, Princess Tulip owed her title to her husband Prince "Brick a Minute" Murphy, who claimed he came from the kings of Ireland—a heritage she chose not to question. Introduced by Tulip's grandmother, Prince Murphy kept his new wife busy for a while bearing princelings that she promptly farmed out to relatives.

Along with the Princess Tulip stories, Virginia had to work on assignments set by *Town & Country* editors, like a profile of the British actor Robert Morley, who was appearing on Broadway in *Oscar Wilde*, a one-man show. Morley could hold his own with Virginia when it came to clever off-the-cuff remarks, so it's harder than usual to tell where the subject ends and writer takes over. Virginia liked Morley, but she hated this kind of work.

In her eyes, it was a step down from her own heyday four years earlier. She no longer had the novelty of being a first-time author, no credits from Hollywood, and no new novel poised to garner reviews and headlines. There was little to show for her first year back in New York aside from a handful of bylined *Town & Country* articles. Even her supply of quips for the columnists had dried up. Leonard Lyons, who came across Virginia playing backgammon at Tony's restaurant, managed to get her only published quote for the year—which reflected her mood: "I've just discovered something that is a profound truth: happiness does not bring money."

It did buy drinks. Even if she didn't have snappy remarks to supply, columnists continued to spot her at places like 21 with other well-known imbibers. Joe Bryan took her to lunch one afternoon in July and when it came time for coffee, she ordered a martini. Seeing his surprise, she asked, "What's the matter? Haven't you ever heard of an after-luncheon cocktail?" Her tolerance for social niceties had worn thin. Bryan recalled her advice on how to break the ice when seated with strangers at a dinner party. She replied, "I ask the gentleman on my right, 'Are you a bed-wetter?', and when we have exhausted that, I remark to the gentleman on my left, 'You know, I spit blood this morning.'" Finally, late in 1939, Leonard Silliman hired her to write for the next version of his *New Faces* revue. The prospect was enough for her to cancel plans to return to Lincoln for the holidays.

The faces in *New Faces* were hardly new. The two leads, Patsy Kelly and Joe Cook, were veterans. Joe Cook had spent decades in vaudeville and Patsy Kelly had been working on Broadway and in Hollywood for almost as long. She was also something of a legend in the lesbian community for her openness about her preference for women. In a 1937 interview with *Motion Picture* magazine, she said she'd been living with actress Wilma

Cox for years and had no plans to get married. Patsy and Wilma were among the lesbian couples Virginia knew from Club Bali and other safe spots in Hollywood. The article also stated, "She would rather walk the plank than go to a beauty parlor. She wears slacks and tailored suits, washes her face and hands and lets it go at that," a style that Virginia's own tastes increasingly matched.

When Eddie and Jean visited Virginia in early April, she took them to dinner with Patsy and Joe Cook, but that was as close to working with them as she ever got. *New Faces of 1940* would prove, in Leonard Sillman's own words, "a disaster on a gargantuan scale." It had started well enough. Sillman hired Virginia, songwriters Baldwin Bergersen and John Rox, and production manager Blanche Lederer and took them to Atlantic City, then in its off-season, to work on the book and songs. *New Faces* was to be a revue rather than a musical, a set of skits that were intended to showcase talents new to Broadway. On the strength of that work, he got backers to fund the show to the tune of $50,000 on the condition that he signed Kelly and Cook—which he did. That was the last thing about this show that went as planned.

From that point on, *New Faces of 1940*—which eventually became *All in Fun*—"grew into a Frankenstein monster which its originator was totally unable to control," as a *New York Times* postmortem put it. Money ran short; the plan to debut in May was scrapped. Kelly and Cook refused to extend their commitments. Sillman brought on new performers—on the condition that they invest in the show. The new performers demanded new material. By the time the show had its first full performance in New Haven in late November, the program listed fifty-one numbers and ran four and a half hours. Sillman even hit up Virginia for a contribution and she later complained that he took her for five thousand dollars. Sillman himself admitted that the show had "more authors than the Bible," but Virginia retained lead author billing throughout. It did her little good.

All in Fun opened on Friday, December 27, 1940. It closed the following night. To reviewers who knew of its bumpy path to Broadway, the show wasn't as bad as it could have been. Brooks Atkinson of the *New York Times* praised dancer Bill "Bojangles" Robinson, a late addition. Robinson's participation ensured the show a place in theater history as the first Broadway show to give an African American top billing. "But like most revues assembled from many hands," Atkinson concluded, "*All in Fun* is scattered and mediocre." The *Daily News* found that "Little of *All in Fun* is completely disappointing. The trouble with it is that not enough of it is as good as it should be."

Virginia could add these to the stack of disappointing reviews of her third book. In late 1939, the newly established firm of Duell, Sloan & Pearce approached her about putting together a collection of her Princess Tulip stories. At the time, she'd only published six, but she had more in the pipeline with *Town & Country*. It was the only prospect she had of seeing her work in book form anytime soon and she took it.

Titled *My Hey-Day*, the book came out in April 1940. Its byline, "By Princess Tulip Murphy as told to Virginia Faulkner," led some stores to shelve it under Murphy instead of Faulkner. The subtitle—*The Crackup of the International Set*—reflected a recognition, however slight, of current events, even if the war in Europe wasn't mentioned. "Time are changing, as I heard somewhere the other day," Princess Tulip states in the introduction. "Many of my oldest friends can now count their yachts on the fingers of a single hand; others are closing their apartments and moving into their homes!" Feeling obligated to check in with her friends, she contacts dozens of them, hoping to wangle a stack of invitations. When none arrives, she concludes, "the International Set was cracking up!"

A few reviewers appreciated the book as simple comic relief, which was becoming a precious commodity. The *Atlanta Constitution* recommended it as "an antidote to the war news." Still at the *New Yorker*, Clifton Fadiman offered a suggestion that put some of his readers in a huff: "It's as wicked as it can be. So, curl up with *My Hey-Day* and a package of marijuana, and have yourself a good debauch." And Charles Poore, in the *New York Times*'s "Books of the *Times*" column, declared that the book "practically makes Miss Faulkner the New-World [Evelyn] Waugh."

But for most reviewers, the humor of the Princess Tulip pieces did not improve in quantity. "Flippant to the point of dulling the point," concluded the *New York Herald Tribune*. The *Miami Herald*'s reviewer found it a failure: "As a take-off on the haut monde, it misses fire pretty painfully." The most withering comment, however, was this two-sentence review in *The American Mercury*: "People who think they are 'sophisticates' are going to think that this is a very witty and naughty book. They and the book belong to the Jazz Age, *circa* 1923." There were plenty of self-styled sophisticates, though, no matter what *The American Mercury* thought. *My Hey-Day* went through three printings in the first two months, becoming one of Duell, Sloan & Pearce's bestsellers in its first year.

Whether or not critics respected Virginia as an author, the public still did. The *New York Post* gave her a half-page spread when the book came out in April. Titled "Nebraska Nomad," it was accompanied by a photo that showed she hadn't lost her sprezzatura. Wearing a house robe, pajamas, and heels, she stretched out in an easy chair, a sly grin on her face. She was heavier, horse riding and tennis now things of the past. Edwin Cox, whose feature "Private Lives: Candid Cartoons of the World's Celebrities" was as popular as Ripley's "Believe It or Not!," included her in a spread alongside Anthony Eden, then British war minister, and Stalin, in one of his Sunday panels in June 1940. The caption below an inset showing her inspecting a manuscript in a chair with a mannequin beside read, "Novelist Virginia Faulkner's pet possession is window display dummy to which she reads her manuscripts. Virginia says its dull stare is a tonic to her own criticisms."

Her own criticisms were increasingly difficult to silence. If she aspired to move beyond being a wisecrack generation machine, nothing she was doing was taking her in that direction. She had started to contribute material to Fred Allen's radio comedy show and quips she'd made years before were now being recycled as column fillers by Sidney Skolsky and others. Joe Bryan had gotten her to agree to write short stories for the *Saturday Evening Post*. The one chance of serious work—adapting a French play, *Le Corsair*, for Florence Meyer's new husband, the expat German actor Oscar Homolka—arose and quickly evaporated. But she was about to meet a woman who would be both collaborator and challenge to Virginia's avoidance of greater artistic risks.

10

Dana

"I am on my way now to have tea with Virginia Faulkner," Dana Suesse wrote her mother on the morning of February 1, 1941. "She is one of the most brilliant girls I have met in a long while. I adore her books." That tea was the start of Virginia's first sustained romantic—and creative—relationship, one that would become the center of her life for the rest of the decade.

At first, Dana's purpose was purely professional. She thought Virginia "might be the one to do the libretto for a modern opera with me. I have a little germ of an idea which she likes." But, as Dana's daybook reveals, their relationship soon became personal and intimate. They met on Saturday. They met on Sunday. Dana saw Virginia before leaving to visit her mother in Niantic, Connecticut, a few days later and four times in the week after she got back. They met for breakfasts, lunches, drinks, and dinners. They went to movies and shows together. They even spent the weekend at Dana's mother's house within the first two months of meeting. In the first three months after that tea, they were together over forty times.

What's odd about some of these rendezvous is that they included "C.B."—Courtney Burr, Dana's husband. He and Dana were still newlyweds, in fact, having married the previous summer. But Courtney Burr and Dana Suesse were a decidedly odd couple. They had been going to dinners and shows for several years, but there appeared to be no special connection, at least for her. Courtney Burr was seventeen years older than Dana and divorced with two grown children. Aside from serving in the Army during World War I, his work consisted of chasing, mostly unsuccessfully, prospects for Broadway shows and people to finance them. At the time they married, he was living with his mother in her Park Avenue apartment.

Though Courtney and Dana moved into their own apartment a few blocks along Park Avenue soon after the wedding, their relationship was barely closer than before. They operated at completely different levels of energy. Courtney was dapper, easygoing, liked by most, trusted with money by few. Although he would eventually have some successes as a producer—most notably *The Seven-Year Itch* in the 1950s—most of his shows never got past the pitch stage. "He was so lazy," the actress and dancer Tamara Geva recalled. Dana, on the other hand, was driven. As much as she loved to socialize, these were never more than breaks between sustained periods of creative work. "When Dana told me she was getting married to Courtney," Geva told Dana's biographer, Peter Mintun, "I asked her 'What the hell are you doing that for?'"

Whatever the nature of her marriage, Dana was powerfully drawn to Virginia. Within months of their first meeting, the two women began looking for a house in Connecticut where they could get away from the city together. Was this a case of opposites attracting? To use stereotypes of lesbian relationships, Dana was more femme, Virginia more butch. Dana was particular about how she dressed, paid attention to fashions, shopped at the better stores. Virginia stuck to the same short hairstyle she'd adopted at Radcliffe, though she was discriminating in her choice of stylists to maintain it. When out in public, she respected the convention that women should wear dresses, having abandoned her Radclyffe Hall affectations; at home, she was happy with a work shirt and a pair of khaki trousers. Dana loved to cook and her letters to her mother are full of reports on recipes she'd tried out. Virginia's culinary interests stopped at heating up something from a can.

They were both fiercely intelligent, voracious readers, and demanding conversationalists, intolerant of pedants, bureaucrats, and trivia. According to Tamara Geva, Dana "was stubborn to an idiotic point. Nothing was right for her. She didn't consider anybody's opinion . . . only hers." Like Virginia, Dana had never found a place where she fully fit in. She married Courtney Burr to conform to the stereotype of a heterosexual woman, but she was unwilling to take a back seat and put his interests ahead of hers. At the same time, neither Dana nor Virginia were prepared to rebel to the extent of risking condemnation. Virginia might have been gay at a time when that was not considered socially acceptable outside a few small circles—but she never failed to pay her dues to the Lincoln chapter of the

Junior League. Dana made sure her mother knew every time her name was mentioned favorably in print.

Dana was slightly older than Virginia. Born in Kansas City, Missouri, in 1909, she was a musical prodigy who made her debut at the age of six. From that point on, Dana's mother seized opportunities to get her much more talented daughter on stage. Dana would later say, "There is only one thing worse than being an only child, and that is being an only child who is also a child prodigy." Children who can play a musical instrument with proficiency aren't that exceptional. But Dana demonstrated a much rarer talent: She could write original music. At fourteen, she performed five of her own compositions on a local radio station, earning billing as "Missouri's youngest composer."

Her musical studies, her increasingly busy schedule of performances, and her mother's protectiveness meant that Dana grew up isolated from other children. She used her time working on various notebooks full of everything from a collection of faces drawn from life and imagination, sketches of outfits she hoped to wear, with detailed notes on fabrics and construction, and quotations and adages from her reading and her own thoughts. "Everything of value in your life will cost you dear and sometime or other you will have to pay the price of it," read one, a premonition that would eventually apply to Virginia even more than to Dana.

In late 1926, Dana and her mother moved to New York City, and within a matter of weeks, she had copyrighted her first song, "I Want the World for You." Soon after that, she was introduced to the bandleader Paul Whiteman, who'd debuted George Gershwin's *Rhapsody in Blue* two years earlier. Whiteman was open to Dana's initial compositions, but music publishers showed no interest in her "serious" pieces. The demand for new popular songs, however, was insatiable. Not only was there a thriving business of musicals and revues on Broadway and for touring theater companies, but also radio and what were known as "prologues"—stage shows that played at cinemas ahead of the feature films. Dana had a few successes, starting with "Syncopated Love Song" in 1928, but it was when she was introduced to the rising young producer Billy Rose that things started taking off.

First hired as a rehearsal pianist for one of Rose's shows in 1930, Dana was soon brought into his circle of songwriters for the long string of revues that would make Rose one of the richest men in the theater business. Her first contribution was a forgettable number about a Brooklynite turned matador called "I Knew Him Before He Was Spanish," but Rose appreciated her work and she soon became his lead composer. Writing popular songs was not what truly inspired her, but she recognized the necessity to put commerce ahead of art—at least until she had made enough money to shift her focus: "There's a lot of glory and fame in being a serious composer," she told an interviewer in 1932, "but no money. Well, I have to earn my living, and I want to write serious music, so I spend fifteen minutes now and then writing a popular song."

Dana Suesse offered Virginia an example of how an artist could pursue both commercial success and creative fulfillment. She never stopped working on compositions that could only ever have been performed in a concert hall. Paul Whiteman included her "Concerto in Three Rhythms" in the fourth of his "Experiments in Modern Music" concerts at Carnegie Hall in November 1932. Leonard Liebling of the *Musical Courier* wrote afterward, "The music of Miss Suesse represents the best type of jazz writing. She . . . harmonizes adroitly and colorfully; and tells her musical story convincingly." But her own feeling about jazz were less enthusiastic. "Jazz is a limited medium," she said later. "This is one-shot stuff."

Throughout the 1930s, she juggled commercial and serious musical work. She wrote the music for Billy Rose's productions, including far-off-Broadway shows like *Casa Mañana*, which was performed on the world's largest revolving stage in Fort Worth, Texas, and his Aquacades—shows combining singing, dancing, and swimming—in Cleveland and at the 1939 World's Fair in New York.

At the same time, she pursued opportunities to have her own compositions performed in classical settings. She joined with Jean Goldkette, Aaron Copland, George Steiner, and other contemporaries in forming the American Symphony Orchestra, an ad hoc ensemble that began holding concerts in New York in 1939. The same year, she collaborated with the harpist Casper Reardon, who had developed a technique for playing in a jazz style. Her piece "Young Man with a Harp" debuted at the Robin Hood Dell amphitheater in Philadelphia, and the two performed a movement of the piece for a gala show at the White House the following year. Dana would have loved to write more for Reardon, but he died unexpectedly about a month after she began seeing Virginia. Even with the loss of a musician she felt inspired by, she was full of ideas for more compositions. "Gosh, I have never been so busy," she wrote her mother in early 1941.

Virginia was busy as well, with her magazine stories and occasional contributions to Fred Allen's *Texaco Star Theater* and *Duffy's Tavern*, the new radio show from her old acquaintance Ed Gardner. But taking on a libretto for an opera would be the biggest step out of her comfort zone since leaving Hollywood. It would be over a year before Dana and Virginia sat down to work together though. Dana was focused on getting the music for Billy Rose's newest revue ready and Virginia was readying her own debut of sorts, her first slick magazine short story since 1935. It came out in the June issue of *Mademoiselle* and proved she had no problem getting back into her old formula.

"Iris and the Ostrich" was about the off-again, on-again marriage of the Cobdens—as usual, a couple for whom having enough money was of no more concern than having enough air to breathe. As usual, both young and good-looking: "Iris was blond and looked exactly like a very young and lovely angel who was having a naughty thought; Cobby looked exactly like the kind of man she would fall in love with, i.e., tall, dark, and far from ill-favored." And, of course, the two of them had blasé in buckets: "'Cobby,' said Iris, 'I want to divorce you and marry somebody else.' 'Come again,' said her husband, putting down his paper with a slight crash. 'I want to divorce you and marry somebody else.' Cobby thought for a while. 'Anybody we know?' he asked, finally."

Cobby voices a view that pervades Virginia's magazine fiction: "Sex is the technical name for the war between men and women." Of the two dozen-plus stories she wrote in the 1940s for major national magazines like *Liberty* and the *Saturday Evening Post*, virtually all involve the same eternal triangle as "The Sitting-Room Safari" back in 1935—husband, wife, and hypotenuse—and end with matrimony triumphant. Not that Virginia ever suggests that her couples live happily ever after. "They gonna divorce?" a character asks about the Cobdens at the end of "Iris and the Ostrich." "No, Kitty," replies Miss Warlock, this story's "other." "Not for a few years anyway."

"Iris and the Ostrich" takes place in a stylish limbo unconnected with contemporary events. The Cobdens could be living anytime between the early 1920s and the attack on Pearl Harbor. World War II occasionally factors in as background, but rarely intrudes upon her characters' lives. The exception is "Personal Footnote," a "short short"—a one-page story—that appeared in *Liberty* in August 1941.

The story's opening line brings the war directly to the forefront: "The shelling was getting much nearer." The setting is ambiguous. A palace in a European country just days after its invasion. The narrator recalls the last moments as she, her aunt ("your Majesty"), and the household servants prepared to evacuate their stately home and join the swarms of refugees. For once, no one has a quip handy. "Now that I am remembering it," the narrator confesses, "I see myself as colorless and static." She was unaccustomed to leaving without fuss and ceremony. "I realized this was actually the Departure. . . . We were just some people going away."

It's by far Virginia's shortest story, under eight hundred words. The narrator, Elizabeth, offers a few thoughts and snatches of conversation with her aunt and two servants. We know they have left, that Elizabeth is grateful to have her aunt's old fur coat to keep her warm. We don't know what fate awaits them. The limit on length—today, we would call it flash fiction—forced her to tap into something beyond her usual wisecracks. Like the reference in "A Room with a Bath" to thousands of slaves killed in the quarries of ancient Syracuse, the sound of artillery serves as a reminder that tragedy is often the backdrop to the best comedies—just as the absence of that backdrop renders so much of Virginia's magazine writing insubstantial and ephemeral. We can only regret that she didn't attempt—or, at least, didn't publish—more such "short shorts."

Superficial though her magazine stories might be, they sold. Sometime during the summer of 1941, she felt confident enough in her income prospects to move to River House, a new and prestigious residence on East Fifty-Second Street with its own pier where owners could park their launches and speedboats. A few months later, Dana decided to move from the apartment she shared with Courtney Burr.

In Dana's daybook, the entry for October 11, 1941, reads, "Move from 15 Park to V's at River House." A few days later, on October 15, after a note about having lunch with Virginia at the Sherry-Netherland Hotel, the following appears in hastily written bleeding ink: "River House incident." And below it, "Mommie—midnight."

No one knows now what the River House incident was. It's unlikely that it involved Courtney Burr making an angry scene as the jealous husband:

If anything, based on secondhand accounts, he didn't have a problem with Dana leaving to live with another woman if she continued to support him financially. Did Dana discover that Virginia was capable of drinking to the point of blacking out and reach out to her mother for help? Or did Virginia panic at the prospect of sharing her space and her life twenty-four hours a day with another woman, a level of intimacy she'd never experienced before? If nothing else, the note in Dana's daybook suggests that a certain thread of uncertainty ran through her relationship with Virginia.

To make things even more intriguing, just after the River House incident, Dana wrote her mother that Virginia had left on a long trip to Lincoln and New Mexico. "Says she prefers to be away from the distractions of New York for a while," Dana reported. We know from various mentions in Lincoln papers that Virginia came to Lincoln in late October and stayed through Christmas. Among other things, she and Aunt Pauline, now divorced from Thomas Howell, attended a luncheon of the local chapter of the Alpha Phi sorority. No matter what her life in New York might be like, in Lincoln she conformed.

Virginia's stay in New Mexico was the first of several visits. According to Dana, Virginia's plan was "to do some writing" and Dana must have decided that she also needed a creative getaway, for in early January 1942 the two met in New Orleans. They rented a house on St. Peter Street sight unseen, which they regretted when they discovered how austerely it was furnished. They were also far from downtown, where they had to travel to stock up on kitchen items and food. Dana hoped to work on a piece titled "Louisiana Legends," but she spent as much time cooking as composing, even after she managed to get a tuner for the piano that had been sitting idle for years.

Virginia came away from their visit with "Inside Creole America," a Princess Tulip piece that treated Louisianans high and low with equal-opportunity condescension. Princess Tulip estimated the vintage of the fashions, political opinions, and plumbing in New Orleans as "respectively from 1920, 1860, and 1492." However, there was hope, she reported, "that by 1945 nearly all of New Orleans natives will know that America is at war, though they may not be sure with whom." She also got a start on several magazine stories. The years 1942 and 1943 were Virginia's most prolific years, with a story appearing in a national magazine, usually the *Saturday Evening Post*, an average of every other month. Part of the reason was Tenterhooks—

their name for the house on the outskirts of Wilton, Connecticut, that they began renting not long after the return from New Orleans.

Back when she left Hollywood in 1937, Virginia had confided to her cousin Sarah Meyer that she thought "the grandest place in the United States" was a farm in Connecticut where she could "putter and paint fences and things." Though Virginia was no more of a handywoman than she was a cook, there's no doubt that she found it much easier to focus on writing when she didn't have the constant temptation to meet someone for a night on the town. In an interview for the *Saturday Evening Post* in late 1943, Virginia went so far as to say, "In 1941, I decided to start life anew under the same name, and have lived mostly in Connecticut, dabbling at light fiction eight hours a day."

What she didn't mention, however, was that she'd made another attempt at a novel. The only remaining trace of it is in a letter from Maria Leiper at Simon & Schuster, just as discouraging as the one she received when leaving London in 1938. Virginia had sent a sample chapter and Leiper had read and shared it with her colleagues. They all agreed it was "slick-paper stuff" and predicted it might turn into something like Ilka Chase's *In Bed We Cry*, a bestselling romantic drama set among New York's sophisticates. But, Leiper advised Virginia, the fact was that Ilka Chase "has more sell in her name" (Chase was an established stage and film actress and radio personality). Leiper felt Virginia could do better, that "she could do a fine amusing book" if she set her mind to it.

Leiper offered her an assessment in the same kind of blunt, critical language that Virginia would later use herself as an editor: "Well, you asked me to tell you what I thought of it. Did you want me to be frank? I know you can write; and so do you. You've got intelligence, perception, style, wit, and emotion, too, though I don't believe you've often tried to use it. In my opinion, however, you haven't made up your mind between the magazines and a novel."

Leiper's letter survives in Virginia's papers as three fragments, cut with scissors from the rest. It's likely that what she discarded was more complimentary: Virginia tended to respect tough criticism over superficial praise. Leiper's feedback echoed, again, what she'd known when leaving the *Washington Post* back in 1934. Faced with the choice between smart, know-it-all, and kinder and truer, Virginia once again chose to stick with what she'd already proven herself adept at. The book is never mentioned again and the manuscript has been lost.

Her Princess Tulip pieces, on the other hand, continued to earn praise, even from *Town & Country's* competitors. After one story, "Without Benefit," which mockingly proclaimed the ersatz patriotism of Manhattan socialites, appeared in the April 1943 issue, Frank Crowninshield, managing editor of Conde Nast Publications, wrote Virginia, calling the piece "one of the outstanding examples of satirical writing which I have read in many years . . . a magnificent and devastating projectile."

"It makes me wild when anyone questions the patriotism of such fine young specimens as Peter Frenzy Fripp or Junior Glockenspiel," Princess Tulip protests. "Why, while bombs were still dropping on Pearl Harbor, Peter rushed to be the first to do his bathroom over in red, white, and blue, and not only that—his valet is a blood donor!" Crowninshield was impressed with Virginia's wit and recalled hearing her name back when she first hit the publishing scene. "You are certainly gifted," he wrote, predicting that her work would appear in anthologies of American humor fifty years from then. He hinted at another motive, proposing to take her to lunch at 21 or "some quieter French restaurant" away from "the rattle of dishes and the clash of personalities." Virginia declined the offer.

The relative isolation of Connecticut helped Dana as well. Billy Rose debuted two new revues with her music, "Venus on the Half Shell" and "Toast of the Town," at his Diamond Horseshoe nightclub in the first year after the move to Tenterhooks. And on the serious side, she composed her largest work to date, the *Concerto in E Minor for Two Pianos and Orchestra*, which was performed for the first time at the end of 1943 by the Cincinnati Symphony Orchestra under conductor Eugene Goossens.

Tenterhooks gave them the space to return to the idea of collaboration that brought Virginia and Dana together in the first place. The project they settled upon, however, was not an opera but a good old-fashioned Broadway musical. Dana threw herself into the work, since it was the first time she'd had an opportunity to contribute the words, and not just the music. They both took the work so seriously that they went "on the wagon," as Dana reported to her mother, swearing off drinking—temporarily.

Only a few pages of the book and lyrics of *That Does It!* survive in Dana's papers in the Library of Congress, along with fragments of piano music. It's unfair to speculate about the show that might have been from these scraps, but it's hard to imagine it being a hit. Set in a seaside resort near Lisbon, Portugal—already known as a hotbed of espionage and secret dealings by Allied, Axis, and neutrals—it opens with a prologue that lets the audience in on the show's one big joke from the beginning. "Calling all spies! Calling all spies!" shouts a character known as "Head of the Spy Ring" in a location referred to in the stage instructions as "Spy Headquarters." One by one, the spies step up to report, in a musical number called "I Spy." "It is important," the instructions advise, "that the audience be able to identify them as spies the next time they appear." So, it's about spying, that much is clear.

There is also a former U.S. presidential candidate traveling around the world à la Wendell Wilkie and his *One World* tour, a movie star, reporters, a handsome naval officer, and beautiful women who are members of G.A.M.S.—the Girls' Aide to Morale Service, or the oldest profession, as it's more often called. Taking place over two acts and a dozen scenes, the show included sixteen musical numbers and a ballet. Although Virginia contributed a few lyrics, most of them appear to be Dana's. They're not bad. One can easily imagine "Goodbye, My Love," for example, among the songs featured each week on *Your Hit Parade*:

Goodbye, my love,
Now you're only a stranger to me.
Goodbye, my love
You're no longer a danger to me.
The way you betrayed me made me see you clearly,
And how it broke my heart you'll never know!

Without the accompanying music, however, "The Circumstances-Over-Which-I-Have-No-Control-Whatsoever Blues" may be amusing but seems unsingable.

Even before they'd finished work on *That Does It!*, Dana began shopping for a producer, starting, naturally, with Courtney Burr. In July 1943, they performed selections for a private audience at the Connecticut home of their friend, *Woman's Day* editor Mabel Souvaine. This led columnist Danton Walker to announce the following week that "Courtney Burr is whipping up a musical for next season with Virginia Faulkner doing the book and

Dana Suesse the score." A few days later, the *New York Times* reported that Monte Proser, a veteran producer and owner of the Copacabana night club, had joined with Burr and Walter Batchelor to produce an untitled musical by Dana and Virginia.

Batchelor was so confident in the show's prospects that he tried to sell it to the studios on a trip he made to Hollywood in September 1943. No one was interested. What he did get nibbles on, however, was the prospect of Dana and Virginia as a writing team, with numbers like fifteen hundred dollars a week mentioned. "Apparently, people have got wind out there that we are a hot piece of property," Dana confided to her mother. They told Batchelor they weren't interested, however. "We wouldn't dream of dropping everything now and going out." It was wiser, Dana explained, "to stay here and startle the East with a really good show before we try our wings out on the Coast." *That Does It!* was done for, but that didn't kill their aspirations to write a show together.

11

It Takes Two

"Finished *It Takes Two*." This, on October 14, 1945, is the first entry in Dana Suesse's daybook after Christmas 1943. A similar gap appears in her steady correspondence with her mother. Partly this is because Wilton and Niantic, where Nina Quarrier lived with her second husband, were close enough to make letters superfluous. But it's likely the underlying reason is simple, if rare for two such creative and intense people: Dana and Virginia were happy.

Virginia thrived on the quiet atmosphere of Tenterhooks, where she didn't have to keep up a frenetic pace of socializing while also carving out time to write. She tended to operate in cycles, approaching her work tentatively at first, then, as her focus on the task tightened, becoming more and more consumed and going for hours and sometimes days without a break, until her body and mind gave out and she collapsed, often seeking peace in a glass of Scotch. Dana was less susceptible to these highs and lows, particularly because she found it easy to set work aside if it meant she could go into the kitchen and cook. Tenterhooks had a big kitchen with an electric stove and refrigerator, plus a basement where they could keep a well-stocked pantry.

Dana took the bedroom downstairs as her study. Upstairs, she and Virginia had separate bedrooms with a shared bathroom in between. There was a large backyard with a table where they could work or entertain guests and a screened porch for the same. Though they made frequent trips to New York City for work, shopping, doctors (Dana suffered from respiratory problems and what today would be called carpal tunnel syndrome) and dinners and shows with friends, it was always a relief to return. "We took the three-forty train back yesterday afternoon and as usual, were so glad to get back home," Dana wrote after a trip in November 1942. "Everything looked fine. We are certainly glad to get that over with."

The house and its location allowed them to socialize at their own pace. They were close to Niantic, close to Stamford, where Gus Schirmer Jr., the son of Dana's original music publisher and one of her closer friends, had begun to produce summer stock plays at the Strand theater. S. N. Behrman and his second wife took a house a short drive away and Dana and Virginia visited several times. They even hosted a "decadent" picnic for the notorious New York madam Polly Adler, whom both had come to know from visits to her various Manhattan "houses" that were popular stops on the late-night rounds of the smart set.

At Tenterhooks, Virginia could spend days, even weeks, with no makeup, wearing workpants and a shirt with rolled-up sleeves. Dana offered Virginia a sense of security she hadn't known since the death of her mother almost seventeen years before. On the first of March 1944, while Virginia was working away, Dana prepared a special birthday dinner for her. "Delmonico steak with mushrooms, mashed potatoes, a special beefsteak sauce, sliced onions and tomatoes and ice cream and cake," she told her mother. Teffy—the pet name Dana was now calling Virginia—"was so thrilled when she saw the cake. She said nobody had actually made her a birthday cake for years."

She and Dana shared little domestic dramas and comedies. Debates over cleaning ladies, frustrations with how hard it was to keep the place heated (Dana's list of gift suggestions for Virginia she sent her mother one Christmas included a carrying bag for firewood and heavy work gloves). One day, Dana surprised Virginia, returning from New York, with a large arrangement of flowers she'd gathered from their yard and a nearby brook, only to be startled when a lizard emerged from the vase and skittered across the floor as they were having dinner. "Poor Teffy was practically hanging from the chandelier when she saw what it was!" she wrote her mother. Virginia reached for the fireplace shovel and handed it to Dana, who dispatched the poor creature into the next world.

Little changed in Virginia's work in 1944. There were more Princess Tulip pieces, more magazine short stories. Carl Brandt, now Virginia's literary agent, negotiated a new project for her, a twenty-thousand-word mystery novel for *American* magazine set on Fred Allen's radio show. She was to write it with Judson Philips, a veteran writer of pulp mysteries who

Fig. 9. Virginia with Polly Adler, Dana Suesse, and unknown man, 1945. Courtesy of Peter Mintun.

used the pseudonym of Hugh Pentecost. Philips would handle plot and structure; Virginia would contribute the dialogue, drawing upon her time as a gag writer for the show. A forgettable work, formulaic in both mystery and comedy, "Murder on the Fred Allen Show" earned them twenty-five hundred dollars each.

Dana had more strings tugging her away from Connecticut. She was still writing for Billy Rose, still looking for opportunities to air her classical work. In February 1945, she went to Chicago to appear on *Hildegarde's Raleigh Room* radio show and in April she joined her old friend on *Paul Whiteman Presents*, broadcast by NBC out of New York. But she was also being careful not to get tied up in any long-term commitments. She had something else in mind.

Their comfort as a couple gave Virginia and Dana the courage to attempt another collaboration, and in the fall of 1945, they began work on a new project. This time, it had nothing to do with music. They were going to write a play. The seed of the idea came from stories about the housing shortages facing discharged veterans and their families, particularly in New York City. Many were forced to sublet and sub-sublet fractions of apartments, adopting Soviet-style communal living arrangements. Virginia and Dana thought there was comic gold in these situations, particularly in the friction between a starry-eyed pair of newlyweds and their world-weary fellow tenants.

The play, *It Takes Two*, came together quickly. They finished the first draft in just three weeks, and before the end of the year, they were shopping it to Broadway producers. Harold Freedman, head of the dramatic department of Carl Brandt's agency, thought the story had a natural appeal for Hollywood, which was eager for material relevant to the millions of veterans returning to the habit of moviegoing. In early 1946, he flew out to the West Coast and quickly returned with a generous offer from RKO.

Even before the play was lined up for Broadway, RKO was ready to buy the film rights, and for a number that still astonishes: $50,000, or roughly $750,000 today. Even better, Freedman negotiated terms that made the deal independent of the stage production. Virginia and Dana signed the RKO contract in mid-March and split the first installment, walking away with $13,230 each. Broadway's reaction to the news of the RKO sale was apathy. This was in part a recognition that with the sale already in hand, there was little chance of making profits from anything but the stage production itself. It took months to find a producer willing to organize and fund a show.

While they were looking, they took the bold step of appearing as a couple—or, as the newspapers referred to them, companions—on Virginia's home ground in Lincoln. Virginia arrived first to attend a dinner marking the twenty-fifth anniversary of the Junior League chapter her mother had helped found, then Dana joined her. The Lincoln papers gave them celebrity treatment, with Virginia's photo appearing in a Sunday society section and another of Dana coming down the staircase of the house on South Street a few days later.

They returned to Tenterhooks still without a prospect for the show. When they did land a producer, though, it should have been cause for celebration. George Abbott was already a legend on Broadway, having staged dozens of successful shows since starting out in 1913. Abbott agreed to take the show in partnership with Richard Aldrich and they set to work with a goal of premiering on Broadway in early 1947. Abbott leveraged the connection with RKO to get the studio to release Martha Scott, and soon lined up Hugh Marlowe and Vivian Vance for the other big roles. The remaining auditions were completed quickly and rehearsals started soon after Thanksgiving.

With a veteran like Abbott in charge, there were none of the fits and starts and crises of *All in Fun*. In hindsight, Dana and Virginia may have wished there had been, so they could blame anyone but themselves. Shortly before the out-of-town premiere in Boston on January 21, the show's name was changed to *Apartment 17-b*—the setting of most of the scenes—but aside from that, everything went as planned. The *Boston Globe*'s critic, Cyrus Durgin, gave the show the benefit of the doubt, chalking up its shortcomings to things that would be fixed before going to Broadway. "Since George Abbott is coproducer and director, it is 100 to nothing he already has begun to do this. If the Abbott touch is still good, and there's no reason to suppose otherwise, the show will shortly realize the promise it showed in its premiere at the Wilbur Theatre last night." He also applauded Abbott's judgment in his choice of actors: "The typecasting of all the roles is just about perfect."

What Abbott couldn't fix, though, was the writing. As a good Boston critic, Durgin shook a finger at "the occasional profanity and some of the sexy jokes" that Virginia and Dana had written in. But the first act was "dull" and though the second and third were "sparkling" and "rousing," there was "a lot of dreary domestic bickering," which he blamed on "the female sex of the authors" (among the show's problems were misogynistic critics). And the pace dragged. And the title "could be changed for the better."

This, at least, Abbott could do. When the programs, ads, and marquee for the play were prepared for the Broadway debut at the Biltmore Theatre on Monday, February 3, 1947, it was back to *It Takes Two* again. A change of title was not enough to bring the script up to the critics' liking, however. Abbott's name and the presence of Martha Scott attracted New York's top reviewers: John Chapman from the *Daily News*, Brooks Atkinson from the *New York Times*, and the dean of drama critics, George Jean Nathan.

Chapman had the kindest things to say. "The authors," he wrote, "have devised several crisply funny lines, even though most of their situations are only normal." Abbott "directed the company with his usual fine sense of pace and the players themselves leave nothing to be desired." This mild praise was, unfortunately, the best of the lot. Atkinson dismissed it with an opening that let readers know he was going to have little to praise about the show: "Two producers and two authors put on a comedy entitled *It Takes Two* at the Biltmore last evening. That is the most amusing thing about it." He was not as concerned about the play's material as the Boston critics. "The authors have written nothing that would upset the gravity of a club of sedate bookkeepers." The only people the play might seem funny to, he suggested, were "some of the backward scholars in the freshman class at Yale."

George Jean Nathan, who'd been taking an axe to plays for over a quarter century, showed that time had done nothing to dull his blade. "It is such occasions that persuade me confidentially to address myself as follows: 'Now see here, George, me lad, why do you persist in wasting your time in this way?'" The show's program said that the play was a comedy, he reported, but "it was a slight exaggeration if comedy means something that amuses one to the point of laughter." He admitted that he'd left after the second act—and wrote that staying that long showed "that I am probably losing my mind." It didn't prevent him, however, from itemizing twenty examples of the play's failed attempts at comedy, including "5. The joke about wanting a martini without any vermouth" and "13. Her indignation when he didn't notice that she had on a new dress." He chose to omit the "thirty or forty more items of a kind" he'd also recorded.

It Takes Two closed on Saturday, February 8, after six performances. Virginia and Dana slunk back to Tenterhooks for refuge. The project they'd devoted over a year to was an utter failure. Not a financial failure. The contract Harold Freedman had negotiated with RKO required the studio to pay the second installment for the film rights upon the play's debut on

Broadway—regardless of whether it ran for a week or a year. But clearly a critical failure and a blow to their hopes of establishing themselves as a writing team.

The weight of the blame had to rest on Virginia's shoulders. She was not only the experienced writer but she'd been through the process of getting a play from manuscript to stage, even if that, too, had been a failure. But more than that: Everything about the play has her fingerprints on it. The silly squabbling husband and wife. The "other" who arrives to form the eternal triangle. The silly character names (Mrs. Loosbrock, Miss Comfort Gibson [the "other"]). And all that wisecracking dialogue that left Atkinson and Nathan cringing.

But they hadn't yet given up hope. Virginia packed up her typewriter and the two of them flew to Haiti, where they planned to rest and start on a second play. Judging by Dana's letters to her mother, however, they spent their time relaxing by the pool, playing tennis, and taking in sights. In any case, by the time they returned in March, Dana had decided to make a change.

Up to then, her work as a composer had drawn on instruction that dated back to her teenage days in Kansas City. When it came time to prepare a piece for performance, such as Paul Whiteman's debut of "Concerto in Three Rhythms" at Carnegie Hall in 1932, she depended on an orchestrator to take her piano part and worked out the instrumentation for a full symphony. Though she gained some experience working with larger ensembles, Dana felt she could not achieve all she aspired to without in-depth study of the art of composition and orchestration. With the money from the RKO deal, she could afford to pay for the best teacher the world could offer: Nadia Boulanger, the Frenchwoman who'd taught hundreds of musicians, including the American composers Aaron Copland, Roy Harris, and Virgil Thomson.

Upon returning to Connecticut, Dana cabled Boulanger in Paris and laid out her case. Although nearing sixty, Boulanger was busier than ever, the war having pent up demand from students outside France. She was reluctant to work with a student who'd already had so much experience with composition and performance. Still, she was impressed by a recommendation from Dana's friend and occasional collaborator, arranger Robert Russell Bennett, and in early July she replied: yes.

Dana began preparing, expecting to spend six months in France but open to staying longer if Boulanger agreed. This left Virginia in limbo: Should she stay in Connecticut and wait for Dana to return? It wasn't clear that she could continue to rent Tenterhooks and she wasn't even sure that she wanted to stay in the house alone for months on end. And having earned such negative reviews for *It Takes Two*, she had to consider where her own career was going. Dana was taking a major gamble in hopes of advancing her artistic career, investing time and money and moving to a different continent, a place she'd never been before. What did Virginia have to compare with that?

When Dana left Tenterhooks in late October for New York and her ship to France, Virginia was down with a cold and unable to accompany her to the dock. They would not see each other again for three years.

12

The Haven

"My lessons are progressing very well," Dana wrote her mother from Paris in early 1948. But after less than two months of lessons, she cautioned that "actual results will take time." Though she was certain she was "learning a lot," she was also sure that an end to her work with Boulanger was "far away."

By then, it was clear that Virginia had to do something. The winter of 1947–48 was particularly bitter. At one point, the furnace at Tenterhooks quit and Virginia had just a hot plate to cook and warm herself by. Faced with the prospect of spending the holidays in the house alone, she decided to return to Lincoln and stay with Eddie and Jean, hoping that she could come back refreshed in the new year. But when she got back to Connecticut in January 1948, she found the house blanketed in snow, the lights and heat off, the furniture covered, shut up for the long term. Even after settling in, she often awoke to find snow piled up as high as the tops of the downstairs windows. The short dark days and isolation wore down her resolve. One day, she felt so desperate she went to the expense of placing an overseas call just to talk with Dana for fifteen minutes.

Virginia stuck it out until spring, but by June she knew she had to move. She let the lease on Tenterhooks end. Dana's mother and her husband came up from Florida and helped her sort out a houseful of two intertwined lives. Dana provided instructions by post from France, but there were so many things to consider. The electric mixer: Should her mother take it? No, on second thought, that had been Eddie's gift to Virginia. The copies of *Gourmet* magazine? Well, if Virginia wanted them, otherwise Dana hated to throw them away. It was hard to know exactly what to do with everything because neither of them was quite sure whether Virginia intended to find another place in Connecticut, move to New York, or put things in storage and travel. However, Nina could take the quilts and the alabaster lamp with the red silk shade in any case, she wrote.

Dana understood Virginia's quandary. She knew that Virginia would not be happy trying to find a decent apartment in New York City in the middle of its sweltering summer, let alone to jump back into the gossip and competition of the smart set without Dana's company and protection. Dana even suggested that Virginia join her in France for a while. "I do think the change of scene would be so good for her—I have been very worried about her," she confided to her mother.

Virginia left Nina and Bob still clearing out Tenterhooks and went back to Lincoln. The stress of moving—never kind to even the most resilient disposition—triggered the start of a manic cycle. She knew that Lincoln was a temporary solution, but it was the only home she had other than the one Dana had abandoned. Even Nina knew something was wrong and wrote to Dana expressing her fears. "Yes, Teffy had told me about her illness last February," Dana admitted. "It's too bad she has cost herself so much money in that direction," she wrote, suggesting that Virginia had already sought some kind of psychiatric help.

After a few weeks in Lincoln, Virginia wrote Dana a cheerful letter. She'd managed to get some writing done, sending *Town & Country* her first Princess Tulip piece in almost two years. "Maldemer Farm: or My Back to the Soil" showed she hadn't lost her touch for toying with potentially controversial subjects. Maldemer Farm was a model collective farm in the fictional country of Ohota that grew three principal crops: "*cannabis sativa* (also known as marijuana, the "mezz," "tea," etc.) and *cannabis indica* (or hasheesh)," and opium poppies. Tulip toured the processing facilities—the Chop House, the Pot House, the Hop House, and the Smoke House ("where all the Maldemer products are tested by purity, flavor, and power before being adulterated for the market"). Truly, the Princess wrote, "I could only bow my head and marvel at the ingenuity and courage" that had turned the farm into "a veritable garden of dreams." This was hardly material to sit well with the Junior Leaguers of Lincoln.

Virginia also announced that she had come up with a new idea: She would build an apartment behind Eddie's house. Whether Eddie and Jean would have agreed was another matter, of course. In any case, she then decided to get away by herself. She booked a cabin at a dude ranch outside Sheridan, Wyoming, for a few weeks in hopes of getting some work done. When she returned in late August, the *Lincoln Star* informed its readers in August that Virginia had devoted "her time to the three r's—readin', ritin', and ridin'."

She found little time for any of them in the next few months. Jean's mother fell ill not long after Virginia's return from Wyoming and, as with Leah Faulkner, an upstairs bedroom was turned into a sick room. To make matters worse, it was now clear that Dana would be in France for a long time. In February, she wrote, "The trouble is that I'm afraid it is further away than you, or I, for that matter, would like." Her best estimate, after consulting with Nadia Boulanger, was that her return wouldn't be earlier than the spring of 1950—over a year away. Whatever arrangement Virginia made for herself would have to work until at least then.

While considering her options in the spring of 1949, Virginia managed to write a short story, "The Illusion of Youth," for the *Saturday Evening Post*, and a Princess Tulip story inspired by the marriage of actress Rita Hayworth and Pakistani nobleman Prince Aly Khan. These would be the last pieces she published as a commercial author. In July, she fled the humidity of Lincoln and headed for Santa Fe again. She had, she wrote Dana, an idea for a play. "If she ever gets it finished it will be a honey," Dana wrote her mother, adding that Virginia was thinking again of returning to New York City.

What happened next is unclear. Sometime in early September, Virginia cabled Dana to say she was staying at a sanatorium in Rochester, Michigan, called the Haven. She followed with a letter saying that she had admitted herself there voluntarily—but the fact that Virginia wrote much of the letter in innuendos and snatches of French that only the two of them would understand "fairly made my hair stand on end," Dana later confided to Nina.

Virginia quickly learned that no one ever enters a mental health facility strictly on their own terms. She and her luggage were searched upon arrival and everything she might use to harm herself or someone else—scissors, nail files, keys—were confiscated. She was put under twenty-four-hour observation and her days regimented with routines in addition to her sessions with the resident psychiatrist. Even her mail in and out was opened and read—hence her subterfuge in writing Dana.

Dana understood that one reason Virginia would have chosen such an out-of-the-way place as Rochester, Michigan, was to keep well away from the New York gossips. "Those vultures would tear her to pieces, needless to say," she wrote her mother. But it's also likely that Eddie arranged it. As president of the Woodmen Accident Company, he was in a position to know where Virginia would get the best (and most discreet) treatment. By the standards of its day, the Haven was one of the top residential psychiatric facilities in the Midwest.

Contrary to the stereotype of a mental asylum as a hellhole—this was just a couple of years after the Oscar-winning *The Snake Pit* portrayed such a facility at its worst, after all—the Haven on the outside looked more like a country estate than a medical institution. It had, in fact, been built as the home of Fred Shinnick, an automotive executive and later owner of the Detroit Tigers baseball team. Located about twenty-five miles north of Detroit, it was a large house in the English Tudor style, with brick walls, steep-pitched roofs and half-timbered fascia. It had three floors and was surrounded by seventy-five acres of ground, including a formal garden and a lake. It typically had around thirty-five resident patients.

The presiding psychiatrist at the Haven, Dr. Leo Bartemeier, was among the most prominent men in his field, former president of the American Psychoanalytic Association (and future president of the American Psychiatric Association). Working under Bartemeier were younger men, including Dr. M. L. Falick and Dr. James Clark Moloney, veterans who'd treated combat victims during the war. Falick and Moloney were also involved in research efforts at the University of Michigan and the nearby Pontiac State Hospital.

As a private sanatorium, the Haven focused exclusively on mental health and particularly on patients needing long-term care. It was also one of the first facilities in the country to move away from the traditional approach of isolating patients during treatment and established an office to improve outreach to family members. A devout Catholic, Bartemeier took a special interest in the mental illness among members of the priesthood and was seen as "a missionary for psychiatry, psychoanalysis, and mental health." He was part of the generation of psychiatrists who had to battle on two fronts: to gain the respect for psychiatry as a discipline within the medical profession as a whole, and to advance its practice as a therapeutic discipline through experimentation with new techniques.

One technique in widespread use at the time was electro-convulsive therapy (ECT). The Haven advertised that it had facilities to administer

ECT and insulin shock therapy. In a feature article on "shock treatment" in the *Detroit Free Press* a few years earlier, Dr. Falick is quoted as saying, "It's a wonderful treatment" and "is being used generally with highly beneficial results." He stipulated that it was only to be used on three types of insanity: "schizophrenia (split-personality), manic-depressive diseases, and involutional melancholia (menopause)." And, he added, "It does not cure alone, rather it opens a door in the patient's mind so that we can talk to them, show them how to control their emotions and how to meet their problems successfully." Falick added that a typical treatment involved fifteen to twenty sessions over the course of six to eight weeks.

There is no direct evidence that Virginia received ECT, but based on accounts of her behavior before and after her time at the Haven, it's likely that she was diagnosed as a manic depressive as well as an alcoholic. She used alcohol to self-medicate in her downswings and alcohol, in turn, helped trigger them. Living with Dana, who was never a heavy drinker and even convinced Virginia to stop at times, undoubtedly helped moderate Virginia's consumption and emotional cycles, but without that constraint she could easily go too far.

Is this what happened on Virginia's return from New Mexico? Whatever it was, it was serious enough that Eddie no longer felt he could leave matters alone. He was no psychiatrist, of course, but he ran a company that was a pioneer in offering private health insurance. He had excellent connections with the medical community in the Midwest, so he knew who to consult and who he could depend upon for discretion. He had always been the big brother who knew how to handle things, whether it was getting Virginia set up with a bank account in Washington DC or arranging the sale of her horse and saddle, but now he became her protector as well. He would have been the one to contact the Haven, to get her there quickly and quietly, to handle financial arrangements, and to act as intermediary between Virginia and anyone trying to contact her. Given prevailing practices, it's also likely that Bartemeier and his colleagues kept Eddie better informed about her condition and treatment than they did Virginia.

Virginia wrote Dana in November that she expected to be at the Haven for six months to a year and then spend another year as an outpatient. By then, she was allowed to work in her room and had taken up her play again, promising to send Dana drafts as she progressed. Other than Dana and her mother—and Eddie and Jean, of course—there were few people she trusted enough to share where she was. "Just say I'm back in the Midwest," she advised Dana to tell anyone who asked.

After that, though, Dana heard nothing more for several months. "I think I'll write to Eddie and ask him if she's all right," she wrote her mother in late January 1950. Not long after that, Dana received a package of books and magazines from Virginia—but no letter. It was not until April that Virginia wrote again. "She begins to sound like her old self again," Dana wrote her mother, "or rather, a new and better self." This last remark could offer a clue to the long period of silence, as the time would have covered a program of ECT treatments as described by Dr. Falick.

By the standards of the day, her treatment at the Haven was humane. One of Dr. Bartemeier's strongest-held beliefs was that psychiatrists should never label their patients according to their diseases. "We diminish the dignity of persons in our care when we speak of them as schizophrenics, manic depressives or psychopaths," he wrote in a paper from around this time. "It is high time we stop calling people names and begin to regard them as persons not unlike ourselves." We can hear this sentiment echoed in something Virginia wrote about a year after she left the Haven: "The one thing all the wizards agree on is, thank God, that I am not a loon." She wrote with pride, "I am not, never was, and never will be, psychotic (or nuts), and I got papers to prove it!" She accepted that she was dealing with an illness—depression—though she was not convinced that he or any of her subsequent therapists had correctly diagnosed its cause. Still, she recognized that the difference was lost on most. "I know only too well what conclusions people draw when you speak of 'depressive phases' and psychiatric treatment."

Another label Bartemeier disliked was "alcoholic." He believed that alcoholism was a symptom, not a disease. Bartemeier compared it to over-eating and over-smoking. In an article on the three forms of excess, he wrote, "Overindulgence is a symptom of some disturbance of the emotional life as certainly as headache or fever or any other symptoms of illness." The alcohol abuser, he argued, "suffers secretly from unspeakable terror which he cannot bear to face. He knows only the device of drowning the fear by drinking." Virginia adopted this interpretation of her behavior. In the past, she admitted, when she began to be depressed, "I used to just give up and

Lincoln Authoress Began Career at NU

VIRGINIA FAULKNER — Her first article was published in the Prairie Schooner.

Former Lincolnite, Virginia Faulkner, now of New York City, who is spending a month's vacation at the home of her brother, E. J. Faulkner, owes her first claim to literary fame to her own home town.

While attending the University of Nebraska, her first article was published in the "Prairie Schooner," English department quarterly.

Writing just "always seemed the natural thing to do," says Miss Faulkner, who also credits her Lincoln high school English instructors with helping her along in the literary field.

* * *

AT PRESENT, the authoress and playwright is working on another play, and will return to New York to continue the work. Among her accomplishments are two novels, "Friends and Romans"—written while a student at Radcliffe college in Cambridge, Mass., and "The Barbarians," published in 1935.

Miss Faulkner received her formal education at the University of Nebraska, in Rome, Italy and at Radcliffe, "although I never got beyond being a sophomore anywhere."

* * *

SHE TOOK up free lance writing in New York after attending Radcliffe, and soon became associate editor of Town and Country magazine. Her other work has included spending two years in Hollywood as a script writer, radio script-writing for the Duffy's Tavern show, and short stories and articles which have appeared in such magazines as Harper's, Saturday Evening Post, Vogue, Cosmopolitan, and American.

In 1947 she wrote her first play, "It Takes Two," in collaboration with Dana Suesse, and starring Martha Scott and Hugh Marlowe.

Barbara Rythes

Fashions . . . On the Beam

Fig. 10. Virginia after her return from the Haven. *Lincoln Journal Star*, June 17, 1951, p. 31.

drink myself unconscious." In this same letter, she also acknowledges that she had been experiencing cycles of depression for years. "Every so often—about every four to six months—there occurs an acute depressive phase, with accompanying physical symptoms." When this happened, it was "all one can do to live, let alone write."

Virginia remained at the Haven for almost a year. By August 1950, she had transitioned to intensive outpatient treatment—"seven days a week," she complained—with a psychiatrist based in Detroit. Eddie wrote Dana to explain that she would be there for some months "taking deep analysis." It was clearly an extended treatment, for she shared with the Radcliffe alumnae journal in February 1951 that she could be contacted at the Hotel Sheraton in Detroit. If she was doing any writing during this time, none of it survives. The only thing we know from this period is that her sessions were suspended for several weeks after her therapist was stabbed by a patient at the Pontiac State Hospital—and that her doctor helped her avoid drinking during her depressive cycles with "barrels of benzedrine."

She left Detroit for Lincoln in June 1951. Eddie and Jean celebrated her return, and two photos of Virginia appeared in Lincoln papers soon after. In one, accompanying an item titled "Lincoln Authoress Started Career at NU," Virginia is standing in Eddie and Jean's library, casually dressed in slacks and holding a book. One thing is unmistakable. The insouciant, slightly defiant look of her photos from the decade before is gone. This Virginia is subdued, guarded. And she has lost a great deal of weight. One of the few times she mentioned the Haven after leaving, she called it "Bartlemeier's Backwoods Buchenwald." Whatever had happened since her return from Santa Fe two years before, no matter whether her treatment was humane and in keeping with the best professional practices, it's clear it was a harrowing ordeal.

13

A House Is Not a Home

"At present," the *Lincoln Journal Star* reported in June 1951, "the authoress and playwright is working on another play, and will return to New York to continue the work." Aside from a passing mention months later—"rehearsals, etc."—in a letter to Ann Watkins, this play disappeared like the third and fourth novels. Either Virginia was working under a pseudonym, or it was a euphemism for something else that was keeping her busy.

After almost three years of study in Paris, Dana Suesse was now back in the U.S., and back to stay. She and Virginia had stayed in touch, despite the constraints on Virginia's ability to communicate. Virginia had written, cabled, telephoned, sent packages of food, books, nylons, and other items hard to come by in a country still recovering from the war. Did she assume that she and Dana would resume the life they'd shared?

If she did, she was going to be disappointed. Dana had moved on, not just as a composer but in her personal life. She was now involved with a man she referred to as her "beau." She had found a musician to replace the much-missed Caspar Reardon, a pianist named Walter "Renz" Hoffman, who roomed with Dana for a while in Paris and moved in with her again after she returned to New York. And though her interest in the theater never flagged (she would go on to write several more plays on her own, though most were never produced), her main interest was in putting her work with Boulanger to use. Though she knew that her opportunities to work as a modernist composer would be fewer and less well-paid than her songwriting, she was ready to take the chance. By this point, she would not have been interested in working with Virginia on another play, especially not another patchwork of wisecracks.

Still, when Virginia arrived at Grand Central Station aboard the Commodore train from Chicago on August 1, 1951, Dana was there to greet her. She was happy to see Virginia looking healthier and in better emotional shape than when they had parted, though she did notice that Virginia had developed a tendency to stutter and blink when speaking. Dana soon made it clear that they met again as friends, not lovers. That first evening, they dined with Renz Hoffman.

Dana had a project in mind for Virginia, but this time, she would only be its facilitator. Polly Adler, once the city's most famous madam and a friend from their wilder days, had left the sex trade behind. To capitalize on that experience, however, she had written her autobiography and was now trying to get it published. Polly wasn't having much luck. Since the summer of 1950, her agent, Ann Watkins, had sent the manuscript to over a dozen publishers. None of them was interested. It wasn't just the subject matter, which was rich with grounds for libel suits. Polly had catered to many prominent men (and women) who preferred to maintain unblemished public reputations. The root problem was simpler: It just wasn't any good. "The writing is bad, the angle is all wrong, and the whole thing sounds phony," complained Lee Barker of Doubleday, one of the publishers who refused the book.

Polly reached out for help to Philip Wylie—a bestselling writer and former client. He turned her down after reading the manuscript. His most damning criticism? "Dullness." How anyone who'd spent the 1920s and 1930s at the center of New York City's most diverse, notorious, and colorful cast of characters while running its most successful enterprise in the oldest profession could write a colorless memoir of the experience was hard to imagine, but there it was. Henry Holt & Co. seemed ready to take the book in January 1951; in February, they were backing away as if it were radioactive material.

After more submissions and rejections, Ann Watkins told Polly it was time to look again for help. What the book needed was to "quicken its pace and reduce its length." For that, a ghostwriter was called for. Once Watkins suggested this, Polly knew who she wanted: Virginia.

Virginia had seen a draft of the book years before, in 1945, during Polly's "decadent" weekend at Tenterhooks. Virginia had typed up fifty-some pages from Polly's handwritten manuscript, though for once she kept her opinion to herself. Polly's attorney, Gertrude Gottlieb, also happened to be Dana's, so there would be women Polly trusted and respected involved. The day after Virginia arrived, Polly met Dana and Virginia for dinner and made her plea. Virginia accepted immediately, but not unconditionally. She agreed to read the manuscript and provide an assessment of what it needed to become publishable.

Two years as a patient had taught Virginia to be cautious. She understood her own strengths and weaknesses better. And she understood Polly's. Virginia knew that she was subject to cycles of ups and near-crippling downs, while Polly only had ups. She could be relentless, petty, selfish, opportunistic, and selective in her memory. "Miss A. is a force of nature," Virginia confided to Watkins. "Anyway, when she gets the conversational bit in her teeth, there's nothing to do but take a seat and hang on." The traits that had helped her survive in business were certain to test the patience of any collaborator, and Virginia was never known for her patience.

Virginia spent the next weeks going through the hundred-fifty-thousand-word manuscript, taking notes, considering how to improve the book. Every few days she surfaced to have dinner with Dana and Renz. At some point, she not only decided Polly's autobiography was a book that could be saved but that she was the right person to save it. She moved out of her hotel, leased an apartment at Sutton Terrace, and sent Ann Watkins a memo outlining her proposal.

Her major criticism was that the book needed cutting and rearranging. "Though this is easy enough to say, still so far as I know the only way it can be done is by the old blood, sweat, spit and polish process: there's no quick way." She outlined eight major points on which rework was required, from Polly's treatment of her parents (something Virginia was more attuned to after many months of psychoanalysis) to inconsistencies in presentation. She did not address the veracity of Polly's recollections, which would prove her biggest source of headaches.

Virginia met with Watkins and followed up with another letter that did confront the matter of facts. "I would hesitate to say the proportion of true and manufactured—and in some cases it's a sort of pastiche of the actual and the apocryphal—but there is plenty which is suppressed or distorted or just plain lied about." It wasn't that Polly invented things, rather that she censored herself in a variety of ways: leaving out details, inventing others, changing names, combining events. Virginia recognized that this

Fig. 11. Polly Adler with Virginia and Dana Suesse at the Club 181, September 1951. Courtesy of Peter Mintun.

created two problems: First, it made it tough to prevent libel when Polly had already mangled the truth; and second, to Philip Wylie's point, her fictitious versions were tepid.

Ironically, to deal with these difficulties, Virginia would have to both check facts and do some inventing of her own. "So long as it is authentic in feeling and spirit, I see nothing against supplying punch lines, rounding off anecdotes, and (where needed to support a point) making a whole goddam brick, even in the absence of straw." Because Polly was still a principal in the ghostwriting arrangement, whatever Virginia wrote had to get her approval as well as Watkins's. Fortunately, Virginia had, she felt, "assimilated Polly's point of view" and felt she could predict what would pass Polly's test. She shared a few passages that she'd doctored with Polly and, she proudly reported to Watkins, "by not so much as a flick of the eyelid did the author indicate that it was all news to her."

Ann Watkins sent the material Virginia had worked on to John Selby, the former syndicated book reviewer now an editor at Rinehart. Rinehart had taken an option on the book, subject to major revisions—the job Virginia was offering to take on. He was impressed. "The difference between the version of Polly I read some months ago, and this last version, is enormous," he wrote. He was in favor of moving forward. He did, however, suggest yet another way in which the book needed improvement: Virginia would need to add "enough of the period"—the 1920s and 1930s—to make Polly's success as a madam plausible. "From time to time the story throughout ought to contain references" to larger events, things like the introduction of Prohibition and its repeal. Now, in addition to fact-checking, she would have to conduct her own historical research as well. But, he concluded, "it is good to know that Polly's book is in your hands. I shudder to think what hash some people could make of it."

Virginia was starting to realize the magnitude of the task she was taking on. "Miss Adler's little opus is really turning into a project and a headache," she confided to Watkins. While she agreed with Selby's suggestion about adding context—had made the same herself, in fact—it forced Virginia to venture from Sutton Terrace to the 58th Street library, where she dug into books on topics ranging from the America in the 1920s to the history of prostitution to Judge Samuel Seabury's investigations into corruption in New York City courts. Her list of sources ultimately came to over three dozen books and even more newspapers articles. On a copy of Selby's letter that she kept with her working notes, Virginia later scribbled next to his comment about adding "enough of the period": "Just took six weeks' slavery is all!"

As she dug into Polly's manuscript with an eye to a finished product that could satisfy all her customers, Virginia also saw that chapters she had thought would just need a little work in fact required thorough overhaul. Polly had written, for example, that she met the gangster Dutch Schultz in late 1931. But he'd been killed in early 1932 and it was obvious that he and Polly had known each other for years.

It didn't help that she was dealing with events that often took place outside the public eye and therefore required more than just a dive into the newspaper morgues. Polly had to move her house frequently to stay ahead of the vice squad. Virginia was able to identify almost thirty different "places of business," for example, but that still didn't make it any easier to confirm when and where something Polly mentioned actually took place. She also had to put Polly's story into some kind of chronological order. She cut up Polly's manuscript and pasted the fragments together according to a timeline and found that it made the story more effective as well as more truthful.

For all her grumbling, Virginia was starting to enjoy the work. "I've got plenty of background dope about the Twenties and some wonderful quotes," she wrote. And even Polly was providing surprisingly helpful: "She really has knocked herself out to supply the dates which I requested" and even agreed to fix the year of her birth. Virginia felt confident enough to venture, "I bet this will be quite a book yet."

Watkins forwarded Virginia's status report to Gertrude Gottlieb to keep the paper trail with Polly in the record. She pointed out that Virginia was "going to need stenographic help" with transcribing all the historical material she was assembling and suggested this was an expense that Polly should cover. Not for the last time, she reminded Polly that Virginia was putting a tremendous amount of time into the project—time that so far had gone unpaid.

The casual arrangement regarding Virginia's work concerned Ann Watkins, and even more so when Virginia disappeared sometime in late 1951. Her correspondence stopped. She'd given up her apartment at Sutton Terrace and left no forwarding address. John Selby at Rinehart asked Watkins anxiously, "What's the latest word from Virginia Faulkner on the Polly Adler book?" She didn't know. The book's future hung in doubt for weeks. Finally, in January 1952, Virginia resurfaced. She was in Milwaukee, at the Hotel Astor.

She had had another depressive cycle. She returned to Lincoln to spend the holidays with Eddie and Jean, and then traveled to Milwaukee to continue her psychoanalysis with a different therapist. She wanted to get at the underlying causes of her depressions. "The current guesser [psychiatrist] is asking—and getting—$25 a day, seven days a week to try and find out," she wrote Watkins. Though she had cut off contact with Watkins, she'd stayed in touch with Polly, and from the one notebook surviving from her work on the book, we can see that Virginia fired off multiple barrages of questions and suggestions to Los Angeles, where Polly had settled.

The broad outline of the book had been settled before Virginia went incommunicado, but on almost every page there remained names, events, and references that needed to be addressed. Libel had been a concern from the start, but now it was time to confront the issue and reduce the risks to a level that Rinehart could accept. Polly had already changed names and details, so Virginia often had first to unravel these changes before she could determine whether they were required. As she worked her way through Polly's manuscript, she compiled a key for each chapter of the characters named and their real identities, along with a growing stack of newspaper clippings. Polly offered her own "Must Not Mention" list that included men from whom she feared lethal, not legal, retribution, as well as specifics of tax evasions that could still attract interest from the Internal Revenue Service.

But the book still needed more than just fact-checking and preventive obfuscation. Polly had approached her life chronologically, from her childhood in Poland and her solo journey to America at the age of thirteen through her limited schooling, initial work in clothing factories, and on to her introduction to prostitution and the art of surviving as a madam. Chronologies are not narratives, however. Virginia understood that Polly's story needed a narrative arc.

The well-used rise-and-fall template wouldn't do. Polly had managed to avoid doing time for her crimes on all but one occasion and even then, she went back to business shortly after her release. In a way, Polly's was a classic American success story, a tribute to what can be achieved with grit, hustle, and lucky timing. But it was also a tale of disillusionment, of the limitations of the American success story. In the end, Polly left the sex trade simply because she was putting more into it than she was getting back. She'd reached burnout.

The fact that Polly's success was in the sex trade created another challenge for Virginia in shaping the story. New York newspapers had described her as "the most notorious woman in the history of vice"—a business that was not only illegal but seen as immoral by potential readers. Polly had a reputation for integrity and prided herself on never cooperating with the police, but most people considered this honor among thieves. Many of her girls had been forced into the trade by poverty, addiction, or abuse; for Polly herself it was tougher to play the victim.

Virginia resorted to a variety of techniques to get around this problem. She used sociology, quoting from objective academic studies of the phenomenon of prostitution. She called on the reader's sympathy, setting poor Polly as the David battling the dual Goliaths of organized crime (everyone from shakedown artists to that homicidal patron, Dutch Schultz) and law enforcement (everyone from vice cops who doubled as shakedown artists to the honorable Samuel Seabury). And she played to the reader's prurient curiosity, devoting a chapter ("Just Lucky, I Guess") to "the secrets of a whorehouse."

It helped significantly that Polly had already come to her own understanding of the role of prostitution in society. What mattered was not morality but human behavior. "I could think of myself as fulfilling a need," she had written, a need one could find in every place and time in human history. "I had a very definite place in the social structure. I belonged, I had a job to do." And she had learned that some of those who condemned her for doing that job were her own customers, "because I was associated with the side of their own nature of which they were most ashamed," that they could rid "their feelings of guilt and self-disgust by making me the target of their ridicule and contempt."

Though Polly would never have considered herself a Marxist, she saw prostitution as a simple question of labor and capital, supply and demand. "A prostitute is just as much a product of our so-called culture as is a college professor or a boot-black, and, as with them, her choice of occupation has been dictated by environmental and personality factors." Virginia topped the creation off with epigraphs for each chapter, drawing upon John Dos Passos, Hemingway, Charles Dickens, W. W. Sanger's history of prostitution, and Harold J. Laski. Most came from Virginia's own reading. Ever since her time as a book reviewer for the *Junior League Magazine*, she had kept up with contemporary fiction and continued to explore the classics.

By early March, Virginia was happy to report that she'd finished the job. "Seems hard to believe, but with luck by this time next week I'll no longer be a white slave," she declared to Ann Watkins. She looked forward to being able "to sit down at the typewriter and write an entire page without once having to use the word whorehouse."

But the job wasn't done. There were more rounds of fact-checking. In May, Virginia left Milwaukee and admitted herself to the Nebraska State Hospital in Ingleside for further ECT—but not before firing off more questions to Polly. She also provided four pages of answers to questions raised by Rinehart's in-house legal counsel. Polly responded a few weeks later, declaring, "This winds up the work." The work, however, was still going. It would be almost a year before the book was ready for the printers.

For the book's last chapter, "Call Me Miss," Virginia chose as epigraph a quotation from Stendhal: "The most shocking fault of women is that they make the public the supreme judge of their lives." It was an observation that allowed Polly to close her story with a spunky dismissal of the mores she'd spent over two decades flouting. But it was something of a declaration by Virginia herself. She'd spent much of the same time trying to write what the publishers and public wanted. Now she intended to take time to figure out what she wanted. To do that, she decided to get as far away from New York City as she could.

14

Pacific Grove

"I wended my way from Manhattan to San Francisco, via Detroit and Milwaukee, with stopovers at gilded loony-bins all along the way," Virginia wrote her friend S. N. Behrman years later to explain her disappearance from the New York scene. "Then I went down to a place near Carmel."

Virginia arrived in Pacific Grove, California, in July 1952. She took an efficiency apartment in the Redwood Lodge on Lighthouse Avenue, a ten-unit motel run by newlyweds Jack and Alice McNeer. And there she stayed "as a girl hermit" for the next three and a half years. She published nothing. She went up to San Francisco now and then—to get her hair done, to meet Polly Adler a few times, and once for dinner with Dana Suess, on her way to Reno to divorce Courtney Barr. Eddie and Jean visited twice.

What was she doing?

Finishing work on *A House Is Not a Home*, for one thing. Virginia's outline had included an opening chapter in which Polly would introduce herself, establishing her narrative voice, and a closing one describing how she left the business and came to write her book. Polly had provided drafts of these, but as with the rest of the manuscript, Rinehart wanted Virginia to apply her editorial touch.

The day she moved into her apartment, Virginia wrote Ann Watkins to apologize for her delay in returning a cleaned-up version of Chapter One: "For the past two months I have not had even two consecutive uninterrupted hours in which to work," due to both her stay at the state hospital at Ingleside and her search for a place to settle in California. A few days later, however, she sent off the two chapters to Watkins, who replied that she was glad that Virginia was better.

Rinehart gave the complete manuscript to John S. Lamont, one of its editors, for an independent check while it sought libel insurance for the book. Lamont loved the book but suggested changes, many based on the advice of Gertrude Gottlieb and Rinehart's lawyers. Virginia spent September working through these. Then Polly had problems getting releases from people she mentioned in potentially compromising ways and Virginia spent another two weeks in November addressing those problems and integrating several more anecdotes Polly had provided. Then she spent a week in December dealing with the last round of questions and concerns from the lawyers.

Finally, in January 1953, Watkins sent Virginia a copy of the manuscript with dozens of changes introduced by Lamont after reviewing the complete manuscript—again. Almost none were accepted as-is by Virginia. She described Lamont's editing as "mutton-fisted and bird-brained." To Watkins, Virginia later wrote that she had "a clear picture of him with two heads and nothing in either."

In the same letter, Virginia outlined her part in *A House* from a business standpoint. There had been no discussion of a fee or royalties when she agreed to work on the book back in September 1951. In March 1952, after Virginia surfaced in Milwaukee, Polly offered her "a percentage" of the book, but Virginia asked to defer that discussion until the book was finished. Polly never repeated the offer and Virginia felt reluctant to stake her claim, given "the delays and confusion caused by my illness."

But working closely with Polly had also alerted her to another consideration: "To be frank," she explained to Watkins, "it is just as well Polly has no financial claim on my services." Polly's demands could be interminable. While working through more questions and changes in the preceding months, "it seemed to me she was unable to go to the bathroom without calling up long distance to consult about it."

More than that, getting her book accepted by Rinehart had piqued Polly's appetite. She was thinking of adaptations: a film? A play? Virginia had experience with both. A series of articles? Another book? Was there enough in the material left on the cutting-room floor to put together a sequel? After more rounds of replies to Polly's brainstorming, Virginia put it bluntly: "All the meat was gotten out of all the material with which I worked. In fact, there's not even enough bones left for soup." To Watkins, she confided,

"As a free agent, I have been able to quash these notions. I doubt if it would have been possible if I were on the payroll."

A House Is Not a Home came out in early June 1953. It was an immediate success, critically and commercially. One of the first reviews to appear, by the *New York Herald Tribune*'s book editor, John K. Hutchens, called the book "a seriously written and, in its fashion, highly moral tale." John Barkham, who'd replaced John Selby as the country's leading syndicated reviewer, credited Polly for acquiring "as great a mastery over the English language as she once exercised over the baser instincts of men." In the *Saturday Review*, Lee Rogow, who wrote that he was reliably informed that the book "was writ by hand by Miss Adler herself," declared it "an extraordinary performance by a nonprofessional writer."

Despite Rogow's assertion, however, in late September, columnist Dorothy Kilgallen, who'd known both Polly and Virginia from her days as a beat reporter in New York, announced that "Virginia Faulkner, a real writing pro, actually put the words together" for Polly's book. Virginia wasn't flattered to see her association made public and suspected someone at Rinehart had talked to Kilgallen. Bennett Cerf repeated the claim in his *Saturday Review* column, but an article in *Confidential* magazine around the same time suggested that some veteran newsman like Quentin Reynolds, Jim Bishop, or Gene McHugh had written the book, "the best job of ghostwriting to come down the pike in many years."

Virginia's link to the book was questioned as late as 2006, when the University of Massachusetts Press reissued *A House*. In a footnote to her introduction, Rachel Rubin mentioned that in a 1961 letter to S. N. Behrman (the "girl hermit" letter), Virginia wrote that she'd ghostwritten the book. Rubin dismissed her statement, however: "There is no documentary evidence of this." Nor was there until Debby Applegate, researching *Madam*, her 2021 biography of Polly, found the full record of the correspondence among Virginia, Polly, Ann Watkins, and John Selby in Watkins's papers at Columbia University.

Applegate followed a lead that one of Virginia's notebooks from her work on *A House* was in the hands of a private collector in Lincoln. The notebook includes not just copies of letters in the Watkins papers but Virginia's meticulous record of her fact-checking and her correspondence with Polly about the book's success, spin-offs, sequels, and other projects carrying on to Polly's death in 1962. Virginia also kept a letter that identified references to T. S. Eliot's poem "The Waste Land" that she had seeded throughout the book as evidence of her work. "My idea then was chiefly to have a 'secret weapon'" in case someone else claimed credit. Between Watkins's papers and Virginia's surviving notebook, more than enough documentary evidence exists to satisfy any skeptic.

At the same time, it's misleading to say that Virginia ghostwrote *A House Is Not a Home*. It would be more accurate to say she did a brilliant job of editing. Her relationship to Polly's manuscript is not dissimilar to Maxwell Perkins's work on Thomas Wolfe's *Look Homeward, Angel*. Like Perkins, she imposed structure on an unwieldy draft by cutting, and in roughly the same proportion. Unlike Perkins, she also added material, mostly to answer John Selby's request that the book present Polly "as the central figure of a good, big picture and not as an independent phenomenon." This was what sent her to the 58th Street library, the "six weeks' slavery" she later complained about. She guided Polly on drafting the introductory and closing chapters and revised them to fit the rest of the book. And she fact-checked. And fact-checked. And fact-checked. Her notebook and the Watkins papers are stuffed with Virginia's notes and references.

What Virginia's work on *A House Is Not a Home* demonstrates is that she was a good writer but a great editor. This becomes particularly clear in her correspondence with Polly about follow-up projects. Virginia recognized that her headaches with *A House* were more than anything else the result of not being able to steer Polly throughout the drafting process. She issued Polly with questions to answer, topics to address, style guidance, instructions on preparing a manuscript. Had she undertaken any of these projects, she would have had greater control from the beginning.

But by the time the Watkins Agency was busily negotiating foreign rights deals—*A House* was ultimately published in over a dozen languages—Virginia had her own project underway, one that would take years and require respite from demands of magazine editors, theater producers, and publishers. A clue to Virginia's decision to move to Pacific Grove and become "a girl hermit" can be found in a quotation she copied at the back of "Adler IV," that one surviving notebook: "In solitude it is possible to love mankind; in the world, for one who knows the world, there can be nothing but secret or open war." It comes from George Santayana's book *People and Places*, and though not used in *A House*, it's worth considering in more complete form: "I was no longer timid or without resource, but rebellious against being roped in and made to play some vulgar trick in a circus. My love of solitude reasserted itself, not that I feared the world, but that I claimed my liberty and my *Lebensraum* beyond it. In solitude it is possible to love mankind; in the world, for one who knows the world, there can be nothing but secret or open war." Virginia certainly saw further work on Polly's various fantasy projects as playing vulgar tricks in a circus. But was that also a judgment she had passed on her own work?

Almost twenty years before, in justifying her decision to leave the *Washington Post*, she had been her harshest critic. "If I'm ever really going to be any good," she had written Eddie, "I'll have to give up this smart, know-it-all line for something a little kinder and truer." Instead, she had kept playing out that line because that was what her readers and editors wanted. On that same last page of the Adler notebook, she copied down another quote from *People and Places*: "If people praise me, I almost always feel that they praise me for the wrong things, for things which they impute to me out of their preconceptions, and which are not in me."

Virginia had spent much of the last three years looking into herself, trying to understand why she was regularly knocked flat by depression, why she turned to alcohol for relief. She had also had time to reflect on Dana's choice to put her commercially successful career on hold in the interest of improving herself as a classical composer. She was ready to make a similar choice. And to do it, she would look to a woman for whom she had developed the deepest respect as an artist: Willa Cather.

An inventory of her personal library prepared after her death shows that Virginia had collected Cather's books from time she was at Radcliffe and had first editions of most of the writer's later works. The early books were harder to get. Cather and her partner and legatee, Edith Lewis, had carefully protected her copyrights and prevented cheap popular editions from being printed. At the same time, while Houghton Mifflin, Cather's first publisher, and Alfred A. Knopf, her publisher from *One of Ours* (1922) on, had treated Cather as a star of their backlists, neither had been diligent in keeping her books in print.

Virginia had also collected every book about Cather that had appeared since the writer's death in 1947. Two biographies, one by E. K. Brown and

Leon Edel, the other by Mildred Bennett; memoirs by Elizabeth Shepley Sergeant and Edith Lewis; and numerous recent critical works that included discussions of Cather's work. Finally, she had a bookshelf of works on psychology, myth, and symbolism that she thought illuminated aspects of Cather.

Just what she intended to do wasn't clear. Several times, she suggested that she was working on an article, but by the time she'd amassed over six hundred pages of typewritten notes, it seemed to have become a book. But what kind of book? A biography? Alfred Knopf, who saw himself as a guardian of Cather's legacy, had said of the Brown/Edel biography, "Here is all the biographical information anyone is likely to gather about Willa Cather." He knew that wasn't true, of course. First biographies, particularly if written soon after the subject's death, are rarely definitive. Source material often emerges years, even decades, later. But more to the point, he knew that Cather had forbidden quotations from her letters in her will, a prohibition that was only lifted in 2011 when her copyrights passed to the Willa Cather Trust.

A biography also requires interviews and archive visits, and Virginia had no intention of doing either. Instead, she seems to have been aiming for something like Sigmund Freud and William C. Bullitt's book on Woodrow Wilson: a psychobiography, a mental and emotional portrait produced through analysis of secondhand materials rather than firsthand knowledge. If she knew of the Wilson book, however, she didn't know that it was dismissed as unreliable as both biography and psychology.

Had she limited herself to an interpretation of her sources using what knowledge of psychology and symbolism she'd acquired by reading, the work would already have been problematic. But Virginia didn't stop there. She applied techniques that would later be described as close reading—except in her case, it could more accurately be called too-close reading. She filled dozens of pages of notes, for example, on a dream that Sergeant recounted in her memoir, in which she saw Cather "standing at the corner of a fine, brown, small field, watching a stalwart young Roman in a white robe drive a primitive plow behind two white oxen." Of just the word *corner* in a passage from *One of Ours* she wrote:

> The corner of the wheatfield is specified as the setting of many of the most important scenes in *O Pioneers!* See C-Notes, 12–3, 13-A [this was

one of the notebooks Virginia kept. There were also D-Notes, E-Notes, H-Notes, J-Notes, and perhaps others now lost]. Also, a corner is at right-angles which is 90°, and nine and zero equal nine which is Sagittarius, the Archer, WC's sign. You also could work this out by writing it inverted—zero-nine—which adds up to the same thing; and parallels the Inversion of initials: Claude Wheeler equals C W equals W C equals Willa Cather.

From Sergeant's memoir alone, Virginia derived over seventy pages of such frenetic notes. She titled the collection "The Dream Bien Meublé," a play on Cather's essay "The Novel Démeublé." Cather argued that the novel had become "over-furnished," novelists obsessed with "the cataloguing of a great number of material objects" and other details. She called for details to be pared back to the essentials: "one passion and four walls," quoting Alexander Dumas.

Virginia's choice of title was an admission that her own critical reading was not just over-furnished but overflowing. She referenced Jung, mythology, astrology, numerology, psychology. She found symbolism in practically every object mentioned (hats were masculine; the colors red and blue referred to female and male sexuality; a corn-knife stands for castration). And most importantly for her project, she found in the texts what she considered the smoking gun of the Cather mystery: the fact that Cather was lesbian.

Once Virginia had seen what she felt was definitive evidence of Cather's sexuality, she could not unsee it. She was so exultant in her discovery that she fired off a letter to Sergeant about her research. She closed it by expressing her gratitude that Cather had in Sergeant "a deep personal friend" who "respected her wish for privacy, but who cared even more . . . about the whole thing—that is, the art of creative writing." But what preceded that statement must have left Sergeant dumbfounded. Sergeant was then seventy-three and Virginia was a stranger to her. What could she have thought of a letter full of sentences such as: "Reading your book has been a unique and absorbing experience and one which is by no mean finished: although I have read it nine times—or perhaps six times more than that—I expect to do a good deal of head-scratching (though not with a hat-pin) before I've finished the exegesis of passages about, for example, hats—little round straws, countrywoman's felts, turreted turbans, and confections adorned with red poppies and blue cornflowers (which no doubt were worn in the spirit of Ceres)."

In the context of Virginia's notebooks, this letter is her almost giddy declaration that she has cracked the code in Sergeant's memoir. On the surface, Sergeant's book is an elegant account of her friendship with Cather. Beneath that surface, however, by interpreting the symbolism she drew from Sergeant's prose, Virginia has found "the hidden story." Sergeant doesn't intend just to hint that Cather was lesbian: "Sergeant wishes to pound it in that WC was a Uranian" Virginia confided to her notes. Uranus is "cold, dry, barren . . . spasmodic, original, errative." And "Uranian . . . is esoteric argot designating a homosexual."

Virginia must have come across as unhinged. There is no evidence that Sergeant replied. But Virginia could not contain her excitement at her discovery. Soon after, she wrote an old friend, Bill Koshland, an editor at Knopf, in the cryptic tones of one conspirator bringing another into the fold. Referring to Alfred Knopf's statement about "all the biographical information anyone is likely to gather," she retorted, "It's rude to contradict, but 'Ollfred' is off the beam."

Not that she was ready to reveal all her secrets yet. "Partly this is because of the touchy nature of some of the material; partly because until I've gone over everything again, I am reserving judgment about what part of it, if any, should be published." Having declared that she wasn't ready to go into details, she proceeds to talk about them in three more dense, single-spaced pages. She apologizes for the length but blames it on her passion: "This is a subject I'm full of up to here, and it's horrible having to keep clammed up."

Virginia knew Koshland from her years with Dana, when he was one of a circle of gay and lesbian friends with whom they could be open about their sexuality—behind closed doors, of course. He kept his own secrets and could be trusted to keep hers. But she was also putting him in an awkward position. Koshland was also one of Alfred and Blanche Knopf's closest associates, a man who would go on to succeed Knopf as president and later chairman. He understood the special regard in which Knopf held Cather's reputation and wishes. And he certainly knew the truth about Cather's sexuality or suspected it.

Koshland's reply navigates a careful path between encouraging Virginia and protecting his own position at Knopf. "I think it would be *infra dig* for me to go on at length about this on Borzoi stationery," he cautioned, but admitted that he was eager "to read whatever results from those six hundred pages." He reminded her, however, that "obviously, your final manuscript is something that never could be published by Alfred A. Knopf, Inc., or Houghton Mifflin."

Virginia also admitted that she'd kept her agent, Carl Brandt, in the dark about her project, and regretted that she couldn't devote more time to it due to other commitments. It's unclear what those commitments were. Ed Gardner from *Duffy's Tavern* had contacted her about turning one of her stories, "So Red the Face," into a screenplay, but she advised Brandt that the story wasn't worth the effort. Nothing was published under her name during her time in Pacific Grove. If she had taken on ghostwriting work for anyone else, there is no trace of it in her papers.

Virginia consulted with Eddie about the projects Polly was proposing. Did she also talk to him about her own Cather project? Had he seen any of her six hundred pages of notes, he would certainly have been concerned that her work was taking on a manic quality. Just as he would have known that she was neglecting commercial opportunities in her focus on Cather. She still relied on him to guide her financial affairs. He may also have seen that she was drinking too heavily when he and Jean had visited.

Virginia was forty-two now, scarred from years of inpatient and outpatient psychiatric treatment. Whether it was by her choice or at Eddie's insistence, she left Pacific Grove and arrived in Lincoln in September 1955. She said it was just a stopover before she headed on to someplace else—Hollywood, maybe, or New York City. Lincoln still had all the drawbacks it had had since her return from Rome: no place to stay other than as a guest of Eddie and Jean or Aunt Milly and Uncle Dick; no work to do; and no acceptance of any but heterosexual lifestyles.

Before packing up her books and notes, she wrote on the cover of one of her notebooks, "A lot of this is a wrong reading" and "The astrological stuff must be all redone." In the year since her frenzied letter to Elizabeth Shepley Sergeant, she had come to temper her own expectations. Though she kept a portion of those six hundred pages, she never again took up the idea of writing a book about Willa Cather on her own.

It is as if Virginia's research had been an exercise in measuring her own worth as a writer against Cather's. In *Friends and Romans*, her pianist heroine, Marie Manfred, declares, "If I could not give up the greatest thing in my life because it could become no greater, then I would be a very small person indeed." One of Marie's friends—a former dancer now mistress of an Italian duke—tells her, "It is so important to have the strength to cut a thing off completely, to be harder upon yourself than anyone else can be." Virginia never again published a work of fiction—indeed, never worked as a commercial writer again. But she was about to discover where her genius truly lay.

Act 2
Back to Lincoln

I don't know where I'm going, but I expect it will be back to the beginning.

—Marie Manfred in *Friends and Romans*

15

Roundup

When Virginia and Eddie left for Radcliffe and Wharton in the fall of 1932, they were orphans, subject to Uncle Bert's tight-fisted guardianship, heading off to uncertain futures. When she returned to Lincoln in September 1955, her future was still uncertain; Eddie's was not.

He was no longer Eddie or Edwin Jr., the promising young man. He was Ed or E. J. He was one of the big men in Lincoln, which made him one of the big men in Nebraska, on a first-name basis with the mayor, the governor, the state's congressional delegation, the heads of the state's big businesses. Like his grandfather A. O. Faulkner, he was a man people trusted instinctively.

Where Virginia's path had wandered, her progress marked with highs and lows, Ed's had been steady, never betraying the slightest doubt that he was on his way to success greater than his father or grandfather had ever imagined. Though he went east for graduate school, he never considered working anywhere but at the Woodmen. He and Jean were always going to return to Lincoln, move into the house on South Street, start a family, and fill the roles in the company and in Lincoln society that Edwin and Leah had played. Only one part of Ed's plan didn't materialize. Jean had a miscarriage in early 1934 while they were living in Philadelphia and was forced to undergo a hysterectomy.

Ed was in his element at the Woodmen. He had a vision of the company becoming a full-service insurer. He helped establish the Woodmen Central Life Insurance Company in 1936, serving as its vice president, and when Bert died in 1938, Ed was named president of all the Woodmen companies.

He was just as much a prodigy as Virginia, though in pursuits that brought less popular acclaim. Not content with steering the Woodmen companies,

Fig. 12. E. J. Faulkner, President of the Woodmen Accident Company, 1940. Courtesy of E. J. Faulkner, Professional Papers, Archives and Special Collections, University of Nebraska-Lincoln Libraries.

he took an active role in insurance industry associations and became a key member of the Health and Accident Underwriters Conference. He also kept in touch with his Wharton professors, and when McGraw-Hill began a series of textbooks on the key topics of insurance, Professor Solomon Huebner recommended Ed to write the volume on *Accident and Health Insurance*. He finished the book in under a year, and after its publication in 1940, it was quickly adopted as the principal text on the subject. It remained in print until 1960, when he revised it to focus solely on *Health Insurance*, which had grown to become one of the largest sectors in the insurance business.

Ed was also one of Lincoln's business leaders. He joined the board of directors of the First National Bank in 1939, the first of over a dozen corporate board positions he would come to hold. He never lost his interest in the Kosmet Klub and his Phi Kappa Psi fraternity and often recruited Phi Psi brothers into jobs with the Woodmen. And he was a natural choice when local charities needed someone to lead a fundraising drive.

Despite these daunting commitments, after the attack on Pearl Harbor, Ed set them aside and volunteered for the Army Air Forces. Commissioned in March 1942, he was something of an exceptional second lieutenant, assigned directly to the headquarters at the newly opened Pentagon. There, he went to work in the Office of Air Support, responsible for the allocation of aircraft to meet the needs of combat forces. Ed remained there, rising to the number two man in the branch with the rank of lieutenant colonel and earning the Legion of Merit.

Upon his return to Lincoln and civilian life, he was elected as commander of the local chapter of the American Legion, the first of many civic organizations he helped lead. Over the decades, he would serve on the Lincoln Chamber of Commerce, the Lincoln Community Chest, the Lincoln Better Business Bureau, the Lincoln Planning Commission, the Lincoln Airport Commission, and the board of Bryan Memorial Hospital. He also became a major voice in the state's Republican Party, helping select candidates and raise funds for their campaigns.

And he was increasingly being recognized as a leader in the insurance industry. Ed joined the board of trustees of the American College of Life Underwriters, and he became a popular speaker on behalf of private insurers in the growing discussion of the need for national health insurance. When the Health Insurance Association of America was established in 1956, Ed was chosen to serve as its first president.

Virginia arrived in Lincoln just as Ed was preparing for his biggest event in years: the 65th anniversary of the founding of the Woodmen and the opening of the company's new headquarters. Ed had decided to move the company from the downtown offices A. O. Faulkner had established decades earlier and selected a plot directly across K Street from the State Capitol. It was a declaration of the company's prominence in the state. Ed hired sculptor Lawrence Tenney Stevens to create a frieze representing a pioneer family in the palm of a giant hand. Two stories tall, the frieze, known as "The Protecting Hand," capped the building's main entrance, mirroring the friezes decorating the Capitol building across the way, and was trademarked as the symbol of the Woodmen. The opening of the new Woodmen building was marked by a ten-page spread in the *Lincoln Sunday Journal and Star*, and the governor, mayor, and most of city's luminaries turned out for the ribbon-cutting. UNL took the occasion to name Ed as the university's outstanding Business Alumnus for 1955.

The contrast between Ed's success and her own uncertain situation, with no publication credits to her name in over six years and no clear way ahead, either for a place to live or a direction for her career, could not have been lost on Virginia when she stepped off the train from California. Ed had brought Virginia home because she was drinking herself to death. That, at least, was the story that people in Lincoln told—and were still telling sixty years later. It was not a promising start.

Virginia took her old room in the house on South Street. But as usual, her relationship with Ed could only stand so much together time. As much as they adored each other, they were also bright, competitive, and argumentative, and each was the other's favorite opponent. Their battles were exacerbated by alcohol. Ed was a typical drinker of his generation, but Jean was already on her way to alcoholism. In theory, Ed's plan to help Virginia by keeping her close made sense. There was no resource in Lincoln he couldn't tap into, and given his influence, with sufficient discretion to protect her dignity and his reputation. But when he and Virginia had to share a roof on a day-in and day-out basis, the differences in their temperaments inevitably clashed.

It wasn't a matter of intellectual disagreements. The two of them could have ferocious debates over questions of history or literature or, most often, language. Ed had a reputation for using unusual words. He would refer to birthdays as "natal anniversaries" and had been mocked at Lincoln High School for never using words of less than three syllables. Clifford Hardin, then chancellor of the University of Nebraska, called him "the Big Eight all-star in vocabulary." Virginia, of course, would never concede ground in a battle over language, and unlike Ed, still had enough French and Italian at hand to switch weapons. But neither of them took these arguments personally.

The problem was that Virginia continued to have her ups and downs and staying at the house on South Street exacerbated the downs. Waking each morning in the same bedroom she'd had when she was nineteen and anxious to escape from the hated stepmother, Betty. Knowing that she had no place to go and nothing to do unless she returned to New York or Hollywood, both places she couldn't stand. Ed, on the other hand, was a creature of routines. Five days a week he got up at the same time, ate the same breakfast, and drove the same route to an office where a constant stream of decisions awaited. He was at the summit of Mount Lincoln and nothing was going to budge him off that peak. Virginia soon took herself to Uncle Dick and Aunt Milly's house, where she disappeared into an upstairs bedroom and only emerged for an occasional meal. She had to get away, she said, from "the house of horrors." Even with Milly's support, though, Lincoln seemed nothing but a way station for Virginia. And then, sometime just before Christmas, she found a project she could put her intellect and energy into.

There are at least two accounts of how Virginia ended up working for the University of Nebraska Press. Her version, as she later related to S. N. Behrman, was that Emily Schossberger, director of the press, approached her. "At a cocktail party [I] met the-then editor . . . who suggested that I might put together a book about Nebraska for them." Another holds that it was Ed's idea, that he came up with the Nebraska book as a lure to bring her back to Lincoln and even provided the funding for it.

This could be true in part. Ed believed in Nebraska, loved to tell prospective Woodmen employees what a great place it was to work and raise a family, and knew that its reputation in the rest of the country was that of a blank spot on the map, a place with nothing but cornfields, pastures, and prairies. A book highlighting the state's history and achievements would be a perfect gift for visiting VIPs, and he knew other companies and civic groups would see it the same way. He did not, however, fund the project. Money, in fact, was its chief obstacle: There was none. The press was reliant on an appropriation from the state budget to cover its operating costs, and that item had been cut for 1956.

When the board of regents decided to charter the University of Nebraska Press as a "non-incorporated agency of the board" in 1941, it only intended to sweep into one office the university's various publishing functions—course catalogs, brochures, bulletins, scholarly monographs, and an occasional book. In selecting Emily Schossberger as the press's first director, the regents put in charge a woman with barely more experience in publishing than themselves. Born in Austria, she had worked in Europe as a reporter, emigrating to the U.S. in 1940 and spending a year as assistant to the director of the Fordham University Press, the job she held when UNL chancellor Chauncey Boucher hired her without so much as an interview.

Schossberger was an anomaly in Lincoln. A single professional woman with no interest in marriage, sophisticated, fluent in five languages, a superb tennis player, she was easily the town's most cosmopolitan resident. Her editorial approach was informal, collegial, continental. In correspondence with Professor George Sarton of Harvard about the press's publication of his 1954 Montgomery Lectures, *Ancient Science and Modern Civilization*, she variously addressed him as "Lieber und sehr verehrter Herr Professor," "Mon très cher maître," and "Gentilissimo e illustrissimo Signor Professore."

What Schossberger lacked, though, was any sense of where to go with the press. For the fourteen years before Virginia arrived, the press stumbled along, publishing an eclectic selection of books. There were biographies of such obscure figures as J. Sterling Morton, the founder of the Arbor Day movement; technical guides on school custodianship and service station management; and featherweight items like Raymond McConnell's *Trampled Terraces*, about the comic happenings in a Lincoln neighborhood. Although there were several works by authors of national repute such as David Riesman, of the forty-four books the press published between 1942 and 1955, only six stayed in print for more than three years.

Money was always a problem. Authors sometimes had to cover production costs, in return for royalties as high as 33 percent, two to three times the industry standard. Even then, the press was often slow and erratic with its reimbursements. Staffing was another problem. The sales manager also served as production manager, press bookkeeper, and Schossberger's secretary. The one full-time editor, Stanley Moon, left at the end of 1955. Schossberger offered Virginia his job, though she needed the board's approval and funding. Virginia accepted and rented an apartment closer to the campus just before Christmas. The Lincoln papers considered it an event worth mentioning on the society page.

Once Virginia had signed up to putting the Nebraska book together, she could look to Ed for help in raising funds in much the same way that he'd led campaigns for Republican candidates and charitable causes. He suggested a brochure to pitch the book to prospective sponsors. With help from Uncle Dick, who was running the Woodmen's publicity department, Virginia created "All About Nebraska," which touted *The Nebraska Reader*, "a book for, about, and by Nebraskans." Although vague—"anything that's interesting, meets high standards of readability, and has a Nebraska angle"—the prospectus promised that the book would be a milestone in the state's history. Written in a breezy, confident style that screams "Virginia!" it describes the book's twelve sections, from "Weather Report" to "Favorite Sons" to "Culture on the Cob."

Ed sent brochures to dozens of his contacts, including Senators Roman Hruska and Carl Curtis, counting on getting the kind of endorsements that would open wallets. Curtis, for example, declared the book "a much-needed project" and hoped that "Nebraska individuals and business institutions will back this worthwhile project." Ed then approached his fellow Bryan Memorial Hospital board member Elwood Thompson, a trustee of the Cooper Foundation, a local charity that provided scholarships and grants and sponsored various community-building activities. The Foundation offered to loan the press five thousand dollars to cover production costs.

By her own admission, all Virginia knew about the state before taking on the project was "that Lincoln is the capitol." She'd been as guilty of dismissing Nebraska as anyone: "For many years I gave the place a wide berth and, alas, contributed my quota of cracks." Collecting material for the book and spending more time around Ed didn't turn her into an evangelist, though. While she acknowledged to Nebraska-born mystery author Mignon G. Eberhart that "there is a hell of a lot more here than meets the jaded eye: by and large, it really is a good place to live," she cautioned, "though not, perhaps, forever . . ."

Virginia was able to find plenty of material from Nebraska's past by digging into the archives of the UNL library and the Nebraska State Historical Society, making liberal use of articles from *Prairie Schooner* and the Society's own magazine. It was a different story with material about Nebraska's present. She confessed that it was "darned hard to find something colorful, attractive and interestingly written about Nebraska during the last 30 years."

Her outline for the book called for a dozen original articles and she leveraged her network and Ed's to line up contributors. Her old New York acquaintance, the columnist and train enthusiast Lucius Beebe, agreed to write a story about the early days of the railroad in the state. Ed's friend Barney Oldfield provided a colorful account of the carnivals and circuses that traveled through Nebraska in the 1920s and 1930s. Mari Sandoz, then Nebraska's best-known living writer, adapted several existing pieces to meet Virginia's requirements.

Virginia's connections came in handy in obtaining permissions to use excerpts from Willa Cather's works. She first wrote to Bill Koshland, who was relieved to learn that Virginia's new project was more grounded and less risky for Knopf than the Cather psychobiography. Koshland's support meant she was safe to approach Alfred Knopf himself, who could, in turn, vet the request with Cather's partner and executor, Edith Lewis. It helped that Virginia also wanted to use material from Lewis's own book *Willa Cather Living*. Lewis and Knopf readily consented, and though Cather's work represents just fifteen of the almost five hundred pages of the book, it's the spiritual glue that binds the collection and makes it something more enduring than a classy bit of boosterism.

Gathering the pieces for the anthology—eventually titled *Roundup: A Nebraska Reader*—also put Virginia in contact with two people who would play major roles in this second act she was still considering just an interlude. She wrote Mildred Bennett, whose Cather book had been a primary source in Pacific Grove, for permission to use "Willa Cather in Red Cloud," a *Prairie Schooner* article that had been the precursor to Bennett's *The World of Willa Cather*. She found that Bennett was not only an enthusiastic contributor but possessed a knowledge of Cather that was at least as extensive as Virginia's. Bennett drew Virginia's attention to the

Willa Cather Pioneer Memorial, the foundation she had established a year earlier to preserve and celebrate Cather's legacy as well as landmarks from her life in and around Red Cloud.

The last piece in *Roundup*, "Nebraska Is Here to Stay," was written by Bruce Nicoll, then assistant director of UNL's public relations department. A UNL graduate and one-time *Lincoln Star* reporter, Nicoll had just stepped down from an assignment as assistant to Clifford Hardin. Virginia feared that this PR man would produce the most booster-ish piece in the book. But Nicoll was a man of few pretensions, a solid sense of humor, and a passion for the history of Nebraska and the west. He tied into the theme of one of the book's major sections, "The Weather Report," and admitted that Nebraskans hadn't always been successful in dealing with weather: "It's nearly a century since we became a state—since plows broke the prairie sod and longhorns moved into our ranges. But what a time—oh Lord, what a really rough time—we've had getting our agriculture squared up with its environment."

Roundup consumed Virginia's 1956. Though in May she assured Carl Brandt that she was "still working on something," that something was set aside and forgotten. By January 1957, as the last few *Roundup* contributions were rolling in, Emily Schossberger confided to Brandt that Virginia was near exhaustion: "not feeling well, hardly eats, and will probably take a week or two of rest when everything is tied up."

In a press with a less skeletal staff, Virginia as developmental editor could now have handed the project over to a production manager who would oversee the design, typesetting, and printing process. Instead, she had to continue along, helping Schossberger, who was still running interference with the publications board and trying to find funding for other books. The Cooper Foundation's loan was exhausted in February, just as it came time to sign the printer's contract. Virginia reached out to Ed, who contacted his friend Morton Steinhart, head of Otoe Foods, who provided an outright gift to cover the initial printing and marketing costs. Then there was a problem with the dust jacket, and the target publication date of April 1957 was slipped to the end of May.

When *Roundup* finally hit the stores, it exceeded expectations. The first printing sold out within a month and two more followed before the end of the year, allowing the press to repay the Cooper Foundation loan and even build a reserve for other books still in development. In the *Omaha World Herald*, Victor Hass proclaimed it a complete success, in large part thanks to Virginia's work: "From more than a thousand books and articles she has taken flesh, muscle and bone and fused them into a single book. . . . It runs to 493 pages, and I didn't encounter a dull page among them." If Virginia hoped her name and connections might win the book reviews in national magazines, she was disappointed. Only *Saturday Review* mentioned the book and then just as one of 325 suggested as Christmas gifts. The American Institute of Graphic Arts selected *Roundup* as one of the fifty best-designed books of the year—one of only five university press books to make the list—and it was one of fifteen books selected as best of the year by the Midwest Book Conference.

Unlike with *A House Is Not a Home*, Virginia's work was credited prominently: "Compiled and Edited by Virginia Faulkner" appears on the front cover and title page. Victor Hass referred to her as "the book's architect"—a term that must have pleased her, considering how hard she'd labored on its construction. Louise Pound, her sister Olivia, and Schossberger took Virginia to lunch at the Lincoln Country Club to celebrate the book. They urged her to stay in Lincoln; she promised to stick around a little longer. The future of the press and her position were still uncertain, but she had her eyes set on other projects and other collaborators.

16

Hostiles and Friendlies

In an item in the program of the Nebraska-Oklahoma football game in November 1957, the University of Nebraska Press claimed it published eight to ten books a year. The truth was, even with the success of *Roundup*, that year it was struggling to publish three. They were all personal projects for Virginia.

To harvest material for *Roundup*, she had read hundreds of stories about Nebraska and came to see that one of the state's most prolific authors was also one of its best. Mari Sandoz had published her first book, *Old Jules*, a portrait of her father, an early settler in the Sandhills, in 1935, within a few months of Virginia's second, *The Barbarians*. Unlike Virginia, though, Mari was no prodigy. She was nearly forty when *Old Jules* came out and her road to authorship had been long and hard. Born into the strain of farm life, she had survived a failed marriage, years of teaching in rural schools, and working her way through UNL when she was ten years older than most of her classmates. With no family wealth to fall back on, she had managed not just to make a living as a working writer but, with nine books and over fifty magazine articles to her credit, to be recognized as one of the country's leading western authors.

Virginia had found enough uncollected pieces by Sandoz to fill a book, and in the late spring of 1957, she put together a proposal. First, however, she needed to get the author on board. It was not an easy job. Sandoz had three books underway and little time to spare for a fourth. She was dubious whether the pieces even justified republishing. And she preferred autonomy to collaboration. As her biographer Helen Winter Stauffer later put it, Sandoz tended to "encase herself in an apparently impenetrable armor of self-protection."

This armor could not withstand Virginia's concerted onslaught, however. In the space of weeks, Sandoz went from skeptic to enthusiast. In the same letter in which she dismisses several pieces Virginia had proposed, she encloses copies of eight others. By August, when the two had agreed on the bulk of the collection and its organization, Sandoz acknowledged that Virginia had "done an appalling amount of work and brought, so far as I can see now, coherence and sense to the hodge-podge."

With Sandoz on board and everything ready to go to the publication board for approval, Virginia faced her next obstacle: The board was on an indefinite break. It not only had no meetings scheduled but the university's administration was reconsidering whether to scrap its publishing arm entirely. Just the year before, Sandoz had written countless letters soliciting donations to keep *Prairie Schooner* going after its budget was slashed and even endowed an annual fiction prize in her name to prop up the magazine's image as a thriving concern. In the face of such tenuous support, Emily Schossberger had quietly begun to look elsewhere for a job. By January 1958, Sandoz wrote Virginia that it had been months since she'd heard anything about "the book you put so much patient work on." She assumed that "the verdict in the board went against you."

As February, Lincoln's coldest month, arrived, the situation seemed grim. Schossberger announced she was leaving in June to work for the University of Chicago Press. Her decision took the publications board by surprise, but her position wasn't advertised, and no interim director was appointed. The board's inaction was taken as a sign that the administration planned to eliminate the press, and these rumors spread well beyond the campus. Leo Jacks, a professor of classics at Creighton University in Omaha and an early Cather scholar, wrote Mildred Bennett, "I am sure puzzled by this university move. I cannot understand all the drive for economy. I wonder what is at the bottom of it." Jacks even confided that he was looking for a place for Virginia at Creighton in case the press shut down.

Virginia was already down, devastated by the murder of two of her friends from the Country Club set, Chester and Clara Ward, and their maid by Charles Starkweather and his girlfriend Caril Fugate. The savagery of Starkweather and Fugate's rampage across Nebraska and Wyoming, which claimed eleven lives in the space of weeks, shattered the sense that Lincoln was a peaceful and friendly place to live. "When the word came," Virginia told Sandoz, she had been typing the introductory note to "The Son," in which Sandoz contrasted the way the Sioux and Cheyenne taught their youth personal responsibility with the rapaciousness of the settlers' treatment of indigenous people. The irony in the context of the Starkweather murders was not lost on Virginia: "I guess I don't have to tell you what I was thinking about our fine white-man's culture."

By late February, with no feedback from the administration, Virginia wrote Sandoz in frustration, "Anything I could tell you about the UNP's future would not be even an informed guess." For her own part, she had had enough. "If the administration refuses to support our program for 1958–1959 . . . then no useful purpose can be served by my remaining an employee." But she also admitted to finding something in the experience of working with Sandoz that she had been missing for years: "It is a marrow-deep satisfaction to have a part in something I know is of value."

Then suddenly, Chancellor Hardin tasked the publications board to meet before the end of March with two tasks: approve the publishing program for the next two years and begin recruitment of a new director for the press. The board approved *Hostiles and Friendlies*, subject to receipt of two reader reports, a standard part of the press's process. Virginia enlisted the UNL English department chair, Dr. James Miller, and Wallace Stegner, then working at Stanford and an old acquaintance of Sandoz's. Both gave the book glowing reports.

The last hurdle was the same the press had faced with *Roundup*: paying for printing. The press's approved budget included funding for its tiny staff alone. Schossberger again obtained a Cooper Foundation loan to cover the upfront costs. As pleased as she was to see the book finally on its way to publication, Virginia was reminded of how small the press was relative to the larger world of publishing when an executive of Hastings House informed her that it would be impractical to coordinate distribution of *Hostiles and Friendlies* with Sandoz's newest book, the western history *The Cattlemen*, given that its initial run would be three thousand copies and *The Cattlemen*'s ninety thousand.

Virginia's second project was "a filial duty," as she later put it. Louise Pound, now professor emerita, met with Schossberger and Virginia in early

1957 to discuss publication of a collection of articles on Nebraska folklore that she'd written since her retirement. Knowing the press's financial woes, she promised to bequeath a thousand dollars to cover the production costs, thinking the book would be published after her death. A few months later, however, Pound decided there was no reason to wait and asked Virginia to begin the editorial process while she was still available for consultation. Writing to the board about the book—in a sentence so lifeless she must have cringed—Virginia argued that, "conversely, and on the affirmative side, to publish the work at this particular time would be beneficial not only as regards public relations but as regards sales."

Unfortunately, *Nebraska Folklore* fell victim to the same delays as *Hostiles and Friendlies*. Virginia assumed that the board would approve the book without the usual procedures, given Louise Pound's prominence. Instead, the board asked for the standard full proposal and two reader reports.

To be rebuffed by what she considered pointless bureaucracy infuriated Virginia. But when Louise Pound died in June 1958, getting the book published turned into a crusade. Olivia Pound offered to lend the press the thousand dollars immediately, rather than wait for her sister's estate to be settled. This did nothing to budge the board or its chairman, Fred Lundy, then acting press director. In November, Virginia updated Olivia in characteristically blunt terms. The board's obstinacy, she wrote, "causes me to exhale flame and smoke." If there was any question of the press publishing Louise Pound's last book, "both the faculty and the citizenry of Lincoln would march on the Administration Building equipped with tar and feathers, and believe me the editorial staff would be right there making sure the tar was kept to a boil."

In her proposal, Virginia portrayed the possibility of the book's not being published in near-blackmail terms. "It would be extremely damaging to the press if we were unable to publish this work." The board couldn't argue that the scholarship was inferior or the subject matter (Nebraska folklore!) was unsuitable. And there was the fact that the local papers had already reported that Louise Pound had made a bequest to the press to help publish the book. "We just plain wouldn't have a leg to stand on," she concluded. The board responded with the objectivity of veteran bureaucrats: they approved the proposal . . . subject to two positive reader reports.

Working on *Roundup* and *Hostiles and Friendlies* had given Virginia confidence in her editorial judgment. As she came to deal with members of the UNL faculty, particularly in the English department, she began to appreciate the caliber of its scholarship. Lincoln was more than the hick town where people complained if a book didn't have enough pictures in it. She became friends with Robert Knoll, a Nebraska native who'd joined the faculty in 1950 after earning his master's and doctorate at the University of Minnesota, and who combined Midwest friendliness with a sophistication equal to that of any Ivy League professor. Knoll used to joke that Lincoln was "Boston on the inside, mud flats on the outside."

Lincoln was also "Boston on the inside" when it came to its sense of social proprieties. Fortunately for Virginia, she had a guaranteed place in Lincoln society's inner circle thanks to her family's position. Through all her itinerant years and despite her declarations that she couldn't wait to escape the town, she'd remained a member of the Junior League and the Alpha Phi sorority. She enjoyed being able to show off Lincoln's best, putting out-of-town visitors at the Cornhusker Hotel and taking them to dinner at the University Club, where they could look out on Lincoln's "skyline" from its perch atop the First National Bank building.

But she was also an anomaly in a town where, as Robert Knoll's daughter Elizabeth later remembered, "every adult I knew was married—except Virginia." She had to keep a low profile when it came to her sexuality. Ed and a few family members knew and accepted that Virginia was gay; a wider circle of her acquaintances suspected it; but that was on the understanding that sex—the Kinsey Report notwithstanding—was a matter best kept behind the bedroom door and certainly not to be embraced as part of one's public identity. On the surface, in 1950s Lincoln everyone was straight.

Virginia's third project, far more than the Sandoz and Pound books, showed what the future could offer if she stayed with the press. *Keats and the Dramatic Principle* was a complete and mature manuscript submitted in the spring of 1957 by a member of the university's English faculty. Bernice Slote was an associate professor who'd been working in the trenches of the department since 1946. On the advice of James Miller, Slote had undertaken to write a work of academic scholarship and criticism as a substitute for earning her doctorate and a way of improving her chance of attaining tenure. Researched over two years, her book was an examination of John Keats's dramatic works and their influence on his poetic approach. When she received Slote's manuscript, Virginia recruited professor Clarence Thorpe at the University of Michigan to prepare the external report on the book, per the usual procedures. Thorpe was a leading expert on the Romantics, but he also knew Slote from her time as a graduate student at Michigan.

Thorpe's report could not have been more glowing. He wrote that he'd been sent two other manuscripts on related subjects—"from top Eastern universities," he made sure to note—and found, in comparison, that Slote's "scholarship excels them all, in range, in thoroughness, in judicious selection of pertinent material." "She has really read her Keats," he added, underlining his words for emphasis. Furthermore, he found the book "more scholarly, more judicious, more valuable than say either of Gittings's recent books on Keats"—Robert Gittings being then the world's leading authority on Keats. And though this was Slote's first work on Keats and virtually her first piece of academic research and synthesis, she had carried it off with "the dexterity and maturity of a veteran."

Virginia wrote the second report herself. Though she acknowledged that, "as regards Keats, I am, I expect, the next thing to a total ignoramus," she gave the book five stars on all evaluation factors. In fact, she worried that her firewalled scores "might tend to invalidate this report." Although she had little more than a year of work as an academic press editor under her belt, it was clear Virginia had a picture in mind of what an outstanding work of scholarship looked like and *Keats and the Dramatic Principle* was it. "This study seems to me to fulfill every requirement of scholarship and literary artistry," she wrote. "Everything that is told has a function and is effectively told; each fact is presented in its proper place and exhibited in its proper relationship; the separate parts build harmoniously to a satisfying whole."

The funding for Slote's book was helped by a Ford Foundation grant earmarked for first works of scholarship. Virginia had few editorial concerns with the book and was able to devote more time to the illustrations and overall design. By the time she wrote at the end of March 1958 to say the book was on its way to the printer, Virginia was addressing its author as "Dear Bernice." Working together over the last year had not only confirmed Virginia's high opinion of Bernice's intelligence and ability but given her a sense that this was a woman she could work with professionally and personally. She proposed that the two of them get together to celebrate in early April—perhaps on Shakespeare's birthday? But that would depend, of course, on Bernice's availability: "Will you be away during the spring break?" she asked. It would be the last time she had to ask about Bernice's plans.

17

Bernice

If Virginia came to Lincoln because of Ed, she stayed because of Bernice. Though Bernice Slote was born within a few months of Virginia and in Hickman, a town less than ten miles south of Lincoln, in every way her life up to the time they met was a contrast to Virginia's.

Bernice's childhood was modest and loving. Her father, John Slote, had come over from the Netherlands with his parents at the age of fourteen, settled with them in Hickman, and took over the family farm after his father died. He and his first wife, Sarah, who came from another Dutch immigrant family in Hickman, had raised eight children. John worked at a variety of jobs, including store-keeping, running a grain elevator, working as a bookkeeper, and serving as the Justice of the Peace. After Sarah died in 1906, John Slote courted Hannah Boell, a Hickman girl thirty years his junior, and they married in 1910.

John and Hannah had two daughters—Bernice, born in 1913, and Belva, born four years later. John was devoted to his second family. Working for the town's school board while they were growing up, he taught the girls to read at an early age and encouraged Bernice's bookworm tendencies. A snapshot from the early 1920s shows Bernice lying on the porch, immersed in a thick book, oblivious to giggling little Belva sitting on her back. He was not a rich man, but he was comfortable, and Bernice and Belva enjoyed piano lessons, rides on the horses John kept, and all the books they wanted.

Both Virginia and Bernice possessed quick and subtle minds, but Bernice had inherited her father's patience and diligence. She started writing stories and poems in her teens, but later said, "I really planned to become a teacher. I loved school." At fifteen, she graduated from Hickman High School, tied

Fig. 13. Bernice reading with her sister Belva on her back, around 1921. Courtesy of Susan Perry.

for best student in her class. John could afford to send his daughters to college but insisted they attend Nebraska Wesleyan University in Lincoln, which he considered more pious than the state university across town.

Like Virginia, Bernice lost her father in 1931. When John Slote died that fall, he was seventy-two, with seventeen grandchildren and two great-grandchildren in addition to ten children from the two marriages. He did not leave behind a generous estate, though, just enough to set up his widow in a small house in Lincoln she shared with the two girls.

Bernice graduated from Nebraska Wesleyan in 1932, the top student in the English department. While Virginia was able to head off to Radcliffe to escape Lincoln and her hated stepmother, Bernice had to go to work. She headed to Malcolm, a hamlet outside Lincoln, and began teaching at the town's only school. She didn't take the job for granted. "It was hard in those days," she told an interviewer years later. "It was the decade of difficulties, where nothing was everywhere."

Bernice would continue to teach for almost fifty years and always considered it her first and favorite profession, but she had to work her way up the ladder one rung at a time. After a year in Malcolm, she took a post teaching English at the high school in Ord, a town of about two thousand one hundred fifty miles west of Lincoln. For the next six years, her years followed a similar pattern: During the school terms she lived in Ord; during the summers she lived with Belva and her mother in Lincoln. Belva was taking the nursing program at Nebraska Wesleyan and Bernice completed the summer master's program at UNL.

While Virginia was in New York and Hollywood, socializing with the likes of Garbo and Tallulah Bankhead, Bernice was supervising the yearbook, playing piano accompaniment for student productions, and organizing ice cream socials. She was the faculty sponsor for the *Ord Oracle*, the one-page high school news that appeared in the pages of the town's paper, the *Quiz*. In photos from this time, she is usually standing to the side of a group of students—plain, bespectacled, conservatively dressed, a typical spinster schoolmarm. Miss Slote was a model of decorum, so her journalism students poked a bit of fun at her in an item in the *Oracle*. It reported that she had kept Charles Keown late one day to write the phrase "I have written" on her blackboard a hundred times, after scolding him for using "I have wrote" in a class paper. His punishment complete, Charles then left her a note: "Dear Miss Slote: I have wrote 'I have written' 100 times and have went home."

In a town as small as Ord, everything soon became public knowledge. Bernice couldn't afford to engage in anything scandalous or even slightly out of the ordinary. When she took an overnight trip to Grand Island with

Fig. 14. Bernice, around 1936. Courtesy of Susan Perry.

other women, it got reported in the *Quiz*. The *Quiz* kept tabs on her trips home, informing its readers when Bernice would be taking her copy of the paper at 5101 Adams in Lincoln. If Bernice was gay, this was not a time or a place when she could be open about it. Whether it was in response to Nebraska mores or simply a reflection of her character, Bernice's public persona was, and remained, modest and self-effacing.

After earning her master's degree in English from UNL in 1939, it took Bernice two more years to find a way to rise up another rung. In 1941 she moved to Nebraska City, a little east of Lincoln, to head the English department at the high school. Two years later, she joined the faculty of the junior college in Norfolk, Nebraska, where she also ran the library and served as assistant to the dean. Bernice enjoyed the work at Norfolk, but the dean enjoyed Bernice's work even more, continuing to load her with additional duties.

After finishing her master's at UNL, Bernice was accepted into the summer course in creative writing at the University of Michigan, among the first graduate programs to focus on the creation, rather than the study, of literature. It might have been more useful for her professional career to begin work on a PhD, but Bernice had long been writing poetry on her own and wanted to hone her skills. The Michigan program benefited from a generous endowment from Avery Hopgood, a successful Broadway playwright, that provided annual awards for outstanding works by students in a variety of genres. Professor Roy Cowden, who directed the awards program, served as Bernice's adviser and encouraged her to apply for the graduate poetry award in 1944 and 1945, which she won both times.

Longing for advancement, Bernice kept an eye on faculty vacancies in Lincoln and applied for an instructor's position at UNL in 1946. Accepted, she started at the bottom of the pecking order. As was the practice, the most junior faculty members were assigned the lowest and largest classes: the mandatory freshman-level introductory composition courses. But Bernice had advantages over her peers. Her years of teaching in high school had given her a good understanding of the needs and general level of competence of freshmen. And she was familiar with the kind of weekly assignments—short essays, or themes, as they were called—that were the bedrock of these courses. She was also the only member of the department who'd studied writing. And while that was seen as a mark against her in the eyes of colleagues, particularly those with PhDs in literature, in the eyes of her students, it meant that her guidance was eminently practical.

Outside of her duties at UNL, Bernice worked on her writing, collecting a stack of acceptance letters that any young writer would envy. Her first credit, in 1946, came from *Prairie Schooner*, the journal she would later edit; the second, a poem entitled "Aeschylus," appeared in one of the country's most prestigious magazines, *Atlantic Monthly*, just a month later. Within a year, she had placed nearly twenty poems in magazines ranging from the *Michigan Quarterly Review* to the *Ladies' Home Journal*. And she continued to publish at an impressive rate, averaging around ten poems a year over the next decade. She kept careful track of each poem's submission history. Some she submitted as many as eight times, but most were accepted eventually.

Bernice assembled a collection of about thirty poems for publication sometime in the early 1950s, but never took the project any further. She had begun to reconsider her decision not to pursue a PhD. When Bernice joined the UNL English department in 1946, it was still common for tenured professors to only have earned master's degrees. Three years later, she and Oliver Evans were promoted to assistant professor in recognition "that their writing is an equivalent to the PhD degree." But the decision was aimed at creating faculty positions that could be dedicated to teaching composition—then the only courses in the department focusing on writing rather than the study of literature.

By the mid-1950s, the rules of the game had changed. Men younger than Bernice were joining the faculty, and all had PhDs: Robert Knoll in 1950; James Miller, who arrived from the University of Chicago in 1953 and became the department's youngest chair three years later at the age of thirty-six; Robert "Bud" Hough, who came in 1956 with a PhD from Stanford; Paul Olson in 1957 from Princeton.

Knoll, who came to be Bernice's closest friend on the faculty, suggested that Bernice pursue the one alternative then considered the equivalent of earning a PhD: namely, publishing a scholarly book, an effort that represented at least as much effort as a doctoral dissertation. During the summer of 1954, Bernice took her first trip outside the U.S. to spend a month in England for research, helped by funding from UNL's Research Council. She visited the British Museum and places closely associated with the Romantics: Windemere in the Lake country and the Wye Valley that Wordsworth had toured in 1798. This led to her first scholarly article, not published until 1957, in the *Western Humanities Review*. In "The Case of the Missing Abbey," she considers one of Wordsworth's best-known poems, "Lines Written A Few Miles Above Tintern Abbey." The mystery in the poem, she notes, is the absence of any mention of the Abbey in the poem, aside from the title.

If Tintern Abbey is missing from Wordsworth's poem, Bernice argued, it is "only because the image, the symbol, has in its turn been interfused with the dramatic situation of the poem." In praising the poem, she cites characteristics that she would come to admire in Willa Cather's work: "a sense of complete, harmonious blending and interaction: past, present, and future; the landscape with its muted, flowing lines; man's work and a natural wildness; all senses, memories, and revelations." By the time this article appeared, however, she was well underway on her Keats book.

Among the materials she reviewed at the British Museum during her second research trip to England in the summer of 1957 were the two plays Keats had written—*Otho the Great* and *King Stephen*. Neither had been produced prior to Keats's death at the age of twenty-four.

What Bernice wanted to highlight in her study was not so much Keats the dramatist but how his poetry reflects what she called "the dramatic principle." As she explained, the dramatic principle was that, as in a typical play, in Keats's poetry the spotlight, the audience's attention, is on the events onstage, not the script itself. She contrasted Keats's approach with that of Wordsworth, who "keeps the poet central, and his voice predominant." In Keats's poetry, on the other hand, "the poet retreats, as does the writer of a play, letting other figures and other voices carry act and meaning. He is both receptive and chameleon."

When we look at Bernice's own poetry, it's clear that she felt closer to Keats than Wordsworth. Many of her poems are descriptive and observational, but the observer stands outside the picture. In "The Revivalist," for example, the poet may be sitting in the revival tent, but she is as detached and objective as a scientist conducting a study:

> He feints like a boxer, right to the soul,
> A dancer nimble with fire and ice.
> He speaks with the rocketing wind of God,
> The Profile promising Paradise.

In "Nude in Tragic Air," the poet is like a docent leading a group through a hall of statuary:

> Note how the body betrays. Her hands,
> They jangle and end, nowhere to go
> But folded. Mouth, a quiver of words
> Criss-cross,
> unshaken to hate or desire.

Exceptions can be found, however, especially among her unpublished work. In a poem titled "1953," she reflects on turning forty and entering middle age:

There are signs.
I awake early, familiar with sun-rise.
(Once my father walked in five o'clock birds,
But he was an old, old man.) I eat less.
I sometimes refuse invitations . . . forget the words
Of a song.

Even though she was about to begin work on the English Romantic poets, she acknowledges that her own tastes were shifting toward the classical: "Now I play Mozart, Bach . . . read Gide and Aquinas." And "one thing more," she adds: "The cashmere girls of the Freshman Class / Do not remember the War."

In Bernice's unpublished poems, we catch glimpses of what might have been a struggle with her own sexuality, though to many who knew her, Bernice had already passed into that asexual state known then as spinsterhood. The most intriguing clues are found in a poem titled "Other Rooms":

What is secret only the door knows,
In dumbness latched from arrogance of eyes,
Second face to the hidden air: the rose
Of darkness, black leaves burst to canonize
The somehow fragrant room (by weathering
A hint flows). Dream that dust and fire
Wed in the multifoliate flower-ring
The gods enclose, but key and lock entire
Lie in the secret, too. Die with the secret you.

A Freudian would have a field day with this. Repressions. Secrets and hidden things. The locked room with its black rose and fragrance. The wedding of dust and fire. Was this soft-spoken, demure, scholarly woman telling herself something she could not share outside her own locked room? Though Bernice was easily the most unassuming member of the English faculty in the eyes of her colleagues, she was not reluctant to hint at a richer life. In a press questionnaire, in response to "Other biographical information (including hobbies, adventures, etc.)," she replied coyly, "I don't have hobbies. I do have adventures, but they are for another book."

Though Bernice continued to have poems accepted as late as 1959, she had by then decided to set aside her aspirations to be a poet. There is no evidence that she attempted a new poem after the mid-1950s and even the poems published late in the decade can be traced back to drafts from years before. Instead, she became a scholar. James Miller later recalled that despite being typecast by most of her colleagues as a drudge capable only of teaching introductory courses, Bernice was familiar with an impressive range of literature and had a sharp critical eye. At the time, Miller was enthralled with the work of Walt Whitman, and he and Bernice would sit in the English faculty lounge, he championing Whitman, she urging him to read Dylan Thomas. Miller suggested they collaborate on an essay in comparative analysis, an attempt to both outline their respective concepts of poetry and to demonstrate the synergies between them.

The paper was abandoned, but the idea of a collaboration continued to germinate. Robert Knoll began to join their discussions, and an acquaintance with the director of UNL's fledgling educational television station, KUON, led to an invitation for the trio to hold one of these chats on the air. Titled "Conversation Piece," the thirty-minute show was broadcast to a handful of viewers at 9:00 p.m. on a Friday in April 1955. The three assumed it was the beginning and end of their television careers.

Still struggling to fill its program schedule a year after its establishment, however, KUON invited them back in November, and over the next few months, "Conversation Piece" began appearing as a regular show. Bernice started to receive fan mail, some of it offering advice on her hair and makeup, but more often praising her deep, soft speaking voice and spirit of quiet enthusiasm for literature. "It was Bernice's program, really," Miller later admitted. Bernice selected each show's theme, chose the poems they read and discussed, and handled the opening and closing of each show. She also moderated the discussions. "Robert and I were particularly good at shouting out critical insights," Miller remembered, and Bernice would calmly but firmly restore decorum. She would continue to anchor "Conversation Piece" well into the 1960s, with her cohosts rotating among members of the English faculty.

Quiet professionalism was the essence of Bernice's public persona. She spoke softly, held her temper, dressed conservatively, and eschewed flash. Her one concession to vanity was her use of black hair dye, which helped on television but less so in person. She loved to talk about literature, but rarely about herself. Miller remembered being struck when, in the midst of one of their lunchtime debates among English faculty members, she pointed at herself and said, "I often wonder how I got in *here*." Her waters ran still, but deep.

Writing to thank Clarence Thorpe for his report on her book, Bernice admitted that she had always intended to do more scholarly writing, "but I turned to writing poetry exclusively for some time and let other ideas simmer." Now, she told him, she was shifting her focus to writing criticism, though "I have very little published." She quickly made up for that. She had papers on the poetry of Edwin Arlington Robinson and Hart Crane, Keats's dramas, and the Tintern Abbey piece accepted and printed while waiting for the Keats book to get published.

Keats and the Dramatic Principle proved Bernice was an exceptional scholar. Reviewing the book in *Comparative Literature*, Richard Harter Fogle of Tulane wrote that Bernice was the first to give the subject of Keats's use of dramatic objectivity "full and systematic attention"—and to do so "against a background of contemporary theory." *English*, one of the oldest journals of English critical study, called the book "a stimulating study, a model of clear analysis and logical exposition." The longest review the book received, by Jack Stillinger in *The Journal of English and Germanic Philology*, took issue with some points but concluded that it was "a distinguished and original production, for which Miss Slote deserves hearty congratulations."

The Explicator magazine, the leading journal of scholarly literary criticism in America at the time, selected *Keats* for its annual award as "the best book of *explication de texte* [a word-by-word analysis]" published in 1958. The award was noted in the Lincoln newspapers and Bernice proudly displayed the plaque in her campus office until she died. The greatest compliment, however, came months later, when L. C. Bonnerot wrote in *Etudes Anglaises* (as translated by Virginia), "Miss Slote, because she herself is a poet, brings to bear a delicate comprehension of Keats, his sensibility, his imagination, and above all, his ambitions." Bonnerot was the only reviewer to identify Bernice as both scholar and poet.

Bernice's book did not, however, change the fact that UNL did not consider her qualified for a PhD. In a letter written on New Year's Day 1958,

Louise Pound explained to Bernice that her lack of a second foreign language ruled out any chance of attaining a PhD. Pound also pointed out that without a doctorate, Bernice could not be considered part of the graduate school faculty and would continue to be loaded up with undergraduate classes. "If you have never had any German, you could hardly gain enough in a short summer session for a reading knowledge of it," she cautioned, adding that she was "a firm believer in the foreign language requirement for a doctorate in English."

In Virginia's mind, however, Bernice had more going for her than anyone other potential collaborator and confidant in Lincoln. She combined a capacity for penetrating analysis with a warmth of spirit. Virginia had always been attracted to women with sharp minds, but Bernice had nothing of the erratic artistic temperament that she'd encountered in women she knew in New York and Hollywood. Virginia began stopping by Bernice's apartment on the way home from the press. She aired her frustrations with the cabal of administrators she was convinced were wrecking the press through uninterest and incompetence, while Bernice gently tried to steer the conversation toward literature. She usually succeeded. Both women were exceptionally well read, but Bernice's work as poetry editor for *Prairie Schooner* had forced her to stay abreast of current literature to an extent that Virginia could not match. Virginia responded by introducing Bernice to Willa Cather, with whom she was then only vaguely familiar.

Visits by a few of the press's authors gave Virginia opportunities to socialize—discreetly—with Bernice in public. They took Mari Sandoz to the University Club and Gene Weltfish, an anthropologist preparing a book on the Pawnee Indians, went with them to Lincoln's one Mexican restaurant. Weltfish later wrote to thank Virginia for "my pleasantest remembrance of Lincoln" and to invite her to visit when she next passed through New York City. "Bernice, also," she added. By the summer of 1958, Virginia could write Mari Sandoz that she was happier than she had been in years, despite the continuing uncertainty over the press.

For Bernice, Virginia served as a catalyst. Where Bernice was settled, Virginia was restless. If she was going to stay in Lincoln, she needed more than just something to keep her busy. She saw possibilities in the press and in her role as chief editor (in all but name), and more specifically, in providing the means to advance her Cather projects with support from the right collaborator. And given Virginia's recognition of her own inadequacies as a scholar and her susceptibility to cycles of manic work followed by incapacitating depression, she knew Bernice would be more than just a collaborator. She would be her partner.

In her last published poem, "Invitation: Debate Between Body and Soul," which enjoyed the rare distinction of appearing in the *New York Herald Tribune* in April 1959, Bernice closes the door on any possibility of a return to her life as a poet:

> If once I can stand
> Where black lines cross on a four-square noon, my face
> Unruffled by leaves, or the motion of sun,
>
> Then I shall never cry for the orange climate,
> The pomegranate seeds of another while.

She never closed the door on the lyrical value of poetry, however. In early 1960, she and James Miller were hired by Dodd, Mead to compile *The Dimensions of Poetry*, an anthology intended as a textbook for students of undergraduate introductory courses. In the book's opening essay, "The Nature of a Poem," she writes defiantly, "Poetry is simply a deep kind of pleasure—like roses, or music, or love." Bernice's capacity to recognize and celebrate such deep kinds of pleasure would immensely enrich Virginia's life and work.

18

The Literature of Possibility

The skies over Lincoln were scattered with gray winter clouds when Bruce Nicoll arrived as the new director of the press in January 1959, but for Virginia and the rest of the staff, it was the sunniest day of the last three years.

In Bernice, Virginia had the ally she needed to take on the projects she thought possible if she stayed as editor with the press. But as the first reviews of *Keats and the Dramatic Principle* began to roll in in early September 1958, it still wasn't clear if the press would even survive. And she had no intention of sticking around if Fred Lundy remained as acting director and chief agent of bureaucratic opposition to her visions. Then Bruce Nicoll came into the picture.

Although the publications board had selected him to be director of the press that fall, his appointment wasn't confirmed until January 10, 1959. "The Board of Regents and the Administration finally got off the dime," Virginia wrote Mari Sandoz the same day. At first, Nicoll seemed an unlikely and unpromising choice. A journalism major, he'd been editor of the *Daily Nebraskan* his senior year and went to work as a reporter for the *Lincoln Star* after graduation. He married a local girl and was planning to stay in Lincoln for the foreseeable future when war was declared. Nicoll volunteered, entering the Army Air Force in July 1942, and spent three years in Europe, serving with the Ninth Air Force in England, France, and Germany.

After his discharge in the fall of 1945, he returned to Lincoln and was hired as assistant director of public relations for the university. The job was a mix of reporting, marketing, and community liaison, and Nicoll's talent for working with people in a low-key but productive manner brought him to the attention of the university's leadership. In 1951 Chancellor R. G. Gustavson pulled him up to the front office as an administrative assistant, which was a polite way of saying he was the chancellor's chief troubleshooter. Nicoll was so good at the job that Clifford Hardin kept him in the position when he succeeded Gustavson in 1954.

This led some to fear that Nicoll was put in as the chancellor's agent to close the press down. But Bruce Nicoll had visions of his own for the press. He had a passion for the history and culture of the west, and he saw the press as a way in which the university could expand its regional influence. Although born and raised in Wyoming, Nicoll was a Cornhusker to the core. In the early 1950s, he and Kenneth Keller, another member of the public relations department, had coauthored *Know Nebraska*, which became a standard state history text for public schools.

At the same time, he had a charge to put the press on a more business-like footing. The board of regents was prepared to cover the press's basic operating costs, but they wanted to move past having to hunt for funding every time the press decided to publish a book. Nicoll felt that the press had an opportunity to solve several problems at the same time: publish more than just a handful of books a year; devote more of its catalog to books with a strong regional connection; and achieve a steady and predictable revenue stream.

Nicoll soon discovered that the press's financial situation was uncertain at best. He later compared his first investigations to a game he used to play in the pastures in Wyoming: lifting up a cow chip "to see if there were any worms underneath we could stomp on." One of these worms was the fact that the press had been paying its authors far less in royalties than they were due by contract. He felt confident enough about the press's financial prospects in future, however, that one of his first decisions was to increase the first print run for *Hostiles and Friendlies* to four thousand and pay for a full-page ad in *Publishers Weekly*. "My, this is a fine office now," Virginia chirped to Mari Sandoz. Within two weeks of coming on board, Nicoll secured approval for Louise Pound's folklore book and two other books and agreement in principle to over twenty more books still in development, most of them brought into the press by Virginia.

"Virginia and I have been blowing soap bubbles on plans for publishing over the next two years," Nicoll wrote Sandoz in reply to a note congratulating him on his appointment. He and Sandoz would become close friends, and she soon began to bring projects to his attention. In March 1959, for example, she wrote him about Amos Bad Heart Bull's pictorial history of the Oglala Sioux, a set of four hundred drawings made on a secondhand ledger book between the 1890s and his death in 1913. Her friend Helen Blish had learned of the book in 1926 while a graduate student at UNL and made it the subject of her master's thesis. Knowing of Nicoll's interest in western history, she proposed that the press publish the history along with commentary by Blish. "Good luck with this most ambitious venture!" she wrote at the bottom of her letter. A most ambitious venture it proved indeed, taking the press over eight years to bring to print.

Nicoll shared Sandoz's desire to better document the experience of Native Americans, and with her help, laid out plans for the Great Plains Indian Library, a series devoted to books on the life, customs, and history of Native American tribes of the region, the first such initiative on the part of a university press. Sandoz also suggested the press publish a memoir by one of her father's Sandhills friends, Charley O'Kieffe. After *Old Jules* was published, O'Kieffe had written several times with his recollections of Jules Sandoz, and she thought his work good enough to merit his own book. The idea fit perfectly with a series devoted to diaries and other autobiographical material of the first generation of Plains settlers that Nicoll wanted to launch, and *Western Story: The Recollections of Charley O'Kieffe, 1884–1898* became the second volume in the press's Pioneer Heritage series.

Bruce Nicoll performed another role that proved vital for the press's survival: as intermediary for Virginia. He shielded her from much of the tedium of the university's bureaucracy and freed her to focus on editorial rather than organizational concerns. But he also shielded the administration from Virginia. Virginia had only one tactic when dealing with opposition: attack, head on and at full steam. The two adjectives that former colleagues most often use in describing her are "intimidating" and "stubborn." No one would ever use those words to describe Bruce Nicoll. He much preferred to avoid conflicts by keeping relations with the rest of the university on a low-key, friendly, and cooperative basis. And yet his values and integrity were rock solid. "Bruce Nicoll has always been on the right side of the angels," Mamie Meredith wrote Mari Sandoz when she learned of his appointment.

Nicoll was an institutional insider attuned to the subtleties of campus politics and personalities. In a rare venture into fiction, "An Incident at the Faculty Club," published in *Prairie Schooner* in 1956, he illustrated the nuances involved in something as simple as a friendship between two professors: "A friend was openly acknowledged as a friend," he wrote, "only after careful recognition of his shortcomings and frailties, a system of social bookkeeping considered essential to the completeness of the liberal tradition." Nicoll was nothing if not a careful social bookkeeper.

As she worked with Nicoll, Virginia came to appreciate this talent. Writing to S. N. Behrman, she admitted that she was beginning to find life at the university fascinating: "The hierarchic set-up, the intrigue, the politics, the mixture of parochialism and true internationalism." In fact, she wrote, the university was not that different from a Hollywood studio: "the caste system, the war with—and dread of—the front office, the intimate knowledge of scores and scores of people whom you've never seen but who are in the 'profession.'"

Nicoll launched his most ambitious initiative for the press in his second year as director. Although *Roundup* was still its bestselling title, it was something of an exception in selling better in the popular than the academic market. University libraries and faculties were still the press's primary customers. He recognized that books like those in the Pioneer Heritage series appealed to ordinary readers as well as to academics. There were two obstacles to reaching this market: packaging and distribution. The press published hardbacks designed for long shelf lives in libraries and its sales agents—all two of them—primarily worked with institutions.

Pocket-sized mass-market paperbacks had come to dominate the popular market, but Nicoll felt this format was too cheap and short-lived to maintain the press's reputation for quality. After talking with several printers, he became convinced that the answer was to publish in a larger format, 5¼ inches wide by 8 inches high, with sturdier covers and white, rather than newsprint, interiors. Not only would these books be more durable, but the size would also allow hardback books to be reprinted in this format through photo-imaging, avoiding the cost of new typesetting. This opened the possibility of reissuing many good books on western history and culture that Nicoll knew of. And in Virginia's case, she saw the potential for reissuing the growing library of Catheriana that she had been collecting.

There were a few hiccups between the decision to start the series, known as Bison Books, to suggest the books' durability, and its actual launch in the fall of 1960. The initial plan was to release eight titles, priced between $1 and $1.95, before the end of 1960 and a further nine in 1961. The press announced these in the brochure for its fall 1960 releases. Virginia wrote Bill Koshland at Knopf about Bison Books and celebrated Bruce Nicoll's leadership. "All the pre-New Deal biogs and 'vanities' and follies (i.e., *Service Station Management*) are being remaindered," and the press would only carry titles "that are real scholarly contributions" or continuing sellers appropriate for a university press.

The first Bison Book listed was *The Hero and the Witness*, a biography and critical study of the work of the Nebraska-born novelist Wright Morris by David Madden. This was to be an original, a book Virginia had been working with Madden on for over a year. Madden's commitment to placing Morris solidly alongside better-known contemporaries as J. D. Salinger and Norman Mailer impressed Virginia and she had come to address him as "my dear Boswell." In turn, he was impressed by her commitment to producing a well-structured, well-argued, and well-written book. His manuscript had grown well beyond the originally agreed target of two-hundred-some pages to a final draft at least four times too long, and Virginia patiently led him through the revision process, helping trim the book back down to size.

Having taken delivery of the final manuscript, however, Bruce and Virginia were dismayed to learn that Madden had never received a PhD—and, in fact, his master's degree, from San Francisco State, was in creative writing. Neither one having advanced degrees—or any degree, in Virginia's case—they felt themselves on the defensive when it came to the perception of the press as part of an academic institution. Virginia informed Madden that the press couldn't publish his book because it would be "bad for our reputation" and the press voided his contract. Mari Sandoz's *Old Jules* then became Bison Book no. 1. Madden was later able to place the book with Twayne, and he specifically thanked Virginia, "who read, word by word, and commented on the manuscript in its 800-page version, amassing a two-inch stack of correspondence," in his acknowledgments.

The introduction of Bison Books offered the press an attractive alternative to hardback printing for academic books. Traditionally, such books appealed to a narrow market, usually college faculty members specializing in the books' subjects and the libraries that supported them. Few instructors assigned texts other than thick survey anthologies (like Bernice and James

Miller's *The Dimensions of Poetry*) or widely available classics. Mass-market paperback editions of classics began increasingly to appear on class reading lists, but there was growing demand for texts in upper-level and graduate courses that were within a college student's budget. Such books could sell slowly but steadily over the course of years.

One of the manuscripts the press had received in the year before Nicoll's arrival seemed an ideal candidate. *The Literature of Possibility: A Study in Humanistic Existentialism* had been submitted by Hazel Barnes, a philosophy professor at the University of Colorado who'd earlier translated Jean Paul Sartre's seminal work on existentialism, *Being and Nothingness*. The book began with a misunderstanding. Barnes had sent Emily Schossberger a proposal that drew upon lectures she'd delivered while teaching at Ohio State University. Schossberger dismissed the idea of simply publishing the talks, which had never been Barnes's intent. She then met with Barnes while passing through Boulder and suggested sending the book to the University of Chicago Press, which she was about to join. Still unsure where to take the book, Barnes was startled to receive a letter from Virginia, who was going through the various projects Schossberger had left behind and wanted to know when Barnes would submit her manuscript.

Barnes wrote to say she would be ready to send it in a few months. Although she would come to be considered one of the foremost authorities on existentialism, this was her first original book and Virginia subjected it to her usual scrutiny. She and Bernice read it, and though neither had studied philosophy, they both found the book interesting, illuminating, and worthy of publication. The thinking was clear, but the writing uneven: "Some of the best passages, incisive and sinewy, are balanced by areas that are rambling and wordy."

Something beyond the book's writing and subject attracted Virginia's attention, however. The letters exchanged between Hazel Barnes and Virginia quickly changed in tone from formal to friendly, almost intimate. It's clear the two women felt a tremendous intellectual attraction. Early in their working relationship, Hazel asked if there might be an opportunity for her to speak at UNL, and Virginia was happy to help arrange funding for Hazel's guest lectureship in October 1959.

Hazel traveled to Lincoln with Doris Schwalbe, another University of Colorado professor and her partner since the early 1950s. Hazel and Doris met with Virginia and Bernice several times during that visit. Hazel wrote Virginia afterward in gushing tones. "Being with you on Wednesday was an unalloyed delight . . . The evening at your apartment still lives with me as a myriad of shifting impressions and recollections climaxing all the events of the day . . . I thank you with true existentialist fervor, which you will remember is totally committed."

That visit established a special level of trust among the four women. All were pursuing challenging intellectual careers while conforming to social norms in their institutions and communities that rejected their sexual preferences. But they also shared a reluctance to confront those norms in asserting their identities. Almost forty years later, Barnes would write in her autobiography, *Stories I Tell Myself*, "When coming out is made into a moral imperative, I grow uneasy. In part this may be simply because I feel that personal reticence ought to be respected. Consensual adult sexual practices, like many other personal preferences, should be one's own business. In principle I object to labeling someone as if a designation of sexual preference expressed the whole person." Virginia and Bernice would later apply this same principle in their treatment of Willa Cather's sexuality. Hazel did not hesitate, though, to dedicate *The Literature of Possibility* to "Doris, who helped make it possible," and she would become Virginia's closest friend outside Lincoln—indeed, more than a friend: a confidante.

Virginia and Nicoll both hoped to attract more books like Barnes's. To prevent receiving more of the problematic manuscripts that had plagued the press in the past, he asked Virginia to put together an informational brochure on its vision and editorial approach, something they could send to guide authors with promising proposals—and to dissuade the others. She took the assignment as an opportunity not just to instruct authors but to serve as a miniature example as well.

Though just twenty-five pages long, *Scholarly Publishing as Viewed by the University of Nebraska Press* was structured in four chapters, three of which were devoted to providing context for the stylistic and thematic guidance in the final chapter on preparation of manuscripts. There were footnotes and a list of sources at the end of each chapter. And a quiet but impassioned defense: "It has been said (perhaps too often) that university presses publish only those works for which a commercial publisher cannot be found"—a remark that implied they dealt in leftover goods—"and does little to brighten the day for those of us who toil in the vineyards."

The powerhouse among university presses at the time was the University of Oklahoma Press. As the UN press's catalog and reputation grew during the 1960s and 1970s, so did a friendly spirit of competition, with occasional poaching of staff and manuscripts in both directions. Before Nicoll began turning things around, however, the advantage lay wholly with Oklahoma. K. Ross Toole was one of several authors who chose to pull their books from Nebraska and take them to Oklahoma instead. After his history *Montana: An Uncommon Land* was announced as a title forthcoming from Oklahoma, Toole wrote Nicoll sheepishly, "It was an acceptable manuscript only by virtue of Virginia Faulkner's hard and perceptive labors. So thorough a job did she do, as a matter of fact, that neither Oklahoma's readers nor editors had anything left to do." In just three years, Virginia had established herself as a masterful editor.

Paradoxically, the best indication of Virginia's regard for a writer—and his subject—was the extent to which she was willing to employ her blue pencil. When James Miller, now head of the English department at the University of Chicago, decided to assemble a collection of Henry James's essays on writing fiction, she gave him her enthusiastic support. Building upon Miller's *Myth and Method: Modern Theories of Fiction*, which the press published in 1960 as one of its first Bison Book originals, *Theory of Fiction: Henry James* drew from over two hundred fifty different articles by James. Over the course of three months, Virginia sent him three dozen pages of "Author's Notes" that ranged from simple copy edits to questions of principle ("Is *The Turn of the Screw* a story, tale, or novel?"). "You take my breath away with your speed in handling the book," Miller told her with a mixture of admiration and humility.

Hugh Luke, a UNL English professor who first encountered Virginia when he wrote the introduction to the Bison Books edition of Mary Shelley's novel *The Last Man*, recalled what it was like to have one's prose come under her scrutiny. "I thought my introduction perfect, and I was proud of it," he wrote years later. "It came back dripping blood. Not one sentence had escaped her sharp eye nor her immense storehouse of factual information." To Luke, it seemed there was more red on his pages than black. What hurt most, though, was the recognition that "she was unerringly right": "Not a single one of her red marks failed to improve those sentences which, only a day before, I had been so proud to have written."

Virginia understood how authors felt at first contact with her editorial notes. "If your initial reaction to editing of your work is the same as mine," she wrote John Milton, author of a study of the western novel, it would be to "find myself shaking with rage if I see so much as a pencil mark." She hoped, however, that after calming down and a drink or two, the author would "realize that the editor and I are on the same side, after all."

She also understood how important structure was to a book—something she'd learned working on *A House Is Not a Home*. Among the many pages of editorial notes on *The Literature of Possibility* that she sent Hazel Barnes, her strongest criticism was reserved for its final chapter. "You are writing your conclusion—your 'wrap-up' of all that has gone before," she advised. "Any more detailed synopsizing is out of key." Introducing new information at that point, she wrote, "is worse than a stumbling block . . . it actually derails us—we lose the thread and get the feeling we're right back in mid-book."

Virginia also used the *Scholarly Publishing* brochure to draw a line separating the press's new way of doing business from its early days: "The UNP does not solicit nor accept contributions from authors to be applied against the cost of publication." It would continue to rely on grant funding when available, but it was no longer going to take on vanity projects. As Bruce Nicoll made clear in an interview with the *Lincoln Star* late in his first year, the press was also not going to get into the business of publishing textbooks. He wanted to focus on two lines of development for the catalog: regional history and literature, especially with the Bison Books; and scholarly works, particularly books written by members of the UNL faculty. Virginia's vision for her Cather projects aligned perfectly with both.

19

The Road Is All

Nebraska had three women defending the legacy of Willa Cather. Virginia and Bernice were two of them. Mildred Bennett of Red Cloud was the third.

Born into a poor Seventh Day Adventist family that moved from place to place in South Dakota, Iowa, and Kansas as she grew up, Mildred was an unlikely prospect to be a Cather champion. Her father forbade the reading of fiction, so she only began to discover literature when she left home to attend Union College in Lincoln. She first encountered Cather when she went to teach in the town of Inavale, five miles west of Red Cloud, where Cather's family had settled after moving from Virginia in 1883. One of her students brought in a copy of *Shadows on the Rock* that Cather had inscribed to her grandmother, and Mildred quickly learned that there were people in the area who knew the writer and her family well.

Mildred married Wilbur Bennett, and the couple moved soon after to Lincoln and then Omaha, where Wilbur entered medical school. Mildred had taken a master's degree in psychology at UNL, but she felt the need to write and attended one of the conferences that Leo Jacks ran at Creighton University to encourage budding Nebraska writers. Jacks, among the first academics to take a serious interest in Cather, mentioned that no Cather biography had been written, and when the couple moved to Red Cloud after Wilbur became one of the town's doctors, Mildred began research on one.

Although Mildred's first book, *The World of Willa Cather*, ends with Cather's departure for the university in Lincoln, it was Cather's first biography per se. Its wealth of detail drawn from Cather's friends and acquaintances such as Carrie Miner Sherwood established Mildred as a leading expert and her book as a primary source. Two years later, Leon Edel completed the critical biography begun by E. K. Brown and this was joined by memoirs written by Edith Lewis, Cather's partner, and Elizabeth Shepley Sergeant, a friend from Cather's years in New York—all books Virginia scoured for hidden meanings in Pacific Grove.

As susceptible to manic-depressive cycles as Virginia, Mildred was at something of a loss for what to do after *The World of Willa Cather*. She took on a variety of commitments, including serving on Red Cloud's school board. She saw, however, that the wealth of artifacts and memories of Cather's life that could still be found in Red Cloud would be lost if someone didn't start to collect them, and in 1955 she established the Willa Cather Pioneer Memorial with the aim of building a museum.

When Virginia laid out her plan for her Nebraska anthology, she knew she wanted not just to incorporate selections of Cather's work but something about Cather as a notable Nebraskan. No author was as familiar with Cather's time in the state as Mildred, so it was natural that Virginia wrote to solicit a biographical piece. Mildred had published "Catherton," an article about Cather and Red Cloud in *Prairie Schooner* several years before *The World of Willa Cather*. "It is exactly what the doctor ordered," Virginia wrote in July 1956, asking permission to use the piece.

One thing Virginia liked about Mildred's article was that it emphasized the cosmopolitan flavor of Red Cloud, a small town far out on the prairie, a place that, like Nebraska itself, was almost universally assumed to be flat, dull, and backward. "Within a few miles of the Cather home," Mildred had written, "were settlements of Russians, French, Irish, Norwegians, Germans, and Czechoslovakians, each with a rich heritage of tradition and superstition." A year later, Mildred convinced Dodd, Mead, the publisher of *The World of Willa Cather*, to publish a collection of Cather's first short stories, works that by then had entered the public.

This drew the ire of Edith Lewis, since she felt not only that Cather had disowned her early writings but that the book was of no critical value. Virginia thought Mildred's approach in editing the book—inserting mostly biographical asides into the texts of the stories—was not up to an authoritative academic standard, but she celebrated the spirit of the act. She, too, wanted to start digging into Cather's early work, since she believed it held keys that could unlock secret messages in Cather's mature fiction.

Virginia and Mildred began corresponding about a project they would take on together. Mildred wanted to take Cather's story forward from where she left it in *The World of Willa Cather*. She wanted to go to Pittsburgh and interview surviving acquaintances from Cather's time there over fifty years before, and then to visit New York and interview Edith Lewis. Virginia wanted to draw upon her work in Pacific Grove and upon the material she was starting to discover in her own talks with Cather's friends in Lincoln, such as Louise Pound and Mariel Gere. Virginia contacted Leo Jacks and persuaded him to write an essay on Cather's use of classical literature. Mildred enlisted John March, a researcher for Collier's encyclopedia in New York who served on the board on the Memorial, to put together a comprehensive bibliography of Cather's published work.

The book they had in mind would be called *The Road Is All*, taking its title from a saying by the French historian Jules Michelet—"The end is nothing, the road is all"—that Cather often repeated. As Virginia envisioned it, the book would be the definitive critical assessment of Cather's work. She wrote with pride to Bill Koshland at Knopf: "The research I did in California is proving quite helpful—the material is being dished out to various scholars, some of whom will contribute to the book."

Maintaining a good relationship with Koshland was critical if Virginia were to realize her plans for her Cather projects. Koshland had become Alfred Knopf's right-hand man and her best connection to Knopf and Edith Lewis, whose hold over the Cather estate—and more than that, whose interpretation of not only of Cather's will but that nebulous thing called her intent—meant they could support or suppress the efforts of anyone who needed to use any material they controlled. Virginia had fence-mending to do, to step back from the melodramatic tone of her letters from Pacific Grove and assure Koshland that her work now had a solid scholarly foundation. But she also had to repair damage from a decade before, when the UN press had published a book edited by James Shively titled *Writings from Willa Cather's Campus Years*.

When the book was reviewed in the *New York Herald Tribune*, Knopf fired off an angry letter to UNL Chancellor Gustavson complaining that the press had published in bad faith. Back in 1948, when Shively had written Edith Lewis for permission to use Cather's student writings as part of his dissertation, she had agreed on the condition that he would not publish the material without her approval—which Shively accepted. "In light of what Mr. Shively wrote Miss Lewis," wrote Knopf, "I find the publication by your press of his book astonishing to say the least." Asked for an explanation, Emily Schossberger quibbled, saying that the book was not "a money-making venture but rather a contribution to scholarship." Gustavson apologized and the press quietly shifted its remaining stock to the backlist. Virginia took care, therefore, to address the question of Cather's legacy directly: "Knopf, H. M. [Houghton Mifflin, Cather's other publisher] and the Cather executors are assured that the press would not do anything to detract from Willa Cather's stature as a writer or dignity as a human being."

Virginia was eager to share her latest discoveries with Koshland. "I have had the opportunity to read dozens and dozens of letters Cather wrote during her university years and in the decade thereafter." She then acknowledged, "Much as I admired her as an artist, I found her personality quite repellent in many respects, and these letters, more than anything, have placed her in a more sympathetic light." The letters she refers to cryptically were ones Cather had written to Mariel Gere and other members of the Gere family between 1891 and 1897. Mariel Gere had been one of Cather's classmates at UNL (and one of Virginia and Ed's teachers at Lincoln High School) and her father had founded the *Lincoln Journal*. After she died in April 1960, her papers and other contents of the Gere home were donated to the Nebraska Historical Society and Virginia was given the opportunity to read and transcribe Cather's letters. Under the terms of Cather's will, none of her personal letters were to be published or even quoted. Virginia knew that even hinting at their publication would put the press at risk of being cut off by Knopf and Lewis.

The impact on Virginia of Cather's letters to the Geres must have been profound. Up to then, she assumed that Cather was a suppressed, even unknowing, lesbian who chose to put on a public face that was neither straight nor gay but simply asexual. But one of the Gere letters changed her mind. In June 1894, Cather wrote to Mariel Gere, "How awfully patient you have been all these years. Patient when I raved over her grace, her beauty, her beautiful playing, her beautiful dancing! Patient and sympathetic when I was in rapture because I had accidentally touched her hand, and still patient when even the happiness of loving her was lost to me forever." The *her* referred to was Louise Pound. Cather had fallen for Louise, the first romantic feelings that Cather put in writing. Pound demurred, leaving Cather distraught. "The thing I had been living for and in was torn away from me and it left just an aching emptiness in me," she wrote Mariel.

This letter told Virginia that there was nothing unknowing in Cather's sexuality. She had experienced the same attraction to another woman that Virginia had felt for Ruth Bernhard, Dana Suesse, Bernice, and perhaps others. But there was little she could do with this knowledge. To suggest anything to Koshland or anyone connected with the Cather estate or family would have put an end to any further cooperation. Even to discuss it outside a tiny, trusted circle—perhaps Bernice alone—would have raised suspicions in Lincoln, where queer people kept a low profile to survive personally and professionally.

But just as Virginia was boasting about *The Road Is All*, the project was beginning to unravel. Her own faith in Mildred's ability as a writer and scholar had been tested by the experience of working on "Willa Cather in Pittsburgh," an article Mildred had submitted to *Prairie Schooner* collecting her initial research. Mildred sent her draft to Virginia just before Christmas 1958, and though Virginia at first responded almost obsequiously, Mildred soon discovered just how sharp the point of Virginia's blue pencil could be. Virginia asked for a revision. Mildred provided it a few days later. In return, she got more notes and a request for a further revision. Though Virginia still deferred—asking forgiveness if "Princess Muttonfist here has bitched up anything"—what she was asking for was really that Mildred start over: There were problems with research, argument, references, grammar, style, and length.

Months later, Virginia still refused to accept the article. She wrote Karl Shapiro, *Prairie Schooner*'s editor, that it might be salvaged with extensively reorganization and additional material. A day later, she took that back: "This article is not worth printing, even with the most elegant and extensive revision." "Willa Cather in Pittsburgh" did finally make it into *Prairie Schooner* in the spring of 1959, but cut severely and only dealing with the first half of Cather's time in the city. Mildred had an attic full of Cather papers, but Virginia didn't trust her to organize, let alone write about it. John March looked through the materials on a trip to Red Cloud and reported to Virginia afterward that it was a chaotic mess. Mildred also disappointed her as a literary scholar. Given a copy of Virginia's notes on Elizabeth Shepley Sergeant's memoir, Mildred confessed that she simply could not detect the interlinear story Virginia felt she had uncovered. All she could see in the book was "straight biography."

And yet, as with Knopf, Edith Lewis, and Cather's relatives, Virginia could not afford to burn her bridges with Mildred. She continued to encourage her to make research trips, and in return Mildred wrote, "If I die on this trip, I authorize you to take all my Cather material to use"—on the condition that any royalties went to the Memorial. Mildred had persuaded Dodd, Mead to release the reprint rights to *The World of Willa Cather* to the UN press, and with the introduction of Bison Books, Virginia saw a perfect opportunity to reissue it—with some updates. But by the fall of 1960, it was clear to both women that *The Road Is All* could go no further.

Having suffered Virginia as an editor, Mildred knew she could not handle her as a collaborator. "After much soul-searching and anguish," she wrote Virginia, "I have come to the decision that for the present at least, I will have to work this thing out alone." For Virginia, this was a nonstarter. She met with Mildred and said the press wouldn't consider moving forward with the book unless she had a collaborator. She had already lined up Robert Hough, a UNL professor whose book on William Dean Howells the press had published. As Virginia later reported to John March, Mildred "asked point-blank if we considered her competent to undertake it alone, and there was nothing for it but to say no." She took John March's bibliography and other material she had collected and worked as much of it into the Bison Book edition of *The World of Willa Cather* as she could without forcing a completely new typesetting.

Virginia was unsympathetic to Mildred's mental health challenges. She found it impossible, she wrote March, "to make allowances for this type of maladjustment after, say, age 40." Virginia seemed to think that she had come through her own crisis and "snapped out of it," and she expected the same of Mildred. Virginia showed no concern that she might find herself struggling with emotional demons again. Most damning, however, was her dismissal of Mildred's potential to ever contribute to Virginia's plans for Catheriana: "Actually, I don't know where Mildred got the idea that she was a writer in the first place." Virginia thought Mildred would do better to

Fig. 15. Mildred Bennett in the Garber Bank building in Red Cloud after its acquisition by the Willa Cather Memorial Foundation, February 1960. Courtesy of *Hastings Tribune*.

turn her energies to her organizational initiatives—"achievements of which anyone could rightly be proud."

The Road Is All was also becoming an unachievable goal due to Virginia's own commitments. From just two books in 1958, under Nicoll's leadership the press published ten in 1959, double that in 1960, and the pace showed no sign of slacking. The first Bison Books had been a considerable success, opening new outlets for the stream of western reissues like J. Frank Dobie's *Voice of the Coyote* and Elinore Pruitt Stewart's *Letters of a Woman Homesteader*. She was working with Hazel Barnes and a fellow University of Colorado professor, Donald Sutherland, on a new translation of *Hippolytus* by Euripides, with a critical essay by Hazel. She was helping Robert Knoll gather material for his selection of the works of Robert McAlmon, *McAlmon and the Lost Generation: A Self Portrait*, and giving his accompanying commentary her usual scrutiny. Knoll's widow recalls him grumbling about Virginia's giving him the editorial third degree, though after the book was published, he sent her a pair of kid gloves, writing, "You do handle your authors with a silken finesse."

Feeling the press was now on solid ground, Virginia felt she could take her first major break after almost five years. She and Bernice would travel together to Europe. Bernice had to visit London for further research on Keats, but Virginia saw other opportunities as well. She wanted to show Rome to Bernice and then to retrace the journey through France that Cather had taken with her friends Isabelle McClung and Dorothy Canfield in 1902. That trip had inspired the poems in Cather's first book, *April Twilights*, and Virginia wanted the press to reissue it with Bernice's annotation and commentary.

The 1903 edition of *April Twilights* was no longer subject to copyright and the press didn't need Lewis's permission to reissue it. On the other hand, Cather had revised the collection for editions published in 1923 and 1933 that were still part of her estate. In the interest of maintaining rapport, Bruce Nicoll wrote Alfred Knopf (and through him, Edith Lewis) to inform them of the press's plans. Lewis's reaction, as relayed by Knopf, was blunt. Cather's best poems were in the 1923 edition, she wrote. The only motivation she could see for reissuing the 1903 editions was profit.

Furthermore, she wrote, "I know nothing about the writing of Professor Bernice Slote; but I feel that any critical writing on poetry demands rather a special familiarity with and interest in the work criticized and that it cannot with satisfactory results be assigned simply as a job." As for any editing of the poems, Lewis felt Cather herself had already done it for Knopf's 1923 edition of *April Twilights*. This conclusion must have infuriated Virginia. Bernice was her all-star pick to place Cather on solid ground with literary scholars and here was Cather's own partner and executor dismissing her out of hand.

Virginia responded via Bill Koshland, in a mixture of defense and deflection. The idea had originated with others, not the press, and had come formally from James Miller, now at the University of Chicago ("nationally recognized as a distinguished teacher and author"). Bernice ("a considerable poet in her own right" in addition to her scholarly credits) was superbly qualified to edit and comment on the collection. And she acknowledged, "I am also jealous of the reputation this press has earned since its reorganization." From the editorial standpoint at least, the reputation of the press rested on her shoulders. She hinted to Koshland that the fact that Knopf had quoted Lewis verbatim without adding any comments of his own showed that he did necessarily share her view.

April Twilights was not the only early work of Cather's that Virginia wanted to reissue, but she and Bernice agreed that it would establish the baseline for the press's approach to publishing authoritative versions of Cather's work. It would be one of four classic works published in the spring of 1962, along with James Fenimore Cooper's novel *Satanstoe* and Charles Maturin's gothic novel *Melmoth the Wanderer*. If the press was going to produce more of these—and there was a growing market for such important if less well-known literary works—it was crucial to earn the respect of the reviewers in influential academic journals like *College English*. The editing, commentary, typesetting, design, and even the covers had to speak for the press's credibility and seriousness.

But there were two other motivations behind the selection of the 1903 edition of *April Twilights*. The first was to demonstrate that Cather was a major author worthy of the same treatment one might expect for an early work by a great such as John Milton or Alexander Pope. For Virginia, it was crucial to rid Cather of the label of *regionalist*. As far back as 1932, her old UNL English professor and *Prairie Schooner* founder Lowry Wimberley had attacked the notion of regionalism in American literature. Not only were technology and transportation making regional distinctions irrelevant, he argued, but the label denigrated any subject to which it was applied: "The expression 'regional' has, as a matter of fact, opprobrious connotations, implying, as it often does, boorishness, provincial-mindedness, and vulgarity." Even the label "American" was to be avoided, since a dismissive imperialist attitude could still be seen in English writing on the literature of its former colony.

Bernice addressed the other reason for starting with *April Twilights* in her introduction to the book. With Cather, she argued, "Nothing in her work is unrelated to the whole." More than most writers, "she worked a single, intricate design in which elements changed names and language and form but always remained a part of the body." When she added a preface to a revised edition of the book in 1968, her tone was even more assertive: "Anyone who is interested in her major fiction and its interpretation will find the 1903 *April Twilights* wholly relevant." Every point she had made in the first edition, she felt, had been "confirmed and strengthened."

It was a bold move to base such an emphatic assessment on such a slight work. Cather's poetry has never been considered as significant as her fiction. One reviewer called the poems "verbally neat, genteel in tone, and almost wholly derivative." But there was no such dismissal of the scholarly merit of the edition. In *Books Abroad*, Robert Gale wrote, "The entire editorial apparatus—a splendid introduction, thorough notes, and a very complete bibliography—is more exemplary than the poems themselves." *April Twilights* was a small realization of Virginia's Cather dreams, but it demonstrated how far she'd moved from her wild notions in Pacific Grove. Unfortunately, the path of Virginia and Bernice's Cather projects was about to take a detour.

20

"Anniversary"

When Chancellor Clifford Hardin announced in early 1956 that Pulitzer Prize–winning poet Karl Shapiro would be joining the university's English department, the Lincoln papers crowed with pride. The *Star*'s lead editorial predicted that Shapiro would "bring distinction to the state and to the university because of the distinction he holds in the nation's foremost literary circles." Hiring Shapiro—who had by then won virtually every prize available to an American poet—was a sign of the state's sophistication: "It is a cultured state that assigns true value to such activities and such performers. . . . Nebraska's real pleasure in its good fortune reflects credit to itself."

The root of all conflicts is a conflict of expectations. Nebraska expected Karl Shapiro to be a shining trophy in its cultural showcase. Shapiro expected Nebraska would be another place where he could pursue his art in his uniquely iconoclastic manner, regardless of what Nebraskans or anyone else thought. Barely six months after starting at the university, he declared in a talk at the Library of Congress that the Midwest was "the most backward part of the U.S." and that most college students were "completely devoid of any intellectual idealism" and "as actionless as old men."

Tapped to take over as editor of *Prairie Schooner* when its founder, Lowry Wimberley, retired in 1957, Shapiro declared that he intended to change the look and content of the magazine and start selling it over the counter in addition to by subscription. Literary geography, he told the *Nebraska Alumnus*, "is too fluid to be mapped out in the old ways, and even literary history, with its pat causes and effects, no longer appeals to us as final and incontrovertible." "Now, there is one fine mess of words. Maybe Dr. Shapiro knows what he is talking about, but we don't" harrumphed J. E. Lawrence in a *Star* editorial titled "Karl Shapiro Again."

Despite his opinions about Lincoln and the Midwest, Shapiro soon came to respect the expertise of his colleagues in the English department. He joined the coffee lounge conversations that had sparked the "Conversation Piece" television program, and soon, he, James Miller, and Bernice began discussing the possibility of collaborating on a critical study of modern poetry. The resulting book, *Start with the Sun*, took its title from *Apocalypse*, a little-known collection of D. H. Lawrence's essays published shortly after his death in 1930. It was not the most solid foundation for what was intended as a rejection of the intellectual, internally focused literature of T. S. Eliot and other modernists. But Miller, Shapiro, and Bernice were inspired by Lawrence's goal: "What we want is to . . . re-establish the living organic connections with the cosmos, the sun and earth, with mankind and nation and family. Start with the sun, and the rest will slowly, slowly happen."

"Where is the song, the incantation, the magic, the passion of poetry?" Bernice asked in her introduction, "The Whitman Tradition." Though she could appreciate "the classical excellence of the Eliot tradition," she argued that it had the effect of estranging the reader, of distancing them from "the pagan joy and wonder" of the body and the natural world. Shapiro, on the other hand, thought that Eliot, Auden, and other modernists were writing what he called "closed" poems—"the poem that clicks like a box—is the type of poem which has lately become a standard in the twentieth century." Miller tried to steer a middle course, less romantic than Bernice, less dogmatic than Shapiro.

Start with the Sun was published in late 1960. With the growing popularity of the spontaneous and visceral poetry of Beats like Allen Ginsberg, there was an appetite for a rebuttal of the intellectual approach of Eliot and others that had come to dominate poetry criticism, if not poetry itself. In *Books Abroad*, Harriet Zinnes called the book exciting and significant. And in January 1961, *Start with the Sun* was selected by the Poetry Society of America for the Chap-Book Award as the outstanding book of criticism for 1960. Writing in *Saturday Review*, however, Robert D. Spector found that "its assumptions are false, its thesis untenable, and its methods bizarre," but credited Bernice for her attempt "to give unity to the book through an introduction and conclusion that judiciously note the limitations of the Eliot orthodoxy."

Fig. 16. Bernice with Jim Miller (left) and Karl Shapiro, 1960. Courtesy of Bernice Slote, English Papers, Archives and Special Collections, University of Nebraska-Lincoln Libraries.

Karl Shapiro enjoyed playing the provocateur. His contributions to *Start with the Sun* included references to psychologist Wilhelm Reich's Orgone Box, the science-mystic P. D. Ouspensky, and the debunked theory of phlogiston, a substance supposedly released by combustion—none of which improved his standing with skeptics. He tried to stir things up on campus with one-of-a-kind events. In 1959 he organized a beatnik poetry session at the campus art gallery. Four local poets read from their work while a jazz sextet played. Bernice read a translation of a poems by Salvatore Quasimodo, and Giovanna Bowsky, the Italian-born wife of history professor William Bowsky, read the originals. It was a very Nebraskan experiment, however. Bernice introduced the performance and assured the audience that "we will leave our shoes on."

As *Prairie Schooner* editor, Shapiro took more interest in its fiction than the poetry, which he was content to leave to Bernice. Even with fiction, however, he preferred to deal with the final decisions and leave the initial culling to others. In 1959 he asked Virginia to become an associate editor and take the lead for reviewing submissions, along with Fred Christensen, who'd been working for *Schooner* since 1929. She thought too many of the stories being published showed the influence of Henry Miller and William Carlos Williams, "whom Karl sits at the feet of," but she was wrong in thinking Shapiro anyone's disciple. "I am an anarchist and full professor at that," he once declared. And he proved true to his word in triggering the biggest controversy of his time at UNL, a controversy that hit the national newspapers and swept up Bernice and Virginia in its wake.

The hand grenade that Shapiro gleefully tossed into the complacent world of Lincoln and UNL in the spring of 1963 was a short story by Ervin Krause called "Anniversary." Krause came to Lincoln the same year as Shapiro. Nebraska-born, he had studied physics and mathematics at Iowa State, served in the U.S. Air Force, and worked for McDonnell-Douglas as a technical writer before entering UNL as graduate student in English. Shapiro encouraged Krause's interest in writing fiction and published six of his short stories in *Prairie Schooner* between 1958 and 1961.

Krause then moved to Honolulu, where he became an instructor in the English department at the University of Hawaii. He continued to write, completing a novel based on his experiences in the Air Force, and in August 1962, he wrote Shapiro to say that he had a story he thought Shapiro would want for *Prairie Schooner*: "Anniversary." There were "fairly stern passages" in it, Krause warned him, "but they are not designed to titillate—in fact, just the opposite, if anything."

Shapiro had already begun to back away from his *Prairie Schooner* duties. He had taken a leave of absence in June 1961 and Bernice had filled in as editor. When he returned for the fall term in 1962, he was named Regents Professor and in early 1963 he wrote Walter Militzer, dean of the College of Arts and Sciences, that he intended to resign as editor at the end of the spring term. Lincoln newspapers reported that Shapiro's reason was "to devote more time to his teaching and writing." The Winter 1962/1963 issue would be the last to list Shapiro as editor.

Shapiro knew that "Anniversary" treaded on dangerous ground. The story centers around a stopover in Lincoln by McDonald, a professor at the University of Missouri on his way to visit relatives during a Christmas break. He calls up Wanda, a widow with whom he had had an affair while working on his doctorate at UNL. They meet and go back to her house for dinner. Eventually, they have sex and then begin arguing. She appeals to him for tenderness. He responds by telling her, "I would not use an animal or a machine as we have used each other."

By today's standards, there is nothing obscene in "Anniversary." In fact, Krause's description of sex is bleak. McDonald is a cynical, bitter man and the prevailing tone of the story is that of emptiness. But Krause's depiction of Lincoln and its major university is not something any city father would be proud of. While Wanda was sleeping with McDonald, she was also sleeping with other men, including a wealthy businessman. Krause writes that the married members of the English faculty affect "crewcuts and virility," snigger with "admiration at the dynamic sex allusions of the visiting literati." The "fairies" in the department approach McDonald "in sly, nuzzling, knee-touching familiarity."

Lincoln was too small a town for such references not to launch speculations. Whether Krause was referring to specific individuals or not, there were gays in the faculty and university administration and just being identified publicly as such was a firing offense. Whether he had a specific wealthy businessman in mind or not, there were powerful men in Lincoln who had mistresses. And whether there was a real-life counterpart to Wanda or not, there certainly were women who slept with more than one man.

What happened next remains unclear, in part because Shapiro's own account changed every time he recounted it. "Anniversary" was set up in galley proof—which at the time was done on campus by the printing shop that was under Bruce Nicoll's management as director of the press. This was just a service to *Prairie Schooner*: Officially, neither the press nor the university had formal editorial authority over the magazine. Then Shapiro received a note from Dean Militzer saying that the story was being removed as "obscene and in poor taste."

When he protested the decision, Shapiro was told the specific problem was "the homosexual business"—the suggestion that there were gays in the English department—and concern that this would lead to an investigation and the firing of some faculty members. Shapiro then informed Militzer that he was moving up his resignation from *Prairie Schooner* to take effect immediately, in protest. He vented his anger in a letter to James Miller at the University of Chicago, for Miller wrote Bernice in late February, asking,

"What's with Karl and the *Schooner*?" Miller agreed with Shapiro's objection to institutional censorship but asked, "Is the Krause really that much dynamite?" After Bernice replied, Miller expressed relief that the matter hadn't "become a political football for the newspapers." It hadn't—yet.

In the meantime, Militzer put editorial responsibility for *Schooner* under a board comprising Bernice, Virginia, Lee Lemon, and Fred Christensen, the other associate editors. Bernice returned "Anniversary" to Krause's agent, citing "editorial changes" due to Shapiro's departure and inviting her to submit another story. She also wrote Krause the same day, with the same explanation. She asked for other stories and offered her best wishes. "The coffee still brews strong in 225 Andrews [the English department coffee room]," she wrote.

Krause would have none of her Midwest courtesy. He fired back, "Regarding your note of March 2, wherein you say you want to use one of my stories, but something other than 'Anniversary'—this mulched in with some other phrases of extraordinary mealy-mouthedness, let me say that you've got a lot of guts." He swore that "you will never get another story from me at any time, under any conditions, until the true situation regarding the *Schooner* is clarified and exposed," and he forbade her to publish anything about him or his stories. "I refuse to provide advertising copy for your rotten comfort."

There was nothing in the spring 1963 issue, the first of *Prairie Schooner*'s thirty-seventh year, that would have struck any of its nine-hundred-some subscribers as controversial: several critical essays and the usual assortment of poems and reviews. There were no short stories, but this wasn't exceptional. Poetry had usually taken precedence in the magazine. In late April, Militzer sent Nicoll a letter laying out the interim arrangements for the *Schooner*. He drew a fine line regarding his responsibility regarding editorial decisions. "These duties are not meant to be duties of censorship nor of supervision but are meant to lie within the realm of establishing bounds rather than of prescripts." He also offered to allocate funding to increase circulation.

Militzer thought he'd put the whole affair behind him when he received his evening edition of the *Journal Star* on Thursday, May 23. The front page reported on budget debates in the state legislature and Willa Cather's induction into the Nebraska Hall of Fame. Eight pages in, however, he was greeted by the headline "Shapiro Says Decision Influenced by Incident."

The lede placed the decision to remove an unnamed story from *Prairie Schooner* squarely on Militzer's shoulders.

What triggered the article was a letter to the *Journal Star* by Bruce Brugman, a former editor of the *Daily Nebraskan*, the campus newspaper, now working as a reporter in Milwaukee. "Even a Pulitzer prize-winning poet, widely acclaimed on arrival, is not safe at Nebraska," Brugman argued. The pressure from the Lincoln establishment, he wrote, was strong and unrelenting. "The moment an unorthodox thought emerges, the vigilantes are out of the chutes like broncos."

Militzer responded with a statement that reiterated the facts as he'd seen them. Shapiro had decided to resign before the decision to cut the story. Militzer had found it obscene and acted out of concern for legal liability—still valid, given the Supreme Court's 1957 ruling that obscenity was determined by "applying contemporary community standards." The *Journal Star* straddled the fence in its editorial on the controversy. No, the magazine shouldn't publish obscene material. "But to have an administrator making the judgment . . . isn't the right tactic, either." The United Press picked up the story, which ran in papers around the country.

Seeing the matter heating up in the press, Shapiro decided to fan the flames. He read the story on KFMQ, a local radio station whose signal barely made it to the Lincoln city limits. "My concern is for the survival of *Prairie Schooner*," he declared. "I hope by some miracle that the guardians of good taste, as they call themselves, will restore the editorial prerogative given me," he added.

They did—but not to him. A week later, Bernice was announced as *Prairie Schooner*'s new editor. And as Shapiro later admitted, after the reading on KFMQ and the various news articles, that "nothing happened." He remained at UNL for another three years. A year after the incident, he signed copies of his latest collection, *The Bourgeois Poet*, at Miller and Paine, Lincoln's biggest department store, where Bruce Nicoll's wife Pat managed the book department. The spring after that, he and Bernice represented the university at a symposium at the Library of Congress. In the summer of 1966, he took another job at the University of Illinois-Chicago. A few years later, he published his only novel, *Edsel*, which combined elements of "Anniversary" and his own experiences in Lincoln and readers were finally given a chance to speculate about fictional characters and their real-life counterparts.

Krause, however, was consumed by the injustice of the incident. He wrote an angry letter to Chancellor Hardin and drafted an angrier one to Walter Wright, the assistant dean of arts and sciences and his PhD supervisor. He even drafted a polemic addressed to the English department. "As for my story, it speaks for itself. I think that none of you has evinced a desire to examine it for yourself."

Krause's resentment continued to burn. He began writing a novel about the incident. *The Censoring* is a bitter book, the work of a man deeply wounded, and vicious in its treatment of almost everyone he knew in Lincoln. Set at "Platte State University," its cast is large and encompasses everyone from lowly graduate students to the chancellor and members of the board of regents. Whether for himself or posterity, he provided a key to the novel's characters.

Bernice is Agnes Grubb. She first appears as she "waddled with heavy dignity across to the English department coffee room." She is fifty-four, "heavy and gray." Although she reminds herself that "her true favorite, Willa Cather, had been both," she tries to cover it up with a girdle and hair dye "so black . . . that midnight or a crow's feather would have been light by comparison." Krause dug into a bag filled with all the rumors he'd heard in Lincoln. Agnes "had never had a lover from what anyone knew," but legend had it that she still carried a torch for professor Tony Hill (Robert Knoll).

In Krause's retelling, Agnes Grubb resents that she has toiled for years on *The Plainsman* (*Prairie Schooner*) and is still just an associate editor, despite her book on Shelley's prose, her many poems, and her book with Frank Reeves (James Miller), *End with the Prairie*. And she resents having to answer to Shafter Charles (Karl Shapiro), the Pulitzer Prize–winning novelist and the magazine's editor. When Charles decides to run a story by Henry Curley (Krause) that she considers "a little physical," she alerts Tony Hill, who shares her concern and elevates the matter to the university administration. Like Shapiro, Charles resigns and like Bernice, Agnes is tapped to replace him.

At a party in the coffee room after the appointment is announced, Charlotte Marks (Virginia) jokingly refers to the fact that Agnes is getting what she always wanted. Agnes, who feels she is above such political acts, gets upset and leaves. Charlotte pursues. Charlotte, Krause tells us, had to return home broke after she ghostwrote a book called *Memoirs of a Call-House*

Cookie. She drives Agnes home. After Charlotte apologizes for her remark, the two women go to bed together and Charlotte puts her arm around Agnes, saying gently, "There, there, Aggie, I loves you."

The Censorship may not reflect the factual truth, but it's an eerily accurate account of the perceptions that Krause was not alone in collecting during his time in Lincoln. As with most conspiracy stories, its conspiracy is too perfectly executed to be plausible, but the interplay of political forces he depicts does correspond to the dynamics of Lincoln, with its state capitol, leading state university, and business community. As a novel it's stilted; as a snapshot of Lincoln in the early 1960s, however, it's a uniquely telling artifact.

The Censorship also reflects the prevailing view of who was responsible bringing "Anniversary" to the attention of the administration: Bernice. In Krause's version, her motivation is prudery, not self-protection. When she receives Curley/Krause's "You've got a lot of guts letter," she is so distressed that she returns to her office and comforts herself by writing a poem, "the poem she had been writing for 37 years, the poem with its 200 small variations . . . the poem of the flesh versus the spirit."

The remaining records in the UNL archives do not reveal who reported the story to Dean Militzer. It could have been Bernice. It could have been Virginia: There was a direct line from her through Bruce Nicoll to Militzer, who, as chair of the board of publications, oversaw the press's operations and approved its budget. Given Nicoll's time working as the chancellor's firefighter, this is a plausible explanation, particularly considering Virginia's opinion of Karl Shapiro's editorial preferences. And Virginia, more than anyone on campus outside the chancellor's office, understood the sensibilities and sensitivities of the Lincoln political and business leaders.

Another way to look at the episode is to ask, who benefited? Not Shapiro: Not only did nothing happen after he read the story on the radio, but he cemented his reputation with the UNL administration as a loose cannon. As Joseph Epstein later wrote, Shapiro "took a number of significant positions that went a long way toward scuppering his career." Not Krause: He published almost nothing after "Anniversary," though he continued to write, even through years of increasing debility from Hodgkin's disease, which took his life in 1970. No, it was clearly Bernice who benefited, attaining the editorship of *Prairie Schooner*, a post she held for the next seventeen years.

She took no pleasure in her reward. She certainly knew that people thought she had orchestrated the whole thing. But she hadn't expected it. In fact, within two weeks of her appointment being announced, she was on her way to England for another summer of research. She wrote her colleague Paul Olson, who was already in London on a fellowship, "I am desperate. I hope I get off so I can tell you all the details of my desperation." By Olson's account, when they met in London, Bernice shared her fears that the rumors about her role in the "Anniversary" episode would scuttle both the *Schooner* and her professional career.

The summer of 1963 also held few pleasures for Virginia. She was hospitalized for extreme hypertension, a reaction to personnel problems at the press: problems she was partly responsible for creating. With the press slated to publish over fifty titles in 1964, the editorial workload was beginning to overwhelm her. Though Nicoll had hired Harry Kaste from the University of Iowa Press in 1961 to work as associate editor and Claire Spatz as assistant editor in early 1963, neither came up to Virginia's standards. Kaste left after too many tongue-lashings from Virginia, moving across town to Centennial Publications, the publisher of Cliff's Notes. Spatz lasted just three months, managing in that time to disappoint Virginia so completely that she sent Nicoll a thirteen-page report that detailed Spatz's failings in even the most basic editorial tasks and questioned her sanity. Over the coming years, the personnel files of the press would be filled with similarly lengthy and critical assessments by Virginia of other assistant editors and copy editors.

Without Bernice to share her evenings with, without Bernice to vent her frustrations to, Virginia was heading for another crisis. But there was one other person Virginia could write to without the pretense of sprezzatura: Hazel Barnes. Hazel and Doris stopped in Lincoln that August and Hazel later wrote that their visit "somehow unified for me all the Virginias I had seen and heard and read in letters." She referred to Virginia as "the many-faceted you" and thanked her for taking them to the University Club: "It was all in a very high key, lifting the evening high up above all its surroundings." But she may also have seen Virginia drinking too much, as she often did there, for she closed with a cautionary, "Do, please, be very careful of yourself."

She must have sensed where Virginia was heading. Among Barnes's papers there is a postscript to an otherwise unexceptional letter from Virginia about press matters dated a month later. Typed, it's full of cross-outs and other errors and raw in its honesty. "It's half-past three" on a Friday afternoon, Virginia writes. It's been a rough week at the press and she's worried about her friends Giovanna and Bill Bowsky. Virginia and Bernice had grown close to the Bowskys since their arrival in Lincoln in 1958. Rumored to come from Italian nobility, Giovanna Bowsky was beautiful, sophisticated, and an expert in contemporary Italian literature. Earlier that summer, the Bowskys' infant daughter had choked on a pill and was left with permanent brain damage due to the extended loss of oxygen. The Bowskys were hammered by the emotional toll, hospital bills, and the difficulties of arranging long-term care for their daughter.

Writing from her apartment on a Friday afternoon, Virginia has opened a bottle of champagne. "This," she tells Hazel, "elevates the anesthetizing process from the sordid. Use the crystal goblets; everything chilled. None of this drinking gin in a dirty kimono." Then she confides that she thinks Giovanna Bowsky is attracted to her, that the "hugs and caresses have, on her part, been getting very business-like." Virginia finds her "a terribly attractive young woman," but—"I'm afraid *young* is the operative word." Though she had just turned fifty, Virginia was still open to the idea of a sexual dalliance, in theory, at least. "Although, as a rule, I think going to bed with somebody—well, in Gertrude Lawrence's words: if you are weak-minded it makes yer 'appy, and if you are strong-minded it don't 'urt yer none—is perfectly okay, I don't think it would be in this one." She trusts that Hazel will understand "that I am talking to you, with inflections, and mostly ironyironyironyironyballs."

Then she goes on to question her big decision, the choice she had taken years before: to return to Lincoln and shut the door on her creative work. "I see now that it was a major mistake for me to stop being a writer and try to be a people. I can't think why I would have anyway, except from despair. So now since 1956 I have tried to be a people and screw that. It is a waste of energy. People are slobs, and they don't care, they never make anything, they are dandruff and snot." Expecting someone to show up on her doorstep within minutes, she closes the letter. "Now I have to be fast, I want to put this in an envelope and mail it." She reflects on the confidence she is sharing with Hazel. "I am responsible for myself; telling you what I feel is a prized luxury. Let me have it. That is all."

Did Virginia ever share these regrets with Bernice? Or did she shield the person most essential if she was to stay in Lincoln and continue with her Cather projects? Ironically, in her own inimitable style, she was echoing to Hazel something Willa Cather had written herself, in an essay on Katherine Mansfield: "One realizes that human relationships are the tragic necessity of human life; that they can never be wholly satisfactory, that every ego is half the time greedily seeking them, and half the time pulling away from them." When Bernice returned from Rome, Virginia put away her misgivings and committed herself to carry on as they had, emotional and intellectual partners. The "Anniversary" episode behind them, they set out on their most ambitious collaboration to date.

21

The Kingdom of Art

Edith Lewis thought little of the press's decision to publish an authoritative version of the 1903 edition of Cather's poems, *April Twilights*, but it bore out Virginia's belief in the importance of getting started on a catalog of Catheriana. After she sent a copy of the book to Elizabeth Shepley Sergeant, Sergeant wrote back asking if the press would be interested in reissuing her own Cather memoir as a Bison Book. Virginia confirmed that Sergeant's publisher, J. B. Lippincott, would agree to release the paperback rights and wrote Sergeant an enthusiastic letter of acceptance. She seized on a comment Sergeant had made about Cather's early work to put forward her own thesis in more moderate language than in her manic letter from Pacific Grove years before. Cather's poetry and early stories, Virginia proposed, "are more revealing than any of Miss Cather's other writings and throw more light than perhaps she would have wished on her other work."

Writing from the MacDowell Colony, Sergeant backed away from endorsing Virginia's plans unconditionally. Cather's college work did not merit reprinting, she thought, and Cather herself would certainly have resented seeing her early poems, essays, and reviews published again. "Miss Cather, as you know, was fiercely determined on the point of being judged by posterity on what she herself chose. She would not even talk of her early work when I knew her."

Sergeant's remarks were not as absolute as those Alfred Knopf passed on from Edith Lewis, and Virginia saw an opportunity to win a key ally in what remained of Cather's circle. "One can sympathize with Miss Cather's wish to be judged only by what she considered her best; one can sympathize with her craving for privacy." But in publishing his writing, "an author forfeits his privacy," and no artist "who leaves a body of vital work can exclude posterity."

It took Virginia months to reach an understanding with Sergeant about how *Willa Cather: A Memoir* was to be reissued. As with other Bison Books, the press avoided new typesetting by using photo offsets from the original hardback edition, which limited how much annotation and correction could be done. Sergeant wanted to revise dozens of pages, adding "patches" of new text; Virginia offered to address the most critical items in a Notes section at the back of the book. Virginia wanted an index, missing from the Lippincott edition, and hired John March to provide one; Sergeant thought this pointless. March visited Sergeant at her home in Manhattan and persuaded her of its value. Sergeant wanted to add a new foreword, then procrastinated about providing it.

In the end, however, the new edition did all involved proud. Sergeant saluted the press and Bernice in her foreword and acknowledged the need to look beyond the bounds that Cather tried to draw around her life as she wanted posterity to see it: "If I were writing a new book I should want to study the mysterious process by which Cather, more than most novelists, used and transformed her own personal experience into the stuff of those great books that are taking their permanent place in American history and literature." She was, in effect, accepting Virginia's argument: If Cather was, indeed, a great writer, then all her work and all her life were legitimate subjects for study. In the world of the early 1960s, it was taken for granted by both women that "all her life" excluded Cather's sexuality, but a younger generation would soon question that exception.

Virginia's Cather production line began to speed up, but there was still the question of the Cather estate's support. In June 1964, Mildred Bennett wrote to inform Knopf and Lewis that the press would be publishing an updated edition of *Early Stories by Willa Cather*, the collection published by Dodd, Mead in 1957 she'd edited, and asked their permission to include nine stories still under copyright. The response was as adamant as the one against *April Twilights*. They hoped "very much indeed that you will not proceed with this volume" and refused to give "even our implied approval."

Virginia's hunch that Alfred Knopf did not fully share Edith Lewis's attitude toward the press's plans to reissue of Cather's early work proved correct, though. Nicoll replied with a letter Virginia drafted. The press had no intention of disregarding Cather's judgment of her own work, he assured Knopf. "But an examination of the entire body of her work is essential if the scholar is to arrive at a just estimate of her achievement and a thorough understanding of the artistic means she used to attain it."

Then he offered an example that put Knopf on the spot: "Surely when you published *The Esdaile Notebook*—to cite a parallel undertaking—it was . . . as a scholarly service and because you share our conviction that nothing should be withheld which contributes to the knowledge of the body of literature and the creative mind of a great artist." *The Esdaile Notebook* was a scholarly edition of the contents of a handwritten notebook of Shelley's early poems published by Knopf in April 1964. *The Esdaile Notebook* was arguably a more minor work than anything by Cather the press was considering: Surely what was acceptable for Shelley was also acceptable for Cather.

Knopf replied that the arguments were sound. He had to: To suggest otherwise would have been hypocritical. He had recommended "that we should stand aside and give your project our blessing"—and Lewis agreed. Lewis later allowed the press to include seven stories still under copyright. The two of them remained suspicious of Mildred Bennett and her involvement, however. Knopf later wrote Virginia that he considered Mildred an example of "what happens so often after a truly distinguished author's death: a second- or third-rate person latches on to his or her memory with great energy and industry."

Although she respected what Mildred had accomplished with the Cather Memorial, Virginia continued to have doubts about her abilities as a writer and editor. The story collection went into the press's plans as *On the Divide*, taken from the title of a story Cather first published in *Overland Monthly* in January 1896. The change of title was meant, in part, to signal a change in direction. This edition would be aimed at both the reading public and academics, so the arrangement would be different—the weaker, less important stories in the back, critical commentary incorporating a broader range of Cather's own work as well as the increasing number of Cather studies, a bibliography, and a chronology of Cather's life, something Virginia had been steadily working on for years.

Virginia approached this project at full speed. Four days after writing Mildred to inform her of the press's decision to do the book, she followed up with a table of contents and more notes about the book's layout. It would follow the model of the *April Twilights* book in every way, down to using the same two-tone style of cloth binding with an imprint of Cather's signature on the front. Virginia intended her Cather books to announce their seriousness and consistency of purpose from the shelf. "But there's no point in yammering on in a letter," she added. "Much more satisfactory to talk things out at the University Club." She needed a drink or two to salve the scars Mildred bore from the failure of *The Road Is All.*

Virginia had two peace offerings for Mildred: First, the press would time the book's publication to coincide with the tenth anniversary of the Memorial; and second, Mildred would be credited as editor. The former was appreciated: The Memorial still relied heavily on sales at the museum's shop. The latter was unworkable from the start. Virginia and Mildred had completely different editorial approaches. Virginia now had years of editing experience behind her and this book was just part of her Cather vision. Editing had become the central purpose of her life, filling her days, evenings, and weekends. Mildred had only two books under her belt, was being pulled by a dozen other commitments, and was frequently debilitated by migraines and manic-depressive episodes. But she set aside her reservations and gamely agreed.

Progress reports from Lincoln began to pour into Red Cloud. Simply collecting reliable reproductions of the stories, which had appeared in magazines and newspapers from Nebraska, Chicago, Pittsburgh, and New York was a challenge. Texts had to be compared, particularly those that had appeared in Cather's collection *The Troll Garden* in 1905, to determine the definitive version. Biographical tidbits kept filtering in. Mildred could not keep up—at least, not to Virginia's satisfaction. And Virginia was adamant that the stories needed to be arranged in *reverse* chronological order to put the best up front for the general reader, a decision that made no sense to Mildred. After several months of frustration, Virginia suggested that Bernice join the effort as coeditor.

This was too much. Mildred refused the offer, which she knew would effectively take the project out of her hands entirely. She would only continue if she continued alone. Virginia tried to placate things but warned that Mildred's decision put the book's schedule at risk. A truce agreed, the work moved on. But it was a temporary ceasefire. As Mildred began to share drafts of her introduction, which Virginia intended to be as comprehensive and detailed as Bernice's for *April Twilights*—a forty-six-page introduction to a seventy-four-page collection of poems—the barrage resumed. Mildred's "excellent point" about the types of women in *The Troll Garden* stories: "Could you develop this a bit more?" She needed to highlight the use of motifs, for example, the turquoise in "Gull's Road." Precursors of heroines who appear in later Cather novels must be identified. Also, she needed to correlate the material with that in *April Twilights*. Also, had she looked at the notes on the Cather letters in the Huntington Library yet? Also, don't forget about manuscript preparation details ("the back of the book notes will not carry a superior number"). Also, "Don't worry about headnotes or introductory matter; one thing at a time and first things first." It poured in at Virginia's usual speed and volume.

By the time the proofs came back from the printer in May 1965, several things were clear. The book wouldn't be ready by the Memorial's anniversary. Virginia was moving forward with her own version of the introduction. And Mildred was heading for a breakdown. Wilbur brought her to Lincoln and she was admitted to the psychiatric ward of Lincoln General for treatment. By 1965, psychiatry had begun to add pharmacological treatment to the electroconvulsive therapy Virginia had received. Mildred's stay was far shorter, but the drugs and their dosages were still blunt instruments and could have severe effects on complex mental processes of the sort required to write a coherent piece of critical commentary. It would be almost two decades before Mildred was able to write at length again. Virginia showed no empathy whatsoever, joking at one point that Mildred had been attending "the University of Paper Hats."

Collected Short Fiction, 1893–1912 came out in September 1965 with no one listed as editor and Mildred credited with just the introduction. Mildred's 1957 collection, just under three hundred pages, had ballooned to almost six hundred with all the appendixes. Mildred would long resent what she saw as Virginia's hijacking of a project she had initiated and brought to print years before Virginia began asserting herself in the world of Cather studies. It was yet more evidence that she was seen as a lowly country mouse by the city mice like Virginia, Knopf, and Lewis, and its memory would hang like a cloud over her dealings with Virginia and Bernice.

One reason Virginia wanted to push *Collected Short Fictions* out was to make way for the book she was sure would revolutionize Cather studies. It began serendipitously in mid-1964, when Bernice decided to link her previous research for *Start with the Sun* with her current work on Cather by writing "Willa Cather and Walt Whitman" for the *Walt Whitman Review*. Working at the Nebraska State Historical Society, she started going through the articles and reviews Cather had written for the *Nebraska State Journal* and the *Courier* while still a student at the University of Nebraska. She found nothing useful in Cather's contributions up to June 1895, when Cather had graduated and, so everyone thought, returned to Red Cloud. The accepted story, as Mildred had written in *The World of Willa Cather*, was that "the worst period of depression for Willa came after her graduation from college, a period of enforced vegetation at home." This period was assumed to have lasted until she was offered a job to write for *Home Monthly* magazine in Pittsburgh in June 1896.

Idly continuing to leaf through old copies of the *Journal* past mid-June 1895, Bernice was startled to find that Cather's column, "As You Like It," continued to appear on a weekly basis into July, when it changed name to "The Passing Show." Then, in its August 3 issue, the *Courier* announced that "Miss Willa Cather, who for the past two years has been the dramatic critic and theatrical writer for the *Journal*" would be joining the staff of the *Courier*. Reading on, Bernice found "The Passing Show" continued as a weekly feature, first in the *Courier*, then again in the *Journal*, until June 14, 1896, about the time when Cather left for Pittsburgh. What's more, she found dozens of reviews under Cather's name as well as others she suspected Cather had written. Bernice, Virginia, John March, and other researchers had already uncovered instances of Cather writing under a pseudonym or anonymously. Bearing this in mind, Bernice began going back through the papers during Cather's student years and identified yet more articles. Over time, Bernice came to feel she had a sixth sense for telling if a piece of writing was by Cather.

As she shared her discoveries with Virginia, the two women agreed that these pieces needed to be collected and given the same careful, even reverential, treatment as the early poems and stories. This collection would reinforce their argument that Cather's early writings were as worthy of study as her mature work—but just as important, it would firmly establish Cather the writer *in* Nebraska and not just Cather the writer *from* Nebraska. It would also have the benefit of being a project they could work on without seeking the approval of Knopf or Edith Lewis (whose names would be noticeably absent from the book's acknowledgments).

These were not typical newspaper reviews, knocked out in haste by an overworked critic. These were considered, reflective essays, and more than just glimpses of the writer Cather would become. Bernice became convinced that in her critical pieces for the two newspapers, Cather had laid out the fundamental principles that guided her throughout her career. Virginia agreed, and they laid out a plan for the book that organized the various articles into thematic groups, as a set of what they called "Critical Statements," culminating in four excerpts they offered as Cather's "Improvisations Towards a Credo."

To put the collection, titled *The Kingdom of Art*, into critical as well as biographical context, Bernice would write what became two extended essays, "Writer in Nebraska" and "The Kingdom of Art." Together, at over a hundred pages, they would be the longest assessment of Cather by a single critic published to date—and the longest work Bernice had produced since her Keats book. But the essays were really a collaborative creation. Among Bernice's papers is a folder of working notes and drafts from *The Kingdom of Art*. Bernice wrote with pen, in the neat, slightly slanted cursive of the high school English teacher of Ord, Nebraska. Virginia preferred pencil and wrote in a hurried, vertical scrawl. From this, it's clear that Virginia drafted passages in the essays as well as in the commentary accompanying Cather's articles.

One of the latter was the introduction to a series of pieces in which Cather attacked the narrow attitudes of Lincoln's philistines. It reveals how Virginia's view of her hometown had changed over the years: "Philistia is usually The Place Where You Live—Eleventh Street in Lincoln, or this side of the footlights. Bohemia is somewhere else—that desert kingdom by the sea, of the Paris of Henri Murger's *Scènes de la vie de Bohème*." But then she writes, "Philistia is primarily a state of mind, a human failure to choose the real thing." In leaving Lincoln for Washington, New York, and Hollywood, Virginia had thought she was leaving Philistia for Bohemia, for a world of culture and sophistication. But once she was immersed in the smart sets of each place, she found that they could be as superficial and narrow-minded as any of Lincoln's churchgoers and club ladies. Her mistake had been "a human failure to choose the real thing."

Unlike Cather, Virginia never had the benefit of an older and wiser writer like Sarah Orne Jewett to advise her. *The Kingdom of Art* reprinted a 1913 interview in which Cather recalled meeting Jewett, "who had read all of my early stories and had very clear and definite opinions about them and about where my work fell short." Jewett was emphatic about one thing: "Don't try to write the kind of short story that this or that magazine wants—write the truth and let them take it or leave it."

Virginia had spent years writing the kind of short stories that magazines wanted and had been well-paid and applauded for it. But few if any of them could be considered memorable, let alone "the truth." Nor would anyone find in Virginia's early work—her stories for the *Awgwan* or her reviews for the Junior League's magazine—any statement of principles or "improvisations towards a credo." Despite her contributions to *The Kingdom of Art* and her occasional attempts to take over the pen of one of her authors, despite the misgivings about "trying to be a people" she had shared with Hazel Barnes, Virginia now closed the door for good on her life as a writer.

The Kingdom of Art garnered uniformly positive reviews when it came out in the spring of 1967. In a sympathetic review in the *New York Times*, John J. Murphy of Merrimack College, who would come to have a warm relationship with the two women, wrote that Bernice "succeeds in demolishing the picture of the young Willa Cather as an untutored Western girl running wild on her pony and talking to old Bohemian women on the Nebraska Divide." Bernice scored an even bigger coup when *Horizon*, the most high-brow national magazine at the time, with its hardback covers and slick full-color illustrations, published an excerpt with an introductory note saying the book "reads as well as many a novel and a good deal better than most criticism."

Virginia's aspiration was for Bernice to follow *The Kingdom of Art* by resurrecting *The Road Is All* and producing the definitive critical study of Cather. As far as she was concerned, no one was better qualified for the job. But it was an unrealistic expectation. Even with all the Cather archaeology of recent years, there was still the prohibition against quoting from Cather's letters, many of which were still unavailable to researchers. And there was the fact that Bernice was weighed down by other duties. She and James Miller had followed up their undergraduate textbook *The Dimensions of Poetry* with another titled *The Dimensions of the Short Story* and then a third, *The Dimensions of Literature*, and Dodd, Mead was pressing for them to provide updates to all three. Having finally been advanced to the status of full professor, Bernice now supervised graduate students and advised their theses and dissertations. Already considered a reliable and uncomplaining worker, she was regularly enlisted to serve on committees for such tasks as reviewing curriculum and textbooks for Nebraska schools. And she was continuing to edit *Prairie Schooner*.

Although Bernice did not care for the satiric and experimental style of much of the fiction and poetry of the 1960s, she saw the opportunity for the *Schooner* to strengthen its reputation as a national literary journal, to address not just current literature but current events as well. In its fall 1965 issue, for example, *Prairie Schooner* included two "Letters from Selma," firsthand accounts of the historic civil rights march in March. One, by a Roman Catholic nun, Sister Mary Paul, had been addressed to her order in Detroit and only came to the attention of the *Schooner* via a student who'd obtained a copy second or thirdhand. The other was by Rowland Sylvester, an Indiana businessman who, outraged by the television footage of Alabama policemen beating the Black protesters, had traveled to Selma on an impulse to offer support and afterward written to a friend just to make sense of what he'd seen. Neither letter had been intended for publication, but their appearance in the magazine attracted so much interest that the feature was reprinted and sold as a broadsheet for several years afterward.

Prairie Schooner achieved another milestone that year, with three of its stories selected for inclusion in the that year's *Best American Short Stories* anthology. Martha Foley, the perennial editor of the collection, singled out the *Schooner* for the quality and quantity of its fiction. In terms of pages alone, Bernice was more receptive to fiction than Shapiro had been. And, as Foley noted, with the decline of the mainstream magazine market—only a few of the magazines Virginia had written for were still in business, let alone featuring short stories—its support for fiction was further solidifying its national reputation. Bernice gave credit to her assistant editors: Virginia, Lee Lemon, and Fred Christensen. She had, in fact, ceded all but the final approval of the content of the fiction section to them, with Christensen continuing to do the lion's share of the initial screening. When he retired in 1972, Christensen estimated that in his thirty-three years with the magazine, he'd read over ten thousand short story submissions.

Bernice and Virginia were now in their midfifties. The pace and volume of their work was taking its toll. After Harry Kaste left, Herbert Hyde was hired as associate editor, but he, too, found meeting Virginia's standards an impossible task. Reporting on his first year's performance, Virginia gave a nod to Midwestern courtesy—"Personally, Mr. Hyde is amiable, literate, well-mannered, and I am sure his private life would be a lesson to us all"—before detailing what she considered his shortcomings (including insufficient "eager beaverism"). Not only did she want Nicoll to find a replacement, but she levied an ultimatum: "I am physically incapable of going on much longer without an associate editor who can carry his share of the load." Two years later, the situation had not improved. In February 1967, she wrote Donald Sutherland, declining his invitation to attend the first performance of his translation of Euripides's *The Bacchae*, saying, "I leave my desk only to take care of the basest physical needs." The reason? "Although the press has grown, the editorial staff has not." Given Virginia's prickly perfectionism, there was little chance it could.

Even when they took time off, it usually involved research (another trip to Europe, a trip to see Cather's beloved Mesa Verde in New Mexico). Bernice received a Woods Foundation grant to return to the British Library and she and Virginia splurged on the trip, taking a cabin on the last voyage of the *Queen Mary*. Prior to Bernice's settling down in London for the fall of 1967, they went to France, Belgium, and the Netherlands, where they visited Harenkarspel, the town where Bernice's father had been born. The trip marked Lincoln's recognition of their relationship, at least in such terms as were allowed in the society pages. When Virginia returned in mid-November, the *Journal Star* reported that she "and her companion, Miss Bernice Slote," had been traveling in Europe.

Aside from these rare breaks, Virginia and Bernice worked. They tended to stick to regular office hours, but inevitably carried folders full of manuscripts to edit and papers to grade. In the summer, Virginia would cool off with a swim and a drink at Ed and Jean's house from time to time. When school was out, there were conferences—the Western Literature Association, the Modern Language Association—where Virginia had to represent the press or Bernice had to serve on a panel, or both. And there were trips out to Red Cloud, for both were now on the Willa Cather Foundation's board of governors. Like the singer Thea Kronborg in Cather's *The Song of the Lark*,

Fig. 17. Virginia, on Bernice's and her first trip to Mesa Verde, New Mexico, 1966. Courtesy of Susan Perry.

they were happy to be consumed by work they considered vital. Anything less would be a failure of dedication. They agreed with Kronborg: "Your work becomes your personal life. You are not much good until it does."

In Lincoln, they rarely spent time socializing. After the roof in Bernice's apartment developed a leak in 1965, she moved into the downstairs unit of a newly remodeled duplex on Fourteenth Street, kitty-corner from the Capitol building; Virginia took the upstairs unit when it became available in 1967, and the two began to host Christmas teas for friends in the English department and their children—the Knolls at first and later John and Ann Robinson. Virginia also began traveling with Bernice on visits to her sister. Belva's daughters remember Virginia as "just another aunt," although one recalls Belva once asking, "Do you think there's something going on between the two of them?"

Though Virginia joked that "I prefer children over the age of forty," she had an easy rapport with them. Robert Knoll's daughter Elizabeth remembers being struck by the fact that Virginia looked her in the eye and listened to what she said seriously, a rare experience for a child of the 1960s. Although she seldom talked about her life in New York or Hollywood, Virginia had a confidence and worldliness unlike that of other women the faculty children were exposed to. And she didn't look like their mothers. She used no makeup, rarely wore jewelry, and kept her hair short, though her clothes were always well-tailored and expensive looking. Bernice, though she stuck faithfully to the unpretentious wear of the schoolmarm, had a warm, welcoming manner and put kids at ease with her gentle voice.

The children also noticed Virginia's drinking. "Aunt Virginia sure likes her Salty Dogs," David Robinson remembers observing to his mother after one of their visits. Most nights, she would only allow herself a Scotch highball, but when entertaining at the University Club, she tended to outdrink everyone in the party. Mary Mignon, wife of Clark Mignon, who joined the English faculty in 1967, recalled Virginia berating a bartender at the club when he struggled to prepare a pousse-café, the dramatic layered cocktail. Bernice pulled her from the bar and steered her, staggering, to the elevator to go home.

But for the moment, in the battle of the flesh versus the spirit—the subject, Ervin Krause had sniped, of all Bernice's poems—the spirit was still winning. Virginia and Bernice had found happiness in the same thing Jim Burden had discovered in *My Ántonia*: "to be dissolved into something complete and great." *Kingdom* would serve as the cornerstone of what Joan Ross Acocella would later call Cather's "Rushmoresque period," when she was viewed as "a great white monument, looming in isolation." Most critics at the time, still treating modernism as the mainstream of English and American literature, considered Cather a marginal figure. Virginia and Bernice treated Cather as an artist outside her time, a writer who had more in common with Virgil and Keats than with contemporaries like Edith Wharton, Frank Norris, or Theodore Dreiser. The problem, as Acocella put it, was that neither side treated her as central to American literature. And neither side treated her as a creature of the flesh either.

22

The World and the Parish

Virginia's biggest, longest, and most infuriating Cather project of the 1960s came to the press through a side door. In late 1960, William Curtin, then professor of English at the University of Illinois, wrote James Miller about a book he wanted to assemble a collection of Cather's journalism from her years in Lincoln and Pittsburgh. "My purpose," he wrote, "is to set the apprenticeship of Miss Cather in a complex literary milieu" and to illuminate Cather's "classical" sensibility toward art. These words would have been music to Virginia's ears. This was precisely part of her plans to reissue authoritative editions of Cather's early work.

Yet even in this first letter from Bill Curtin, Virginia could have found clues to the frustrations to come. He misspelled *Pittsburgh*, *aesthetic*, and *sends*. He addressed Miller as editorial adviser for the press, unaware of who held the real responsibility. But his letter also brimmed with enthusiasm, and through the decade it would take to bring Curtin's project to print, his resilient optimism would prove the one force capable—*usually*—of withstanding Virginia's editorial fury.

After Curtin addressed a new request to Virginia on Miller's recommendation, her response was favorable but cautious. There were already other Cather projects involving UNL faculty, she informed him, and if two books appeared to overlap, the press would always pick the one from "the local boy." Still, she promised his manuscript would get a fair shake. It took Curtin a year to reply. The reason, he explained, was that he had decided it was essential to transcribe the hundred-plus pieces he had located and now had over eight hundred pages of material. After looking over the articles and Curtin's introduction, Virginia gave a tentative yes: "This is a book we will want to do, but it is apparent that it needs a lot of work, both as regards selection and editorial contribution." But one thing she was certain of: "This will be a BIG book." It would turn out to be two big books.

Curtin did not expect so equivocal a response to his submission. Although relieved to hear the press was interested, "I am," he wrote, "hurt and dejected by how very easily my limitations are observed and judged." It was early days, though, and he assured her that his disappointment would soon pass "in the whirl of work." Curtin made his first trip to Lincoln and Red Cloud in the summer of 1962 and wrote Mildred Bennett that he looked forward to "a lifetime of pleasure in our mutual Catherorgy."

Curtin's visit encouraged Virginia tremendously. He was young, enthusiastic, intelligent, and self-effacing, not the typical condescending academic she loathed. The collection, she felt, would not only be "indispensable to Willa Cather students, but a model of its kind in the treatment of primary material." More importantly, *she* was excited: "I am anticipating with relish every step of the road between now and pub. date—the headaches will be horrendous, but oh brother the satisfactions!" Considering the need to get advanced review copies out months before publication, she estimated the book could be out by spring 1964: "But nobody is holding a gun on you."

Little did Virginia realize that Curtin's next update would be only the first of many speed bumps on the road to publication. "It seems that each time I write to you I'm trying to throw off a depression," Curtin apologized. He had been down with mononucleosis and was still recovering slowly. He offered tidbits about the book, then shifted to chit-chat: had she read Walker Percy's *The Moviegoer*? "A most remarkable novel." And she responded with rare empathy. "Please, under no circumstances, let the book weigh on you."

A year later, after another Curtin visit, she was still his biggest supporter. As more Cather articles rolled in, her confidence grew. "The book is wonderful and you are a great man." A year later, in the spring of 1964, with the "Anniversary" episode behind her and *Collected Short Fiction* underway, she could exclaim, "Just think how glorious—we'll have all the early Willie—poetry, nonfiction, short stories." Not meaning to pressure Curtin, she suggested that it would be nice to bring out his book in the summer of 1965. Three months later, she wasn't suggesting anymore: "It is imperative—repeat: imperative—that it come out in 1965."

She tried to motivate Curtin by asking him to sense the hot breath of other scholars "working with the same materials" on his neck. As with Mildred, she offered to take on work herself: writing headnotes, providing a biographical chronology (Virginia did love adding chronologies to her Cather books). Then she made matters worse by comparing him to Bernice, saying she could have written ten times as much commentary on the poems as she did, "but she stuck to her knitting." She quoted from a particularly praiseworthy review of *April Twilight* to illustrate. Virginia didn't know, as any teacher would, that using a model student as an example usually stokes resentment, not aspiration.

Curtin and his family sailed to France at the end of September 1964 to spend a year in Aix-en-Provence, where he had a yearlong assignment at a French university. He sent Virginia a cheery note from New York acknowledging her offer of help and she replied with a letter full of more details to address. Publication in 1965 was still within reach. "Godspeed, take care, and have fun," she closed.

Three weeks later, everything changed. The good news, the big news, was Bernice's discovery of Cather's articles from 1895 and 1896. The bad news was that Curtin's book was going to have to be revised substantially—not the Cather pieces, but his commentary, because Cather had incorporated, directly or indirectly, chunks of her *Journal* and *Courier* work into her pieces for the Pittsburgh papers. He was going to have to read all the new material, which Virginia would try to ship to France, and then rewrite dozens of his headnotes as well as his introduction. "With luck we can still get her out in 1965," she wrote optimistically.

Virginia briefly thought the rediscovered articles could be added to *The World and the Parish*. That was certainly Curtin's impression when he replied that he was both excited and depressed by the news. The 1965 publication date was out of the question, he wrote. The whole book would have to be reorganized, something it would be almost impossible to do in France. And then, in blithe disregard to her concerns, he devoted another three single-spaced pages to a travelogue on Paris, Chartres, and Provence.

By mid-November 1964, Virginia and Bernice had worked out what needed to be done: "*The World and the Parish* is going to have a little brother, selected and edited with commentary by Bernice." This would be

The Kingdom of Art. She estimated it would be short—less than a quarter of the length of his book. The press was going to proceed with both books, Bernice's slated for 1965 and his "in the first half of 1966." Ultimately, *Kingdom* took over a year longer, but her estimate for Curtin's collection was even more optimistic.

Curtin and his family returned from France in the summer of 1965, but his situation in Illinois had become uncertain. He wrote Virginia that "I may be looking for job next year." Her reply was oblivious to his apprehensions. Instead, she devoted three pages to her new plan for the book, along with a complaint that she was still having to juggle too many other chores for the press and living "this gypsy life": "I just get the material laid out at home and then I have to scoop it up and bring it to the office."

With Bernice's discovery and Curtin's year abroad, the dynamic had shifted and Virginia, rather than Curtin, was now in the lead. "I have very little comment on your commentary," he wrote after receiving another update and a folder full of rewritten headnotes. Though he'd been assured of a promotion at Illinois, Curtin was finding, like Bernice, that increased faculty rank came with increased demands on his time. "I've just been appointed to my seventh committee!" he complained.

In her letters to Curtin over the next year, Virginia also made it clear that relations between Lincoln and Red Cloud had changed—irreversibly. "So much of the Gospel according to St. John [March] and St. Mildred has been shown to be partial, distorted, or wholly untrue," she wrote, and any of their work "should be used with the utmost circumspection." Then, after hinting that she'd gained access to a secret cache of Cather letters, she added without a trace of irony, "Cather seems to breed a cloak-and-dagger atmosphere."

By the summer of 1967, though assuring Curtin that she was not scolding him, Virginia observed icily that errors in the material he was sending her "do enormously increase the time that must be spent in editing." His copy was so rough that she was retyping (and rewriting, though she did not say that directly). Their collaboration was again complicated when Curtin returned to France in 1968 for another year, this time in Dijon. "It is too soon now to work out a schedule for handling the ms.," she wrote early that year. When he failed to reply, she followed up in April asking again for an update.

It would be over a year before he replied. In addition to the challenges of trying to work without the resources of his home campus, Curtin had had to deal with family crises that forced him to set aside his work on *The World and the Parish*. When he returned from Dijon, he would be moving from Illinois to take a new position at the University of Connecticut. But, he wrote Virginia, he was ready to pick up where he'd left off. She responded with an ultimatum: "Either the book goes into production this fall or we may as well forget it." She also bristled at his suggestion that she had taken unreasonable liberties with his text over the last few years. "I think I'll just let that one lie there," she huffed. In her mind, fault was all Curtin's, not hers. "The number and kind of new errors" she had found in his manuscripts "suggests that neither you nor your assistant reviewed the newly retyped material." And she had yet to receive a draft of the introductory essay. She expected a major piece, on the order of Bernice's two essays introducing *Kingdom*. Instead, Curtin delivered a piece of under fifteen hundred words. At this point, in Virginia's mind it was her book. Given his silence over the past year, she informed Curtin that she had consulted Bruce Nicoll and the two of them had decided that "if the book were to be published at all, we would have to get on with it."

Her response also demonstrated that Virginia's view of the collection's purpose had shifted since its inception. Now it wasn't meant for "the serious scholar specializing in Cather." They would have to go through the primary sources, the newspapers themselves. They were not providing authoritative texts, in other words, but "reading texts," works for college libraries, students, and the public. Thus, there was nothing to be gained by "perpetuating misspellings, erroneous names and titles, accidentals" and the vagaries of archaic newspaper house styles. In fact, she had prepared a memorandum on the editorial principles she had applied in editing Cather's work—something she was so proud of that she included it in the book's second volume.

Virginia's drive to finish the book took its toll on her as well as on Bill Curtin. Bernice had slipped on a stepstool in her kitchen and wrenched her back, leaving her prostrate in her apartment. Virginia took over the housekeeping and nursing duties, which quickly left her exhausted and in need of bedrest herself. James Woodress, who was working on a Cather biography, read the manuscript and returned it with a bushelful of pink correction slips.

She and Bernice then went through the complete proof—now nearly a thousand pages long—and came up with further changes and corrections. As a peace offering, she also sent a proof to Mildred. Even when Curtin sent her his acknowledgments text, she rewrote it ("You have to specify why you are thanking people"; "I have used conventional 'acknowledgese' wording").

The World and the Parish came out in two volumes in April 1971, the same time as Woodress's biography, *Willa Cather*, published by Pegasus. The two books were reviewed together in the *New York Times* and national magazines. The reception was not what either publisher had hoped. Robert Gorham Davis, the Columbia professor who wrote the *Times* review, felt that Woodress added little to the existing biographical works by Edel/Brown, Sergeant, and Lewis. And he dismissed the notion that Virginia and Bernice had been putting forward for years about Cather's early writing: "There is strangely little here to foretell the later artist of great achievement and suffering."

This was mild criticism, however, compared to Gerald Weales's eight-page review in *The Southern Review* the following summer. The "use of juvenilia is standard among literary scholars," he acknowledged, "but the Cather specialists have the disease at its worst." He took direct aim at just what Virginia was most proud of: "The thing that annoys me about *The World and the Parish* is that the editing gets in the way of our perception of Cather as a practicing journalist." The conceptual divisions were "pointless," the editorial approach "designed to obscure the material." Instead of presenting Cather's weekly columns as they were written, Curtin—working at Virginia's direction, of course—chose "to break them up and scatter them through the book or to drop sections entirely."

Weales's criticism is justified. Anyone trying to trace Cather's evolution over a sequence of articles would have to track them down at various places in the book, piece them together, and identify the missing parts (or worse, not know something was missing). Over the years since the book was published, some Cather scholars claim to have cut up and rearranged the texts back into their original order of appearance.

Weales was also unwilling to view Cather with Virginia's unwavering awe. Cather's proclamations about art at times veered into "the high flatulent" (e.g., "to feel greatly is genius and to make others feel is art") or "calculated gushiness." He was willing to call *The World and the Parish* an ornament to Cather's work as a journalist but pointed out that "she can be boringly repetitious and fakeily clever." Bernice could take solace in the fact that he had favorable things to say about her work in *The Kingdom of Art*, but Virginia had some choice words about Professor Weale and his review, aired over a few Salty Dogs.

Her dissatisfaction with the reception of *The World and the Parish* pales, however, in comparison to the impact of its preparation on Bill Curtin. In November 1970, as Virginia was doing the final checks on the two volumes, scheduled for publication the following spring, he wrote her a long, agonized, self-castigating letter. It was not a letter of author to editor. It was the crawl of an abject sinner toward the pulpit at a revival, a confession of his faults and failures. "The experience of the last ten years has shown me myself in a terrible way. . . . What I have learned about myself has made me increasingly miserable." He would never be able to accept praise for the book: He didn't deserve it, he thought. But it's also about the pain of Virginia's rejection. "When I met you, I was overwhelmed. (I guess I loved you, in my way; but I don't anymore.)" He'd seen her early delight turn into frustration, then irritation, and finally, he felt, contempt. He invited Virginia to write her own angry letter and unload her feelings toward him. For his part, however, he was done: "I don't want to know you in a personal way anymore, Virginia. I can't stand how much you can hurt me." He no longer had faith in his ability to take on another scholarly project. "I am haunted by the superficial and irresponsible person which I have been," he wrote and closed by begging, "Please forgive me, and forget."

Curtin's pain was so raw that he could not bring himself to send the letter. He put it away in his desk and tried to go on with his life. Then, in 1973, after receiving a letter from Virginia asking him to take part in the celebration of centenary of Cather's birth, he found the strength to pull out the letter and send it. "I am still afraid of you," he confessed in the cover letter he added. He recalled a time in Virginia's office at the press when she pulled out a file drawer full of manuscript drafts, proofs, and correspondence, and explained how she had accumulated sufficient evidence to protect herself against any complaint, "legal or otherwise," he might take a notion to raise. "I certainly have no case, but I am afraid you have a file," he wrote.

"What all this points to," he confessed, "is that you were right: I am not a scholar." Curtin wrote that his ordeal with Virginia over *The World and the*

Parish had led to "my utter loss of self-confidence." He felt he had become "a merely average teacher." He had struggled to meet her deadlines and to do a thorough job of reviewing proofs because he was dealing with family problems that kept him up "long sleepless nights." His letter closes with not the usually "Yours" or "Sincerely" but with a disturbing "Goodbye."

Bill Curtin found a way past this moment of withering self-doubt. He survived Virginia by over forty years, passing in 2021 at the age of ninety-four with a stellar professional record. But his agonized letter managed to crack her mean lady editor facade, if only a bit. In her reply, she shouldered some of the blame. "I look back with no pride to some phases of our relationship as author and editor," she wrote, regretting that she didn't have more experience or perspective to draw upon. She did not, however, agree to look past Curtin's failures to review proofs and his "relegating" work to others, adding, cuttingly, that there was a reason why an inaccurate text was referred to as "corrupted." She closed with a begrudging, "For what it may be worth to you, I wish you well."

23

Willa Cather's Imagination

By the end of the 1960s, the work that Bernice, Virginia, and a supporting cast of Cather scholars were doing had begun to pay off. When Jackson Byers of Duke University undertook to compile *Fifteen Modern American Authors*, a survey of research on the leading twentieth-century writers (as chosen by a poll of almost two hundred American literature specialists in the Modern Language Association), Willa Cather was the only woman represented, and the scholar he chose to write her chapter was Bernice.

Even a glance through the chapter, at forty pages the longest in the book, shows that Cather's critical legacy was still a work in progress. There was no authoritative biography, the one by E. K. Brown and Leon Edel having been written a decade before Bernice's archival finds and without access to the embargoed letters. There was no uniform edition of Cather's work, thanks to her major works being split between Houghton Mifflin and Knopf and continuing resistance to publication of public domain works and recovery efforts like *The Kingdom of Art*. Her first novel, *Alexander's Bridge*, had been out of print for decades. There was no book-length critical study of her work. Wright Morris had a volume in the Twayne's United States Authors Series, thanks to the press having passed on David Madden's book; Cather would not get her Twayne's book (number 258 in the series) until 1975. And no collection of letters, of course. So, Bernice's article was a catalog of fragments.

What it also demonstrated, however, was that a growing number of scholars were taking an interest in Cather and that no one was doing a better job of keeping track of their work than Bernice (and Virginia). In part, this is because they were cultivating a new generation of Cather researchers. Hardly a year passed without at least one of Bernice's PhD students undertaking a dissertation about Cather. And Virginia continued to encourage authors to bring Cather studies to the press.

She had been working with the first of these, Richard Giannone, since 1964. Giannone had approached the press about turning his dissertation on the role of music in Cather into a book, and though Virginia tended to discourage authors from thinking there could be a straight line from dissertation to book, she was happy to make an exception in this case. If he were willing to do the necessary reading and research ("at a guess, about three years' work"), he might have a book.

From the very beginning, Virginia took a noticeably gentler tone in her correspondence with Giannone than she did with Bill Curtin. Though he was just a babe in the woods when it came to the full scope of Cather's writing, she didn't consider this a permanent condition. Giannone bristled a bit at her suggestion: "It goes without saying that I've read all of Miss Cather's own work, except the uncollected non-fiction." But he added words guaranteed to win Virginia's heart: "All of this is not to say, however, that I do not need the stern comment of an editor." He welcomed her recommendations and assured her of "my willingness to co-operate with your editorial judgment."

Although Bernice expressed reservations about Giannone's manuscript, Virginia was enthusiastic about his prospects. He arranged a visit to Lincoln and Red Cloud in the summer of 1964 and she was delighted by his promise to "really do it up to the king's taste." Giannone's first exposure to the Cather materials available in Nebraska was hardly sufficient for him to complete the book, though, particularly given the disarray of the material in Red Cloud. And then there was Bernice's discovery of Cather's forgotten newspaper work. Sharing this news and the changes in plans for the press's Cather collections, Virginia reminded Giannone that she'd told him "that life among the Catherites was wildly melodramatic." "It was an understatement," she joked.

Virginia's initial estimate of three years for Giannone to finish the necessary research and complete his book wasn't far off, at least in comparison with *The World and the Parish*. But her hunch about his potential to produce a study to her standards, certainly more demanding than a king's taste, proved correct. For one thing, he heeded her advice to pay closer attention to the classical references in Cather, even though she was miffed when he suggested that Nils Ericson's flute in "The Bohemian Girl" was linked to the pipes of Pan, the Greek god depicted as a satyr and often associated with sexual symbolism. Still, she had to have been pleased when he wrote in the spring of 1966, "Your ideas about myth work out with remarkable consistency." He was teaching Hemingway that semester and he contrasted the two writers: "Follow an allusion in Cather and you're brought back into the heart of the novel. Follow a Hemingway detail and you go nowhere."

Giannone delivered his manuscript that summer. It was "packed with new insights and fresh and valuable interpretations," Virginia was happy to report, though she then warned him that "these are about the last kind words you will hear from me until the manuscript goes to press." "From experience, I've come to prefer negative criticism," he replied. He got plenty of it. Over the course of the next year, Virginia sent him comments, corrections, and cautions as she and Bernice worked through his draft chapter by chapter. She reminded repeatedly him "to keep the focus on your subject and not to feel that you have to pronounce on Willa Cather's art as a whole." At times she sounds a bit like a mother telling a child not to swim too far from shore: "Willa Cather's art is very complex—we have just begun to realize how complex—and some of your general statements could be quickly demolished by a reviewer."

Virginia felt Giannone worked "at a pitch of poetic intensity" and sometimes became so convoluted in his analysis that even she found it hard to follow. At one point, she wrote that she and "Aunt Bernice" had spent two hours trying to work through a chapter on *The Troll Garden* stories. "None of it had to do with substance, only with stylistic matters." By May, Giannone had had enough. He questioned whether Virginia was truly only concerned with "textual and stylistic matters." Some comments showed that she disagreed fundamentally with his critical interpretations, and he felt a line had to be drawn there. "If, in fact, you cannot trust my judgment, does that not put an end to the whole business? Where do we go from here?"

His letter was brief. Her reply was not. The problem, in her view, was his "departure from scholarly procedure in critical writing," and she proceeded to specify examples from his manuscript. But unlike her exchanges with Bill Curtin late on the tortuous path to *The World and the Parish*, this letter ended with an olive branch and a pep talk. "Editing is not nice work," she admitted. It was tedious and as hard on the editor as the author, if not harder. The author accrues the advantages of the book's reception; "the editor is just older." But she would not be putting in this effort unless she believed that his book was "a truly original and significant contribution." Giannone had telephoned Virginia several times after sending his letter to complain further, telling her he wanted to be rid of the whole thing. She begged him not to give up now, when they were almost done: "You are so close to a book to be proud of."

Not quite that close, however. And as the editing and revision process dragged into the summer, the dynamic between editor and author shifted. Comparing the correspondence on Giannone's book with that on *The World and the Parish*, it's Virginia who's clearly the more harried and disorganized. Giannone's letters are crisp, professional, with nary a typo. Virginia's are rushed, full of cross-outs and corrections, overflowing with extraneous details. Several times she went on at length about problems at the press—personnel turnover, the challenge of keeping up with the increasing volume of work (over sixty books scheduled for 1968), "visiting firemen," administrative headaches. The only neatly typed letter from the press is a note from Kay Graber in June informing Giannone that Virginia was in the hospital and would not be back at work for at least ten days. This, Virginia later wrote, was due to her hypertension medication, which included a depressant. It likely triggered a down cycle after months of her working at fever pitch.

Music in Willa Cather's Fiction finally came out in late 1968 and received favorable reviews. Most found Giannone had convincingly made a case for music as a central element in Cather's work. "Giannone makes it clear that Cather's most inventive experiments with fictive form correspond to her deliberate and sustained adaptation of musical form," wrote Marilyn Zimmerman in the *Journal of Aesthetic Education*. Moreover, he'd produced a definitive study. "No one is likely to find anything further of new and central significance to say" on the subject, John Edward Hardy wrote in *The Kenyon Review*.

Giannone's book was a test run for Virginia. She had her mind set on building not just a body of Cather's work but of work about Cather. If the University of Nebraska Press were not to be the premier place for Cather publications, then who? For any university and academic press outside of Nebraska to take the lead would fundamentally undermine the state's

Fig. 18. Virginia, Bernice, and Ron Hull in front of Sandoz Hall dormitory, 1967. Courtesy of Virginia Faulkner, Editor Papers, Archives and Special Collections, University of Nebraska-Lincoln Libraries.

credibility as champion of its own literature. Though Mildred Bennett was building up the archive in Red Cloud to be the largest collection of Cather's papers outside private hands, its organization was still short of what a serious center for study would need. Both Virginia and Bernice agreed that Red Cloud was the proper place for the collection and steered contributions its way but gritted their teeth over its slow progress. *Music in Willa Cather's Fiction* was an important building block, but its focus was too narrow to gain attention among American literature scholars.

Luckily, the opportunity to publish a broader critical study of Cather's work presented itself not long after Giannone's book came out. David Stouck, a Canadian scholar, introduced himself to Virginia and Bernice at the Western Literature Association conference in Provo, Utah, in 1969. Stouck had become fascinated with Cather's work as a graduate student at the University of Toronto. In 1965 he traveled to Red Cloud to visit the museum and met Mildred Bennett and surviving Cather acquaintances, but he'd been discouraged in pursuing a Cather dissertation by Northrop Frye, the head of the Toronto English department. Frye, whose 1957 book *Anatomy of Criticism* had provided the theoretical basis of New Criticism approach adopted by most English departments in the 1960s, told Stouck that he didn't consider Cather's work worthy of a dissertation.

Stouck and his wife Mary Ann, a specialist in medieval English literature, retained their interest in Cather, however, and after meeting Virginia and Bernice, they both submitted articles to *Prairie Schooner*. "These pieces confirm my feeling that we must have a book from you," Virginia wrote, and she suggested the press could bring it out in 1973 to coincide with the Cather centenary. In Virginia's view, Stouck was the first Cather scholar—aside from Bernice, of course—who got it. Instead of her usual caveats, she bubbled with enthusiasm. "How I wish we could sit down and talk!" she wrote. He touched on points she had been trying to make since the mid-1950s, "before I came back here and before I had any idea of an association with a university press": the importance of *Lucy Gayheart*, the richness of references in *Alexander's Bridge*. Indeed, it was Virginia who put herself in the student's seat. Stouck's analyses delighted her, "for they establish new connections and reveal new patterns." And she applauded his shaking off secondhand opinions: "You get your ideas and work them out from the writings themselves. And that's the way it has to be."

Stouck quickly agreed to work with the press and the book began to take shape over the next few months. Although drawn in part from articles he had already published, it was going to encompass the full range of Cather's work. But not too full. "I don't think anyone will be in a position" to write such a book, Virginia advised him, meaning anyone but Bernice. In fact, she wanted to downplay any implication that it would have biographical elements, rejecting his first title, *Willa Cather, the Unsentimental.* She suggested "something like *Imaginative Modes in Willa Cather's Fiction*," though she admitted it didn't "have much pizzazz." They eventually met halfway, settling on *Willa Cather's Imagination.*

Virginia was less willing to compromise when it came to discussion of Cather herself. In April 1974, she sent Stouck her markups on his completed manuscript. What irked her most were what she called his "received conjectures" about Cather's personal life and her relationship with Isabelle McClung. "Received conjectures" was her unsubtle insinuation that Stouck was starting to listen to the younger scholars calling for more direct reference to Cather's sexuality. "Since your book is primarily literary criticism you should (in fact, must) stick to what can be solidly documented from primary sources." And that, she emphasized, didn't mean "merely one letter, written perhaps in a moment of extreme emotional distress"—in other words, a letter like the one to Mariel Gere mourning Olivia Pound's rejection that a decade earlier had helped Virginia recognize Cather as lesbian in fact and not just symbolism.

Virginia's letter reveals the lines of defense she was preparing against the growing calls to abandon the myth of Cather the great artist who existed above or outside sex. First, there was the documentation hurdle. "Unless and until you have read every single available letter by Willa Cather, have dug more into what can be recovered of her life from 1890 until her death," neither Stouck nor "anyone else in God's world can, with integrity, classify her relationship with Isabelle as you have done." Then, there were the decoys: "the Moore boy, S. S. McClure, and that young man in New Mexico." Finally, there was the bunker. "I should add also that you should have read and studied every published scrape of writing at the very least ten or twelve times before attempting to make certain categorical assumptions about the degree of autobiography which appears in the fiction." Who else could answer that challenge at the time except the woman making it and her partner?

One reason that Virginia opposed probes into the nature of Cather's sexuality was that she thought that the biographical approach to a writer's work was inherently superficial. Bernice had said as much in her Keats book: "The life of a poet is hard to find in his work." They were both disciples of New Criticism and believed that the text, not the author, was the only proper subject for study. "In the personal view," Bernice had written, "one must depend on that surface, defining the poet-speaker by what is known of him." The biographical facts, she argued, are just the islands that appear above the water: beneath them, "there are far greater continents and a deeper sea-change in the creative life than anyone can measure."

In working with the two women, Stouck found their manner could not be more different. "Everybody liked Bernice and wanted to work with her," he remembers. Although she had obvious demands on her time and seemed to have difficulties meeting deadlines, Bernice put time with students—and Stouck considered himself one of them—ahead of everything else. "She gave of her time generously: a gentle, gracious, motherly woman." Virginia, however, "was the opposite." She seemed just as overloaded as Bernice but made no effort to disguise her impatience. Like many of her authors at the time, he was subjected to her fierce, intense look as she leaned forward across her desk, cigarette in hand, demanding, "Whaddaya got?" In their correspondence, on the other hand, Virginia took pains to set her expectations, explain her advice on structure and critical approach, and detail every correction and suggestion. "She was painstaking in a way that few editors today match," Stouck recalls.

Virginia found a respite from her intense focus on the Cather projects in her work with Wright Morris. Bruce Nicoll had first thought of approaching Morris in 1967 about reissuing his 1948 novel *The Home Place*, set in Nebraska and filled with Morris's own stunning black-and-white photographs. Nicoll thought it fit neatly into the state/regional literature he'd made the focus of Bison Books. Soon, however, Virginia saw the opportunity to pick up more of Morris's titles as they fell out of print—and her respect for his writing grew quickly. Over the next dozen years, the press would publish over twenty books by Wright Morris as Bison Books.

The job of working with Morris quickly evolved from business to friendship. Like Cather, Morris never quite fit into the main currents of the literature of his time and even now is considered a neglected American master. Unlike Cather, however, Morris was relaxed in the management of his oeuvre. He recognized that the University of Nebraska Press was his best bet for keeping his work in print, since most of his books had sold no more than moderately and only a handful had gone into mass-market paperback editions.

Fig. 19. Virginia and Bruce Nicoll, around 1970. Courtesy of Virginia Faulkner, Editor Papers, Archives and Special Collections, University of Nebraska-Lincoln Libraries.

This was a new role for Virginia. Morris's books were not only already written but well written. She had none of the misgivings she'd felt with the less-polished Bison Books. All Morris's required were acquiring the rights and agreeing on the covers—and even the covers soon settled into a simple but striking two-tone (black and one other dominant color) design scheme still used today.

Virginia and Morris had much in common. They had both spent time in Europe in the 1930s, both had sophisticated tastes in art and literature, both enjoyed good liquor and lively conversation. Their dealings ran on a casual track, never putting editorial or business matters ahead of friendly feelings. Several years into the press's work with Morris, for example, Virginia sent him their standard promotional questionnaire, having discovered that the press had nothing on file from the man she considered Nebraska's best living writer. With the woman she considered Nebraska's greatest writer, however, she could not afford to be so relaxed.

24

The Art of Willa Cather

Virginia began thinking about Willa Cather's 1973 centenary long beforehand. As she came to better understand the time required to produce Cather books to her standard, she became more conservative in her estimates. She wanted a whole program of activities: not just the usual annual conference in Red Cloud, but an academic conference hosted by the university, a concert of music related to Cather like the one Bernice narrated at back in 1963, some kind of tribute that could tour the state, plus whatever Cather books the press could herd into print. And she was happy to sweep up an initiative started in Red Cloud, a letter-writing campaign to get the state's congressional delegation to lobby the post office for a Cather commemorative stamp.

Whatever she did, however, had to be done with Mildred's cooperation. There would have to be a celebration in Red Cloud and the foundation would have to have a hand in it. At the same time, having attended a decade's worth of annual conferences, she felt that the foundation lacked the organizational and physical capacity to host an academic event of the scale and seriousness she had in mind. She and Bernice had learned that in the fall of 1971, when the Western Literature Association held its annual meeting in Red Cloud. Though not large, the WLA outstretched the town's lodging capacity, and some attendees had to stay in Hastings, forty miles away.

The choice of Red Cloud did reflect the clear choice by western literature scholars to place Cather in their pantheon. The WLA devoted its spring 1972 issue of *Western American Literature* to Cather, with feature articles by the likes of David Stouck and others of the generation of academics now following in Bernice's footsteps. Soon after the journal was published, Bernice received an invitation from John Murphy at Merrimack College to

Fig. 20. Virginia, around 1972. Courtesy of Virginia Faulkner, Editor Papers, Archives and Special Collections, University of Nebraska-Lincoln Libraries.

deliver the keynote address at a Cather seminar he was organizing. Murphy's would be a much smaller affair than Virginia had in mind, but it was another demonstration of the growing recognition of Cather's importance. Bernice accepted, of course, and wrote that Virginia would also be attending. She had to send her reply by special delivery, however, an indication of just how harried she was in keeping up with her many responsibilities.

Among the projects Bernice was working on for the centenary was *Willa Cather: A Pictorial Memoir*, an illustrated book on Cather's life and world. Despite all her experience with Cather research, obtaining reproductions, borrowing originals, and requesting permissions for dozens of historical photographs and images was a significant task that she and Virginia often worked on in their evenings together. The book would include original photographs by Lucia Woods of the landscapes around Red Cloud and settings incorporated in Cather's work, such as the Silas Garber house that was the basis of the Forrester mansion in *A Lost Lady*. Woods's Lincolns roots were tightly intertwined with Virginia's. Their fathers and grandfathers had been friends and done business together and the Woods Charitable Fund had provided grants that helped with previous books Virginia had edited. An exhibition of the photographs at the Sheldon Art Gallery on campus would also provide a centenary event to coincide with the seminar.

Another event during the summer of 1972 marked a turning point in the dynamics of Cather studies. Cather's companion and literary executor Edith Lewis died in August. Cather's literary estate, including all unpublished papers, passed to Cather's closest surviving relatives, her nephew Charles Cather and his sister Helen Cather Southwick. Lewis had always been careful to respect the letter and spirit of her partner's wishes and wary of the press's motives. Only in recent years had she grown more comfortable with the use of some material still under copyright.

With Charles Cather, who became the executor, and Helen Southwick, however, Virginia, Bernice, and Mildred Bennett all had warm friendships sustained through years of letters, birthday cards, and visits. These bonds eased the process of obtaining permissions but would also prove constraints. Both Southwick and Charles Cather opposed what they considered unseemly insinuations about their aunt's sexuality and relationships with other women, particularly Isabelle McClung and Edith Lewis. Prior to Lewis's death, their authority had only been informal. Now, they were in a position to cut off cooperation completely.

Late in October, Bernice and Virginia flew to Boston to attend the Merrimack College symposium. It was Bernice's first time traveling by air, and she held tightly onto Virginia's arm as their plane lifted off, worrying about the danger of falling from such a great height. She soon relaxed, however, and admitted it was a pleasant experience. Virginia was pleased, as she later wrote Wright Morris, because she'd had "a bellyful of steam cars and good trains have become extinct in America."

Bernice delivered her keynote, "Willa Cather: The Secret Web," on Saturday evening. The secret web, she explained, was the complex set of relationships that defined Cather as an artist and that resisted easy interpretation. She summed up Cather's art as "apparent simplicity, actual complexity"—the same banner Virginia had been carrying since her immersion in Cather in Pacific Grove.

On Sunday morning, they took a bus with Murphy and other attendees to Jaffrey Center, the New Hampshire town where Cather had worked on *My Ántonia* and *One of Ours* and where she and Lewis were interred at the Old Burial Ground. Lewis's grave next to Cather's was still so new that there was yet no headstone. Virginia and Bernice had brought pieces of turquoise and tiger's eye from Mesa Verde National Park in Colorado, which Cather and Lewis had first visited in 1915 and which played a large part in the "Tom Outland's Story" section of her novel *The Professor's House*. As Murphy watched, they reverently pressed the stones into the still-soft earth around the graves.

When Virginia and Bernice returned from their trip, they learned with disappointment that *Willa Cather: A Pictorial Memoir* would not be released on schedule due to printing problems. The press had published relatively few books with color illustrations and getting to an acceptable product proved harder than expected. And Virginia and Bernice had less energy and patience to deal with unexpected setbacks. "Us old ladies," Virginia wrote Wright Morris, were spending too much time on "Work, Willa, Weather, Meetings, Foul-ups, and Flu." Virginia lost a week in hospital after returning from a trip to New Mexico with the flu, and Bernice had just been drafted into serving on a selection panel for the National Endowment for the Humanities.

Though Bernice was by now a senior member of the English faculty, she was as much a target of ad hoc taskings as she had been as a junior instructor twenty years before. Partly this was because she was too polite to object and had a tremendous capacity for work. But it was also a symptom of the sexism that was as endemic to the university as it was to most male-dominated institutions of the time. "The department was a good old boys' club," recalled one of Bernice's graduate students. And as an unmarried woman, she was assumed free of outside commitments.

Fortunately, as the centenary approached, others began to pitch in. Ron Hull from Nebraska Educational Television took the lead in organizing the year's first official Cather event, a concert of music mentioned in Cather's books performed by the university's symphony and chorale, conducted by Emanuel Wishnow of the music department. He enlisted the actress Sandy Dennis to narrate a program of readings selected by Bernice. The Cather concert crossed the state from Scottsbluff to Omaha before ending with two shows in Lincoln in early April.

Virginia's brother Ed lent a hand with the Cather commemorative stamp. As one of the biggest fundraisers for the state's Republican Party, he was able to ask Senators Carl Curtis and Roman Hruska to sponsor the necessary bill and obtain the support of the Postmaster General. The bill passed easily, and the post office arranged with Red Cloud's postmaster to hold a First Day ceremony on September 20. Over a hundred postal workers and volunteers issued over six hundred thousand stamped postcards that proclaimed Cather "one of America's masters of creative writing."

Although April opened with the Cather concert and saw the release of *Uncle Valentine and Other Stories: Willa Cather's Uncollected Short Fiction, 1915–1929*, edited by Bernice, as well as her pictorial book with Lucia Woods, the responsibility for putting together the conference, the main event of the centenary, at least as far as Virginia and Bernice were concerned, weighed on them. Virginia told Morris that it was "the grayest, gloomiest spring I can remember," and her outlook couldn't have improved when she slipped on a stair and broke her ankle. Ed began stopping by their house on the way to work and taking Virginia to the press before looping around to arrive at the Woodmen offices, a habit he kept up until she retired.

"The International Seminar on the Art of Willa Cather" finally took place in late October. The emphasis on "International" was deliberate. Not only were the invited scholars from as far away as Japan, France, and Italy, but the tiresome "regionalist" label was to be cast off for good by positioning Cather as a great world writer. To reinforce this message, no one from Nebraska, not even Bernice, was asked to deliver a paper. And it would not be the expected gathering of literary academics. Marcus Cunliffe, an English historian, put Cather into the context of Frederick Jackson Turner and myths about the American frontier. Eudora Welty spoke from the perspective of one writer's admiration for the work of another. Alfred

Fig. 21. Bernice and Virginia with Leon Edel and Alfred A. Knopf at the presentation of the plaque to Willa Cather. *Lincoln Journal Star*, October 25, 1973, p. 1.

A. Knopf, visiting Nebraska for the first time, recalled their relationship as author and publisher. Leon Edel reflected on the challenge of writing the first biography of a woman legendary for protecting her privacy. Even the American academics asked to speak, including James Miller and James Woodress, Cather's most recent biographer, avoided talking exclusively in the context of American literature. One attendee, Ellen Moers of Barnard College, did, however raise a concern that the conference was ignoring a label more important that "regionalist," remarking in one discussion, "We haven't even opened up . . . the whole feminine side of this book [*My Ántonia*] and all the books."

Knopf's attendance was something of a milestone, a clear indication that the days of distrust were past. Although retired now and walking with a cane, Knopf took part in most of the conference, including the unveiling of a plaque commemorating Cather's work for the *Journal Star* on the first day of the conference. The ceremony was featured on the front page of the *Evening Journal* along with an article by Bernice about Cather and her prolific work (over two hundred fifty articles, reviews, and columns had been identified by 1973) for the paper.

Knopf was so impressed that upon his return to New York, he wrote Bernice to congratulate her for "a magnificent conference." He followed up several days later, sending her a copy of a 1932 letter from Cather that, he wrote, "explains far better than any words of mine could what my relationship with Miss Cather was like." Given the strictures against the use of Cather's unpublished letters, this demonstrated just how Knopf's respect for Bernice and Virginia's work had grown. Bernice returned the letter via the stamped and addressed envelope Knopf had provided, but—ever the researcher—not before transcribing it for her own records.

On a personal level, even more special than Knopf's attendance was the fact that Bill Koshland, now chairman of the board of Alfred A. Knopf Inc., took time to come to Lincoln as well. Koshland came purely as a gesture of friendship and respect for Virginia, whom he'd only seen once or twice since her years in New York. He, James Miller, and Eudora Welty were among the select few at the cocktail party Virginia and Bernice hosted at their house on Fourteenth Street the night before the conference.

On Sunday morning, the participants, including Knopf, piled into two buses and rode west to Red Cloud. The weather was dry, crisp, and clear, and Catherland showed itself off in its finest fall colors. Upon arrival, they were greeted with cauldrons of coffee and homemade breakfast rolls, then ushered back aboard for a tour of Red Cloud and the surrounding area. Before heading back, Mildred fed everyone a Midwest Sunday fried chicken dinner at the Zion Lutheran Church. What most impressed attendees, though, was not the hospitality but the depth of knowledge and appreciation of Cather's work and the lengths to which the foundation was preserving her legacy. Ellen Moers, who was then researching her landmark work of feminist criticism, *Literary Women*, later wrote Mildred, "I think the sort of thing you and your remarkable Red Cloud collaborators are doing for Cather is the height of sophistication."

For Virginia and Bernice, however, there was little chance to sit back and enjoy the satisfaction of having brought off the Cather conference so successfully. First, there was the drudgery of chasing down publishable versions of all the talks and papers. But more profoundly, there were the consequences of Bruce Nicoll's departure to deal with.

When the board of regents met in August 1973 to agree on the university's budget for 1974–75, it also decided to bring the press under tighter control. Among the measures it approved was the establishment of a board of directors with Nicoll as its chairman. To the public, this appeared a promotion, an acknowledgment of his achievement in raising the press to a position of prestige within the university, the state, and the world of academic publishing. In fact, it was an intervention. In recent months, Nicoll had been experiencing memory problems and he was scheduled for surgery to determine their cause. Nicoll's children now believe their father was in the first stages of early onset Alzheimer's. Within a year of the regents' announcement, Nicoll would be in a nursing home.

But there was another problem the regents needed to confront: the fact that the press had accumulated a debt of nearly half a million dollars. Fred Link, a professor in the English department, was appointed as acting director at the start of September, with an assignment to report back to the board on the press's role in relation to the university and with a clear picture of its financial health. The former was easy. The press had, under Nicoll's leadership, published the work of dozens of UNL faculty members, enhanced the university's reputation, and improved its ability to attract academic talent. The money, however, was another matter. While Nicoll had pulled the press out of the financial problems of Emily Schossberger's era, its performance in balancing profits and losses was erratic. Nicoll and Virginia tended to program more out of optimism than market analysis. And Link found that bookkeeping and cost accounting practices were inadequate: The press hadn't even hired a business manager to oversee these functions until the late 1960s.

When Chancellor Hardin rescued the press by assigning Nicoll as director back in 1958, he had left its business model undefined. Although Link was not a businessman, he understood that Hardin had viewed the press like another university department rather than as a business unit. Each year, the administration allocated an operating budget based on Nicoll's estimates rather than treating it as a cost center with its own revenues and expenses. Nicoll assumed the Nebraska taxpayers were covering the press's losses; the university's accounting department kept wondering how its deficits were going to be eliminated; and no one, other than Milan Frey, the business manager, knew that sales never came close to covering the press's annual production costs.

Link presented his assessment to the regents in November 1973. He offered three options: continue with the current arrangement and hope that the deficit would somehow be resolved; close the press; or fund it properly. Knowing the regents favored the last option, he compared the press with counterparts and recommended that the press adopt a hybrid model like that of other university presses, a combination of subsidies and traditional business profits and losses. His final recommendation was delivered separately: The press needed a director who was a publishing professional.

The regents agreed to keep the press but instructed Link to see what could be done to reduce the deficit while the process of recruiting a new press director got underway. Revenue had to increase and costs had to be cut. The ads and catalogs for 1974's books were revised to reflect higher retail prices. Everyone was asked to look for ways to bring the overhead down. A sidewalk sale was held to clear out the mustier corners of the warehouse and luxuries such as the liberal use of full-color gloss printing in the Cather pictorial memoir were cut from plans for books still in preparation. Original poetry, of which the press had published fewer than a dozen titles, was eliminated completely; books on music, which involved expensive specialized printing, were abandoned. Aside from the new director, new hiring was stopped. Meanwhile, the editorial workload remained. "The fact is," Virginia wrote Wright Morris, "Old Lady Faulkner usually has had it when the whistle blows here at the jute mill and all I want to do is go home and take my shoes off and curl up with a jug of Scotch."

For Bernice, the success of the centenary brought an invitation to lead a seminar at Marquette University in Milwaukee, where she lectured on "Willa Cather's America," and new graduate students eager to work on Cather. *Prairie Schooner* devoted its summer issue to a "Cather Portfolio" that included essays by James Miller and others, and at the same time, she and Virginia were putting finishing touches on the proceedings from the centenary seminar, *The Art of Willa Cather*.

Focused on the problems before her in Lincoln, Virginia was abruptly pulled back into the world she'd left almost a quarter of a century before. After years without contact, in May 1974, she received a letter from Dana Suesse asking for help. Dana was organizing a concert of her works at Carnegie Hall and was looking for funding. She and her second husband, Ed Delinks, were investing their own money in an event they hoped would resurrect Dana's reputation as a composer. It had been over two decades since her last concert in New York City. Virginia offered to send her "a yard" (a hundred dollars) and suggested Dana try "putting the arm on a few of those rich dykes that used to abound" when they lived in Connecticut, "if any are still ambulatory." Virginia confessed that "I have been completely out-of-touch with the so-called Gay World for many years."

Virginia added that she had recently been named a full professor in the English department, a step that John Robinson and Fred Link had pushed through. Having received inquiries about Virginia from other university presses, Link wanted to dissuade her from considering a move, even though this was improbable given her age and the strength of her ties to Lincoln, the university, and Cather. Aside from being able to sit on thesis and dissertation committees, she would have no classes and no graduate students to supervise. Even though she was entitled to march with faculty at commencements, she wrote Dana, "Since I haven't even an A.B., it's a case of nothing to wear."

Dana's concert took place on December 11, 1974. Frederick Fennell conducted the American Symphony Orchestra and pianist Cy Coleman performed Dana's "Concerto Romantico" and "Jazz Concerto in D Major." Dana herself, with great trepidation, performed one number. Although well-reviewed, the concert was sparsely attended, and Dana wrote Virginia afterward to bemoan the financial loss. She followed up a while later with an update on the problems of trying to get a recording released. Just before closing, she took a moment to look back at their days in Connecticut. She mentioned some of their old lesbian acquaintances, but then cautioned, "All these past associations are, as you might imagine, a closed chapter for me." Except for Virginia, with whom she hoped to remain friends. Yet she added a further "note in passing": "I am married to a very good and innocent man, and I trust he will stay that way," making it clear she intended to keep that closet door shut.

If Dana was concerned that Virginia harbored any longings for a closer relationship, she had nothing to fear. By now, she and Bernice had become partners in everything they did. They lived together, socialized together, traveled together, and worked together on the Cather projects. Though they projected an asexual identity to the public, people who worked with them assumed they were a couple.

Gay life was coming to Lincoln, even if Lincoln was slow in welcoming it. Louis Crompton, the first openly gay member of the English faculty, had conducted a seminar on "homophile studies" in the fall of 1970 that prompted a state senator to introduce a bill to prohibit the teaching of any course dealing with "aberrant sexual behavior" (which included homosexuality and lesbianism) at any state-funded university. The campus paper the *Daily Nebraskan* published a series of articles about the difficulties of living as a queer person in the city, including a story about a gang of bikers assaulting gay men and lesbian women at the only bar known to allow same-sex dancing. On the other hand, when Phyllis Lyon and Del Martin appeared at the student union ballroom as partners to speak on the topic "Lesbians Are Human," a capacity audience turned out.

Early in 1974, Jonathan Katz, a writer in New York City, wrote Bernice asking if she could "give me some information about Willa Cather" for a book on the history of homosexuals in America. She didn't answer. Katz shouldn't have been surprised. Two years earlier, his *Coming Out: A Documentary Play About Gay Life and Liberation in America*, performed off-off-Broadway, had portrayed the relationship between Cather and Isabelle McClung as a lesbian romance, and the Cather grapevine was too reliable for Bernice not to know about Katz's play. She would not have been prepared, though, to see how the Cather stamp was perceived in the gay community. An article in the Austin, Texas, gay and lesbian newsletter *The Rag* proclaimed, "Willa Cather: Gay Woman Adorns Stamp." Like Katz's play, the short piece declared that Cather and Isabelle McClung had been lovers and that McClung's marriage in 1916 had so affected Cather that "for several months she couldn't write at all." The writer credited "dedicated herstorians" with uncovering facts about Cather's sexuality and relationships that were omitted from her "official male biographies." Ironically, Mark English's design for the stamp incorporates the same symbol that Gilbert Baker would later incorporate in his LGBT pride flag: the rainbow.

Late in the summer of 1974, Virginia and Bernice took their first long vacation since the trip to Europe several years earlier. The visit to Cather's grave during the Merrimack conference had reminded them that they'd never visited two places close to Cather's heart: Quebec, the setting of her novel *Shadows on the Rock*, and Grand Manan, the island off the coast of New Brunswick where she and Edith Lewis had built a summer home in 1928. They arranged to meet Helen Cather Southwick and her husband Phil on Grand Manan in early September after spending over a week driving along the St. Lawrence River. While on the island, Virginia and Phil attempted to retrace the walk taken by Henry Grenfell, a character in Cather's story "Before Breakfast," only to discover that Cather had taken license with geography. Arriving exhausted back at their hotel, Virginia joked that she was having second thoughts about championing Cather.

"We certainly returned to reality with a crash," she wrote Wright Morris from Lincoln in September. The press was still in suspense about its next director and there were signs everywhere, from publication delays to new administrative procedures, that the salad days were over. *The Art of Willa Cather* wasn't released until late November. In its review, *Choice*, the journal of the American Library Association, offered an insight into how Virginia and Bernice's Cather projects were perceived outside the state: "Although the emotional context of the Cather factory at Nebraska often seems dangerously close to cult worship, it has produced scholarship of a consistently high order, and this present volume is no exception."

Even within Nebraska, however, there were criticisms of the extent to which work on Cather had monopolized the press and the English department. The novelist Shirley Schoonover, having only recently left Lincoln for Rochester, New York, published a "Letter from Nebraska" in the *New York Times* that asserted, "There are a couple of women associated with the University of Nebraska Press who do endless research on Willa Cather. And if you don't love Willa Cather's work you are not included in the literary life of the university."

Just before Thanksgiving, David Gilbert, then associate director of the University of Texas Press, was announced as Bruce Nicoll's permanent replacement, starting in January 1975. The University of Texas Press was one of the biggest academic presses in America. Although the University of Nebraska Press was now among the top fifteen academic presses and widely recognized for the success of the Bison Books series and the merit of its scholarly publications, it had also been something of a mom-and-pop operation, as Fred Link's investigation had revealed. Virginia had good reason, then, to wonder how Gilbert's arrival would affect the work that had become the central focus of her life.

25

Out to the Wind

In early March 1975, Virginia sent David Gilbert a memo pitching a new Bison Book, *Willa Cather on Art*, drawn from *The Kingdom of Art*, *The World and the Parish*, and other sources. He returned it with skeptical comments. "Who is the new audience here? Is it just because we pull out a slice and put it into paper?" He confessed that he "needed a brief basic course on the Cather canon (again)," although he reassured her that "you haven't been wrong yet." But the days when she could count on instant approval for anything related to Willa Cather were over.

Interviewed soon after his arrival, Gilbert remarked that "Virginia Faulkner is the hidden gem of this organization. She has that kind of intelligence which is extremely rare in an editor." Gilbert had a different vision for the press, however. He wanted to broaden the catalog, publishing more books on natural history, folklore, agriculture, and economics. "Something like a book on feeding the world," he suggested. While Virginia had always recognized the place in the catalog for technical books, she never considered them anything more than the dues she paid for the opportunity to work on the literary projects that were her passion. Subjects like ice drilling, Nebraska wildflowers, and farm policy held little interest, and she often found the authors of such books ham-fisted if compliant.

The press had to adapt to changing needs. In early 1975, Virginia commented in an internal memo to Gilbert that it wasn't worth publishing an edition of Goethe's *Wilhelm Meister* because "kids come to college so ignorant now that you have to spend your time with Homer, Voltaire, etc.—central figures." On the other hand, the increasing number of feminists among literary scholars was creating a demand for more editions of works by women—not just American and English writers but continental ones as well, as she wrote in support of an edition of one of Georges Sand's novels. Gilbert agreed, and the press published Sand's *The Country Waif* in 1976 with an introduction by Dorothy Zimmerman, a UNL professor of English.

Up to then, Virginia had to admit, the press's actual market research efforts had been limited. "If we had the money to undertake it properly," she wrote Dorothy Skardal, author of *The Divided Heart: Scandinavian Immigrant Experience Through Literary Sources*, "it would involve sending out questionnaires and interviewing a representative sampling of libraries and scholars." Instead, they spoke with a few knowledgeable scholars, usually members of the UNL faculty, and looked at the catalogs of other academic presses. If anything, she conceded, the arrangement worked to the author's advantage, since academics tended to be more generous than hard data. Gilbert would not accept such a haphazard approach and asked Virginia to take a harder look at initiatives she had previously taken pride in, such as the series devoted to Renaissance and Restoration dramas. From his time in Texas, he had a better grasp of the practical considerations of the academic market and initiated a separate discount schedule aimed at sales to university libraries and bookstores.

On the other hand, Gilbert supported her plan "to keep Bisonizing" Wright Morris's books as the paperback rights became available. She was delighted when Robert Knoll announced that Morris, who'd just retired from teaching at San Francisco State University, had agreed to come to UNL as a visiting professor in the fall of 1975. Drawing upon his experience in helping organize the Cather centenary events, Knoll arranged to turn the Montgomery Lectures for that year into a conference on "The Art of Wright Morris" and enticed the small but enthusiastic cadre of scholars following Morris's work to speak. He collected the talks and discussions from the conference in *Conversations with Wright Morris*, which the press published in 1977.

Jo and Wright Morris dined with Bernice and Virginia at least once a week during that semester, often as Virginia's guests at the University Club. They had a special reason to celebrate in early October, when Bernice was one of twelve "Great Teachers" in American universities featured in the October 13, 1975, issue of *People* magazine. The article quoted her on the synergies between her teaching and her research: "I can talk with students because I am still studying. You can't teach well unless you are learning at the same time." Virginia had her own triumph a little later when Bill Koshland at Knopf wrote to suggest that the press reissue one great prize of Catheriana that had eluded her from the beginning: Edith Lewis's memoir, *Willa Cather Living*.

The fall of 1975 brought Virginia her first opportunity to dust off her skills as a creative writer in over twenty years. Robert Beadell, a professor of music at the university, had accepted a commission to write a dramatic composition as part of the school's celebration of America's bicentennial. His idea was to create a piece based on Cather's story "Eric Hermannson's Soul," first published in the April 1900 edition of *Cosmopolitan* magazine. He approached Bernice to write the lyrics, but she declined, saying she was overcommitted, and suggested Virginia instead.

The plan was to present *Out to the Wind*, a "musical drama" in May 1976, as the culminating production of the school of music. Bernice suggested the title, which came from "Eric Hermannson's Soul." Margaret Eliot, a young woman from Boston, upon seeing the Nebraska prairie, wants to let her soul run "full length out to the wind." Beadell had so far only written some incidental music, and Virginia wrote of their deadline, "God knows how we'll make it."

They didn't. The process of writing and staging *Out to the Wind* would come to make her experience with Leonard Sillman and *All in Fun* seem quick and painless. No one had quite the same understanding of what the work was intended to be: a drama set to music? A musical? An oratorio? Would there be spoken scenes interspersed with songs or would the entire work be set to music, like an opera? Beadell wanted Virginia to provide the lyrics first; she knew from working with Dana that songs were better written collaboratively between composer and lyricist. Neither of them had the luxury of time to devote to the work. By March 1976, it was clear this was not going to be a bicentennial event. Instead, the process stretched out for another two years. "The opry is, I think, going to be something like the diary of Anaïs Nin," Virginia wrote Wright Morris after the first year. "We shall never see the end of it." It wasn't until the summer of 1978 that anything resembling a score and libretto finally came together.

In the meantime, there were yet more books to edit and fewer authors she looked forward to working with. "We have an unusually unprofessional and cantankerous batch among the current crop," she told freelance copy editor Dorothy Clair. "And nothing in the works that I can get excited about." The only Cather project was a Bison Books edition of *Alexander's Bridge* with an introduction by Bernice. This was something of a milestone: the first work still wholly under the control of the Cather estate and made possible through the trust Virginia and Bernice had established with Charles Cather and Helen Cather Southwick.

When Joan Crane, a librarian at the University of Virginia, approached the press in late 1976 about a Cather bibliography, a project she and Bernice had long considered a missing but essential piece of Catheriana, Virginia knew enough to respond with caution. "Looming large, as always, is the question of funding," she advised Crane, remembering the lean years before Bruce Nicoll's arrival. "A thorough consultation with our director," along with a detailed cost estimate, were required before a decision could be taken. The Cather foundation provided a grant to cover Crane's initial work, and she was given a go-ahead from the press in early 1977. *Willa Cather: A Bibliography* was ultimately published by the press in 1982. Cather books were long-term affairs.

For the first time in over a decade, there were no original works of Cather criticism underway with the press. Considering the effort Virginia had invested in working with Cather scholars, this may have been a good thing. There were few aspects of her job that still excited her and many that had grown old and tiresome. Writing "blurbese," for example. She joked to Morris that she was writing a new edition of the press's catalog and was tempted to write things like, "A real dog," "Yucky," and "Recommended by the author's mother." "If I just spoke Russian, I'd apply for a job as society editor on *Pravda*," she added.

Virginia chafed at the emphasis on process and administration after the years of Bruce Nicoll's relaxed approach. She returned to her habit of dealing with depression by drinking. Elizabeth Knoll recalls greeting Virginia and Bernice one evening at the University Club. Bernice smiled and nodded; Virginia simply stared at her, glassy-eyed, without recognition. Checking in some mornings, Bernice would find Virginia passed out on the couch in her apartment. She recognized when Virginia was losing her fight with the black dogs. If she could afford the time, she would cancel her classes for a few days and two of them would head out to a town like

York or Grand Island. Bernice would rent a motel room, and she would work on her papers while Virginia slept, watched TV, and sobered up. Then they would return to Lincoln and resume their normal schedules. It was behavior Gilbert wouldn't have accepted from a more junior member of this staff, but given Virginia's seniority and critical role, he gritted his teeth and looked the other way.

Virginia knew she was stuck. She hadn't worked as a writer for over twenty years, and at sixty-three she wasn't likely to be hired by another press. In fact, what loomed in the not-too-distant future was retirement. If Virginia couldn't see it, Dave Gilbert could. He hired Steve Cox, then with the University of Tennessee Press, gave him the title of executive editor, and told him directly that his job was to ensure a smooth transition when Virginia retired. Neither Cox's hiring nor the choice of job title sat well with her.

To make matters worse, Gilbert gave Cox a desk in Virginia's office in hopes of fostering the transfer of knowledge. For the first few weeks, she tried to barricade herself behind a cloud of smoke from her unfiltered Camel cigarettes, but gradually Cox's easygoing manner and solid grasp of the business wore through her defenses. Soon, she was routing memos and reports through Cox, who also established a better rapport with Gilbert. Even more remarkable, Cox was able to coax Virginia into talking about her time in New York and Hollywood. She admitted she missed the caliber of people she knew in the studios and their laissez-faire attitudes. "We only worked as hard as we needed to," she told him.

Virginia needed something to inspire her. One prospect was the opportunity to pay tribute to Mari Sandoz, her first collaborator at the press. Several years earlier, Helen Winter Stauffer had proposed to turn her dissertation on Sandoz into a biography, and Virginia had urged it be accepted, even though she felt "if it is to be made into a publishable book Mrs. Stauffer will have to start over." After earning her PhD at UNL in 1974, Stauffer took job in the English department at Kearney State University and with that work and further research on Sandoz, it wasn't until 1977 that she was able to begin writing.

Stauffer submitted the first version of her manuscript in mid-1978, but *Mari Sandoz: Story-Catcher of the Plains* took four years to reach print. The delay was partly due to Stauffer's workload as a professor, but an equal factor was the care with which Virginia treated the book. If the press was going to publish a biography of Mari Sandoz, it was going to be as close to perfect as she could make it.

Her effort started with the review of Stauffer's manuscript. Virginia acknowledged that she knew Sandoz too well to be completely objective and insisted that a second reader who wasn't personally acquainted with "the dramatis personae" review it as well. That she asked Steve Cox demonstrated how far he'd risen in her estimation. Unfortunately for Stauffer, they were unanimous in their opinion: It was too long, illogically organized, not objective in its critical assessments, awkwardly written, and parochial, considering Sandoz only in the context of other Nebraska writers. But it was also clear that if a Sandoz biography was going to be written anytime soon, Stauffer was the person to write it.

Their advice was simple but bitter to swallow. Stauffer needed to take a lesson from Sandoz and "write as many drafts as she needs—4 to 10 if necessary." Virginia didn't simply kick the ball back to Stauffer. She sent along detailed notes that ranged from corrections and suggested tweaks to advice that could serve any would-be biographer. Stauffer had interviewed so many people, read so many letters, pored over Sandoz's books and reviews, and the draft was awash in details. "Writing a book is not unlike prowling around in an attic," Virginia advised. "You can learn a lot from what's in the old trunks and boxes, but you have to be able to decide what's junk and what is pertinent and revealing."

She also discouraged Stauffer from simply quoting recollections of Mari: "You wind up with something like how the various blind men described the elephant," she cautioned. Stauffer had included a lengthy preface. Ditch it, Virginia instructed. "It's not until the book is finished that a writer know what he has actually done." But she also no longer had the patience to hold an author's hand to the extent she had with Bill Curtin and others. "There's no way that I can continue this intensive review," she concluded after page one hundred twenty of over five hundred. "This is an authorial chore and it's not what the university press pays me to do," she informed Stauffer.

The root of the problem, Virginia felt, was that Stauffer's draft lacked a narrative. She needed to figure out Sandoz's story at its most essential, then build the book around that framework. In her own words, she was recommending the same approach later described by Pulitzer Prize–winning biographer Robert Caro: "Boil the book down to three paragraphs, or two, or one. . . . Then, with the whole book in mind, go chapter by chapter." In her internal memo on Stauffer's progress, Virginia provided such a synopsis, and reading it one wishes she'd had the time and energy to write Sandoz's biography herself:

> The pattern—again oversimplifying—was a running battle with just about everybody and everything: she never put her dukes down, not for a minute. She never forgot an injury, real (and there were plenty of them) or imagined (and I think there were plenty of those, too). She battled for her artistic integrity, which God knows we must respect, and for the poor, the downtrodden, and those minorities she fancied; she battled against the social and political system of virtually the entire world and God knows she was probably right there, too—but it did mean that she wasted an awful lot of energy. . . . Her physical and moral courage were incredible; and she could be patient and generous beyond belief in helping would-be writers, whether they were any good or not. She did live in a black and white world (and that was why we called that collection *Hostiles and Friendlies*).

Stauffer took the criticism seriously. She set aside her manuscript, started again, and focused on telling Mari Sandoz's story. It would be nearly two years before her next draft arrived at the press.

After decades of accepting every task that came her way, Bernice was finding it necessary to decline out of sheer exhaustion. The University of California Santa Barbara invited her to come for a term as a visiting professor in early 1977. Though flattered, she turned the offer down: "The energy crisis takes many forms: to cite but a single example, I haven't any," she confessed.

The summer of 1977 was intended to be time for her to work on her application for a National Endowment for the Humanities grant that would enable her to begin the culminating project of her years of Cather research: an authoritative—no, *the* authoritative critical biography. But as Virginia wrote Wright Morris, if Bernice was on vacation, "she seems to be the only person who knows it." If she wanted to keep working at the pace she'd become accustomed to, however, her body now refused to cooperate. In July she was hospitalized for a week and diagnosed with cardiac arrhythmia. Virginia took time off to visit each day and worked from home after Bernice was released. Though she was able to return to teaching at the start of the fall semester, within the first two weeks she came down with flu, which she passed along to Virginia. They both dragged themselves through to Christmas, when they flew out to California to spend the holiday with Bernice's sister Belva.

In the spring of 1978, they had a chance to put the worries of Lincoln behind them. They flew to Calgary to attend a conference held in Banff in the Canadian Rockies, a place they'd long wanted to visit. Organized jointly by the University of Alberta and Idaho State University, "Crossing Frontiers" brought together Canadian and American academics to explore common themes in the literature of the west of the two countries. Virginia and Bernice looked forward to spending time with old acquaintances and discourse as elevated as the altitude.

Instead, on the third day, they sat in shock as Robert Kroetsch, a Canadian writer and academic then at the State University of New York Binghamton, delivered the day's major paper, titled "The Fear of Women in Prairie Fiction: An Erotics of Space." In it, Kroetsch looked at *My Ántonia* and a Canadian novel, Sinclair Ross's *As for Me and My House*. "We conceive of external space as male, internal space as female," he asserted. "More precisely, the penis is external, expandable, expendable; the vagina: internal, eternal." Designated to respond to Kroetsch's paper, Sandra Djwa from Simon Fraser University broke up the room with her opening comment: "It's hard to know how to respond to these . . . ejaculations." But Kroetsch had set the theme, and she had no choice but to stick with it. She referred to a key remark: his description of Cather's use of Jim Burden, the male narrator of *My Ántonia*, and Ross's use of a female diarist in his novel as examples of "a kind of transvestitism." Then, in the question-and-answer period, Kroetsch was asked to explain how Cather's lesbianism related to his argument.

This was too much for Bernice. She objected to the suggestion and reached for the same defense that Virginia had employed to dissuade David Stouck: namely, that no one had a right to put a label on Cather's sexuality unless they'd read every letter she'd ever written, talked to everyone who knew her, analyzed every metaphor, symbol, and reference in her work. In other words, until they'd spent the better part of a lifetime on Cather research. Everyone knew that the only people who'd come close to doing this were Bernice and Virginia. And everyone knew they were never going to touch the "L word."

The subject of Cather's sexuality was not going away, however. Jane Rule had declared Cather a lesbian in her 1975 book *Lesbian Images*, and from that point on, the closet door could not be shut again. In July 1979, the *Minneapolis Star* ran a five-page feature on Cather that brought it up. Asked to comment, Mildred Bennett remarked, "If you're in the East, they'll tell you she was a lesbian. And maybe she was." But she added, "I don't know how anybody is ever going to prove it." In the same article, however, Bernice dismissed Cather's "mannish image" as "overemphasized": she just dressed "comfortably but simply." Cather didn't marry "because she was working on her career so much," which was a remarkable feat of dissemblance on Bernice's part, given that the same explanation could apply to her.

The opportunity to make the definitive case for their view of Cather arrived the summer of 1978 when Bernice was awarded the NEH Senior Research Fellowship. For years, it was taken for granted that Bernice would write the "big" Cather biography. The *People* magazine article back in 1975 mentioned that her apartment was crammed with boxes of research material for the book. But as she outlined in her fellowship application, there was more material yet to be collected. Trips would be required: to Pittsburgh, New York City, Washington, DC, Vermont, and London, where she expected to spend at least two months at the British Library.

Their commitments only allowed a short break, but Virginia and Bernice seized the opportunity to make a quick visit to England in August. Little about the trip turned out as planned. They found London dirty and inhospitable, and time spent in the British Library unproductive. Hoping for respite on their return voyage on the *Queen Elizabeth 2*, they were tossed around the cabin in the roughest seas either had ever seen. Back in Lincoln, Virginia came down with a viral infection that kept her out of the office for weeks. "I'm still largely in a fog about what's going on here at the press," she confessed to Morris.

Her mood was not improved by the news that *Out to the Wind* was finally scheduled to be staged in early February 1979. To Virginia, it had become "the f___g opera" after "umpty-ump" revisions and she just wanted to be rid of it. She was too professional, however, to share her feelings with

Fig. 22. Bernice, Mildred Bennett, and Virginia at the premiere of *Out to the Wind*. Courtesy of the National Willa Cather Center, Red Cloud, Nebraska.

Robert Beadell, who'd spent his summer finishing the score. As Robert Knoll later recalled, Virginia accommodated all Beadell's requests: "If he needed a four-beat line, she gave it to him; if he needed an extended dialog to prepare for a musical interlude, she delivered it"; and if scenes needed to be rewritten to ease stage direction, she rewrote them.

The musical drama, as it was finally labeled, premiered on Thursday, February 1, 1979. Reviewing the production for the campus paper the *Daily Nebraskan*, Peg Sheldrick was qualified in her praise: "To call it anything less than a fine, entertaining evening is unfair; but to call it an unqualified success is inaccurate." Sheldrick felt that part of the problem stemmed from the decision to videotape the show for Nebraska Educational Television as it was being presented in the theater rather than to arrange a separate performance in a television studio. It was also the most ambitious theatrical production that had been attempted within the resources of the campus: eight sets, nine set changes, and a cast of over forty.

It was a case of too much and not enough. Cather's story mentions the visit of a third-rate opera company, but *Out to the Wind* expands this into two scenes and four songs, all spoofs of opera at its worst. "All of them were funny songs but with so many together it was hard to appreciate them," Sheldrick wrote, in an echo of the criticism editors at Simon & Schuster had leveled at Virginia's novels forty years earlier. And the central story was weak, undeveloped.

As a student production, *Out to the Wind* lacked the financial risk that led Broadway producers to keep composer and librettist on hand all the way to premiere and sometimes after. Beadell and Virginia attended just a few rehearsals. "We have all done the best we can," she told Sheldrick in a half-hearted endorsement before the first performance. Knoll later asserted, "In this last work, Virginia Faulkner came home, bringing all that she had learned, here and elsewhere." In reality, *Out to the Wind* demonstrated how little of the fierce commitment to giving her best remained.

26

Breaking Down

To Virginia's family and friends, *Out to the Wind* was a splendid success. Ed and Jean held a dinner in her honor at the University Club. Mildred Bennett came from Red Cloud for the premiere and presented a bouquet on behalf of the Cather Foundation. Old acquaintances popped up with letters of congratulations. Virginia told a few that "Bob and I are going to work on it some more in due course," but due course never arrived. *Out to the Wind* had had its last performance.

Whether Virginia or Bernice were considering retirement, the kind of honors that accompany the end of a career began arriving. Bernice received the university's first award for Outstanding Research and Creativity, making her the first member of the faculty to win the school's highest honors for both teaching and scholarship. Axis, the association of business and professional women in Lincoln chose Virginia as its "Woman of Achievement" for 1979. Axis solicited letters testifying to her accomplishments, and Ed was delighted to list them in detail, starting with that day when she was escorted into his third-grade classroom. The same month, she took part in a colloquium on "The Private and Public Responsibilities of the American Publisher" held at the Library of Congress. Of the thirty-some invitees, many of them presidents of America's biggest publishers, Virginia was the only one with the title of editor.

At the Cather foundation annual conference in May, Bernice and Virginia were given awards for "outstanding research and scholarship" and a few months later, Bernice was one of ten recipients of the Nebraska Governor's Award for the Arts. With Virginia's help, Hugh Luke and Hilda Raz, who had taken over the day-to-day responsibilities for *Prairie Schooner*, began soliciting articles and reminiscences that would fill a special double issue in Bernice's honor they slated for spring 1981.

It helped distract Virginia from the increasingly tense atmosphere at the press. She was finding it harder to disguise her feelings about Dave Gilbert's direction. It was, she wrote Wright Morris, "complicated paper shuffling which seems to have little to do with the great World of Letters." For the last year, she had been discussing the possibility of joining the staff of the Center for Great Plains Studies with its current director, Paul Olson. Established by the regents in 1976, the center was the brainchild of Max Larsen, a mathematics professor who believed the university needed to encourage multidisciplinary studies that brought the sciences and humanities together. The venture proved a success, at least in terms of attracting grants and hosting conferences on such topics as "Ethnicity on the Great Plains," and the center needed help with its growing number of publications. Virginia thought she could not only take on this work but get the center to sponsor Cather books that Gilbert was reluctant to take on.

The move made sense for Gilbert as well, and by the start of summer, everyone concerned was informed that Virginia would be shifting to part-time with the press, spending at least three days a week at the center. The long-standing confusion over responsibilities between her as editor in chief and Steve Cox as executive editor ended: Cox would now head the editorial department and Virginia serve as editor emeritus. She held onto the few projects she still felt a strong commitment to: Joan Crane's Cather bibliography, Helen Stauffer's Sandoz book, and further Wright Morris reissues.

Virginia had settled into her new routine and Bernice was laying out a more realistic plan of work for the Cather book when their world was upended in early November 1979. Bernice suffered a massive stroke as she sat in her office discussing plans for *Prairie Schooner*. Rushed to the hospital, she lost consciousness and lapsed into a coma. Virginia spent the following weeks at bedside, anxiously looking for any sign of reawakening. As the days drew on, she became more and more distraught, and Ed began to suspect that she was drinking herself to sleep each night.

Rumors that Bernice's condition was not going to improve ran through the faculty and the Catherland community. The governing board of the Western Literature Association, of which Bernice was then president, appointed Helen Stauffer to act on her behalf while giving Bernice the title of president,

O.S.L. (on sick leave). She was moved to the Madonna nursing home, and Virginia continued to come and sit by her side each day. One afternoon in early January 1980, Bernice opened her eyes and, seeing Virginia, gave her hand a faint squeeze. "She's back!" Virginia exclaimed, and ran to fetch the nearest nurse. Once it was confirmed that Bernice could see, hear, and respond with a slight movement of her hand, Virginia called Ed, Robert Knoll, Hilda Raz, and everyone else she could think of, her voice trembling with excitement.

Bernice was back, but just barely. She spent another month in rehabilitation before being allowed to return to her apartment. She needed a cane to walk and was easily fatigued. By May, she was talking about returning to work on the Cather book, if not classes. Wright Morris, in town for an exhibit of his photographs, paid a much-appreciated visit. He had recently been advised to cut back on his drinking and watch his blood pressure, so the three of them shared their health woes and sipped diet sodas like good patients. Virginia and Bernice had to pass on attending the Cather conference in Red Cloud, the first either had missed in twenty years.

Virginia was now based at the center, working on proposals for three Cather books that she felt were being blocked at the press: a collection of writings on literature, a complete collected poems that would draw upon still-copyrighted material, and a variorum edition of *The Troll Garden.* Though she warned that there could be stiff fees for the necessary permissions, she predicted that Bernice could persuade Charles Cather to keep them reasonable.

She also knew she could count on Helen Southwick's support. After their time together on Grand Manan Island, Helen had come to rely on Virginia in the defense of the Cather legacy. Southwick had memories and family legends to draw upon, but she looked to Virginia for tactical support. The first assault was launched in her own backyard of Pittsburgh when *Hearts and Diamonds*—billed as a "documentary drama"—premiered in early March 1980. Written by University of Pittsburgh drama professor Attilio Favorini, the drama interwove the stories of two women who had spent time in the city around the turn of the century: Willa Cather and the actress Lillian Russell.

What set off Helen Southwick's alarm was the fact that Favorini depicted the relationship between Cather and Isabelle McClung as a romance, with

Fig. 23. Bernice and Virginia, 1979. Courtesy of Bernice Slote, English Papers, University of Nebraska-Lincoln Libraries.

the two reading love letters to each other in one scene. This sent Southwick to the thesaurus, where she looked up "romance." After listing synonyms, it said, "See 'love,'" which led her to another string of words representing everything from platonic to sexual love. She was willing to look at it as just a poor choice of words, but it still seemed wrong. What existed between Willa and Isabelle wasn't romance but a "lovely, deep, true, and constant friendship."

Helen demanded to see a copy of the script. Favorini complied. "I got the impression that the letters were made up," she wrote Virginia—which they were, of course. Nevertheless, she had a heated meeting with the playwright, who said that he had relied on James Woodress's biography as the source for his interpretation of the relationship between Willa and Isabelle. This she relayed to Virginia, who could, in turn, confirm it with Woodress himself.

Virginia informed Southwick that the view of the Cather-McClung relationship as lesbian could be traced back to Mildred Bennett and John March in the 1950s. What was more, there were at least two more assaults in preparation. Phyllis "somebody or other" (Robinson), had a contract with

Doubleday for a Cather biography and another author (Sharon O'Brien) was working on a "psychosexual" study. The latter had avoided contact with anyone at the press or the university, but Virginia vowed to take a close look at her work and, "if her scholarship is defective or incomplete, blow it out of the water."

These words have been used to argue that Virginia and Bernice were the primary source of opposition to open discussion of Cather's sexuality, and that their motive was, in part, to protect their own. Given her history, especially her time in New York and Hollywood, one could hardly suggest that Virginia was naive or prudish, but she did come from a generation for which homosexuality was a private matter and, even then, only acknowledged in a few settings where the risks were acceptable. And in writing Helen Southwick, she was addressing someone whose cooperation was crucial for the continued success of her Cather projects.

Virginia suggested that "it's a historical fact that the homosexual label is attached to nearly every great woman." But she also felt that the younger feminist scholars were among "quick-buck, self-promoting types" who grab for "every sensational straw." Yes, Woodress did write that Isabelle McClung was "the one great romance of her life"—but he added that Cather "was convinced that art and marriage did not mix." A better response, however, Virginia argued, would be to prove that there was *another* relationship that was the true "one great romance" of Cather's life—and that "it was an enduring one." This, she suggested, Bernice would do in her Cather biography. For the moment, she asked Helen to treat the information as confidential, though she added, teasingly, "When you stop and think about it, it is pretty obvious who that man was and I know that Bernice is anxious to be the first to present this truth, buttressed with her deep knowledge and impeccable scholarship."

Over forty years have passed since Virginia wrote this letter and virtually every scrap of information about Willa Cather's life that survives has been gathered and scrutinized by several generations of scholars. We know that whether or not Isabelle McClung was "the one great romance" of Cather's life, her one enduring relationship was with Edith Lewis, with whom she lived for almost forty years and to whom she left her literary estate as a living legacy. Which leads to a sobering conclusion about Bernice Slote's "impeccable scholarship" when it comes to the matter of Cather's sexuality. Willa Cather took great care to protect her privacy, during her life and afterward, but no one familiar with the body of biographical research would say that her one great romance was with a man.

Did Bernice intend to make a case for Cather as heterosexual as a way of diverting attention from her own relationship? There is little in the record to support this interpretation. Bernice may have been guilty of deceiving herself, but she was not practiced in deceiving others. A simpler explanation is that she wanted to preserve for Cather the same public image that had served her all the way back to her time as a beginning high school teacher: the smart woman too intent on her career (art for Cather, teaching and scholarship for Bernice) to have time for a man.

By then, Bernice and Virginia were fully invested in their mission to continue advancing Cather as a figure above and beyond sexuality. Virginia declared to Alfred Knopf, in a letter intended to secure his support for the proposed poetry collection, "We have shown ourselves to be honorable and responsible and capable of maintaining the highest standards of scholarship, as well as being completely dedicated to Miss Cather and her work." Anything that diminished Cather's standing—as they felt the label "lesbian" did—also diminished the significance of their own work.

Unfortunately for Virginia, the future of her place at the Center for Great Plains Studies was now in doubt. Paul Olson had resigned as director. The regents then appointed Fred Luebke, a historian, as acting director while a replacement was recruited. Olson's encouragement of the Cather books had always been conditional, dependent on the availability of funding, and Luebke looked to Virginia to raise it. Dave Gilbert had transferred what remained of Virginia's workload at the press to Steve Cox and his editorial staff, aside from the Sandoz biography and a few other books, so there was no place for her to return to. It was agreed that Virginia would retire at the end of June.

Hazel Barnes and Doris Schwalbe made a rare visit to Lincoln in July. En route to New York, they spent the day with Bernice and Virginia, who treated them to lunch at the University Club. "You were looking wonderful—no sign at all of the previous year's strain and worry," Barnes wrote afterward. In a snapshot of Bernice and Virginia taken during the visit, Virginia's eyes have a sparkle missing from all the news photos taken to publicize *Out to the Wind.*

Despite her retirement, Virginia was convinced she could find a way to move forward with the collection of Cather's writings on literature, even without funding in place. She laid out her plans in a letter to Alfred Knopf, who replied in late August, "Everything you say and write is very persuasive indeed." He was confident that they could work things out "so that all are satisfied and that the proper job is done for the greater glory of the lady in question." But, he added, he was heading off to vacation and since the book had been in development for several years, "a few weeks more will not make that much difference."

A few weeks were all Virginia had left. She died on September 15, 1980.

In a letter he wrote to Jo and Wright Morris the day after Virginia's death, Robert Knoll explained that the confidence Hazel and Doris had seen in July was quickly lost. "She had retired as you know on the first of July, and ever since had been distraught." Age had slowed her body, but her mind was still swift, sharp, and voracious. Without the press, without constant demands on her time, she became restless and anxious. The remaining Cather books were not enough to keep her occupied. Having cared for Bernice since her stroke, Virginia now became the one who needed care, and it was more than Bernice could handle. Bernice reached out to Knoll for help. On the evening of September 15, he came over to the house after Bernice and Virginia returned from dinner at Wendy's. He looked in to say hello to Virginia, who was watching Monday night football on television, then headed upstairs to Bernice's apartment.

Still recovering, Bernice was exhausted. Not only did she have her usual workload awaiting a return to full-time duties, but she felt the Cather book looming over her as a huge unmet commitment. If anything, the demands on Bernice's time were greater than before the stroke while her resources were substantially diminished. Where Bernice had a schedule that more than filled her days, Virginia had almost nothing. She was experiencing days of manic highs when she wanted to talk with Bernice for hours about the Cather biography, to plan research trips, think up yet more projects they could work on.

Bernice had decided that the situation was unsustainable. Virginia was unable to get herself out of her cycles of highs and lows and Bernice was risking another stroke. The only answer was to check themselves into a hospital—Virginia for psychological observation, Bernice simply to recover her strength. Knoll promised to talk to Ed and arrange for them to be admitted to Bryan Hospital, where he still served on the board of directors.

That night, however, after Knoll left, Bernice went to check on Virginia and found her in her chair. Assuming Virginia had fallen asleep, Bernice tried to wake her, only to realize that she was no longer breathing. Virginia had died while they were discussing what to do about her. Frantic, she called Knoll and Ed, both of whom rushed to the house.

Bernice was devastated. Weeping, she had trouble answering their questions. Ed contacted the coroner and the funeral home. Virginia's body was taken away and cremated as soon as the coroner had signed the death certificate. Ed arranged for memorial service on Wednesday the 17th: Just a few people, mostly family, were invited. Robert and Virginia Knoll took Bernice, who was still too upset to speak to anyone.

Ed took responsibility for clearing out Virginia's apartment. Although he didn't mean to be brusque, Virginia was his sister, he was her executor, and he felt those were closer and more formal relationships than whatever had existed between her and Bernice, which in any case had no legal standing. Even if Bernice hadn't been down to her last reserves, it wasn't in her nature to confront Ed over differences in how to respect Virginia's wishes. She watched without objection as he gathered up Virginia's letters and personal papers and took them to the Woodmen headquarters to be incinerated. The only papers left for posterity were those in her files at the press and her letters that survived his basement flooding. Just one suitcase, the one containing her notebook from *A House Is Not a Home*, escaped the incinerator, hidden away in a closet and only found decades later when the Woodmen moved from its headquarters building across from the Capitol. Ed donated her library to the English department and arranged for a room to be established in her name. He also provided an endowment to *Prairie Schooner* for an annual Virginia Faulkner Award for excellence in writing.

Seeing Virginia's presence removed so completely from the space they had shared for over a dozen years was too much for Bernice. She flew to California to stay with Belva. With Virginia gone, Bernice had lost her primary source of inspiration. As difficult as she could be to live with at times, Virginia had been the one who steered Bernice away from Keats and toward Cather. She spurred on her research and gave her outlets via the press, the Cather Foundation, and her connections to the WLA and other groups. And it was Virginia who never lost her conviction that Cather was an artist worth dedicating the whole of one's life to. "Willa goes on and on," she would remind scholars undertaking studies into Cather's work, and Bernice more than anyone.

A special edition of *Prairie Schooner* honoring Virginia was published in early 1981. It included "The Case of Richard Strauss," a Cather article for *The Pittsburgh Gazette* from 1904 that Bernice had discovered just prior to her stroke. It was the last article Virginia had edited for the magazine, and out of respect for her twenty-plus years on the *Schooner* staff, the issue's masthead still listed her as an advisory editor.

Bernice did not give up completely. She agreed to attend the Cather foundation's spring 1981 conference in Red Cloud and delivered a paper that effectively spanned her own research, from the introduction to *April Twilights* and all those brittle copies of the *Lincoln Journal* and *Courier* for *The Kingdom of Art* to her most recent finds in Pittsburgh. She visited the *Prairie Schooner* offices occasionally but no longer took an active role in editorial decisions. Robert Knoll would stop by the house to check in and often found her at work, surrounded by Cather papers and taking notes, but he had the impression that she was going over material she was already familiar with. "She was lost without Virginia," Virginia Knoll recalls.

The double issue of *Prairie Schooner* paying tribute to Bernice came out in the summer of 1981. It opened with a letter from Governor Charles Thone whose language bore the unmistakable signs of Ed's love of the ornate: "Distinguished daughter of the Plains, you have listened to the wind and flourished in the sunlight, bearing enduring and celebrated fruit which enhances the literature of the world." From Chicago, James Miller contributed a reminiscence. He could still write that he looked forward to reading Bernice's "definitive biography of Willa Cather," for which her "whole lifetime in Nebraska and her career as poet and critic have been a fine preparation." No one knew better the extent of the materials involved, the number of archives to be visited, the depth of information required to justify the label "definitive."

The *Journal Star* ran a column by Herb Hyde titled "Celebrating Bernice Slote" to mark the issue. He concluded by declaring that Bernice had "enriched my knowledge of the literary world more than she can ever know." The paper also profiled Bernice on the front page of its Sunday entertainment section, calling her "the world's leading Willa Cather scholar," though she refused to make such a claim herself. It noted that her work on the Cather biography had been set back by illness and "the death of her close friend and colleague Virginia Faulkner," but also her assurance that "I'm back to work."

She did seem to have revived. She attended the annual Cather conference with Ron Hull in the spring of 1982 and agreed to serve on the committee appointed by the governor to select the next Poet Laureate of Nebraska, replacing John Neihardt, who had died in 1973. Along with Ted Kooser and Roger Welsch, she read at a special tribute to the Lincoln-born poet and science writer Loren Eiseley held at the central library in August. The same month, she was one of five winners of the Bronze Sower award from the Nebraska Committee for the Humanities. Prodded by Mildred Bennett, she agreed to deliver a paper at the Cather conference in 1983.

As winter approached, however, she lost steam again. Sue Rosowski, a member of the UNL English faculty, had begun helping with research for the Cather book. She found that Bernice was reluctant to make arrangements for the trips she'd long considered essential. Then, in late 1982, barely three years after her first stroke, she had another. Its immediate effects were less severe, but when Belva and her husband George came out from California, they decided that Bernice's capacities were too diminished for her to live by herself. Bernice was moved once again to the Madonna nursing home and Belva and George spent the next two months in Lincoln. When they left, Sue Rosowski took over, coming regularly to check on Bernice and help feed her. Bernice never lost consciousness as she had before, but there was no Virginia sitting beside her now, and she steadily declined.

Bernice died at the Madonna home on February 22, 1983. Belva and George returned and were immediately faced with the question of where she would be buried. Bernice had said that she wanted to be buried next to Virginia in the Wyuka cemetery. But Virginia was interred in the Faulkner family plot, alongside her parents, uncles, aunt, and grandparents and Ed would have to agree. He refused. They found a spot in the cemetery in Hickman where her mother and father were buried.

At her memorial service, Reverend L. Brent Bohlke, one of Bernice's former graduate students, noted how essential her work had been to him and generations of Cather scholars: "If Cather was the first to bring the muse into her country, Bernice Slote was among the first to give Cather to the world. I have great difficulty thinking of Cather scholarship without her." He quoted the line from *My Ántonia* that appears on Cather's gravestone: "That is happiness: to be dissolved into something complete and great." In her memory, the English department at the university established the Bernice Slote Award for the best new writing to appear each year in *Prairie Schooner*.

Bernice's poetry has disappeared into the back issues of the dozens of magazines where it appeared. Little of what Virginia accomplished prior to her return to Lincoln has been remembered. Her books are long out of print and scarce, her stories uncollected and forgotten, her one movie credit, *Bridal Suite*, a rarely purchased DVD, her play with Dana Suesse never produced again after its one disastrous week. The most recent reissue of Polly Adler's autobiography *A House Is Not a Home* still questions Virginia's role in its writing.

Instead, what survives are their Cather projects. Few writers have been so devotedly served as Willa Cather was by Virginia and Bernice. *The Kingdom of Art*, *The World and the Parish*, and *The Collected Short Stories* remain foundational works for Cather scholars today. In a 1983 tribute to the two women, Robert Knoll wrote that because of Bernice's careful research and closely argued analysis, "no Cather scholarship from Nebraska will ever have to be done again: these are the definitive books." While later Cather experts may disagree, Virginia's meticulous editing and Bernice's commentary continue to serve as benchmarks. Starting in 1992, the press, in partnership with UNL, began publishing scholarly editions of Cather's work, with thirteen volumes to date. Robert Thacker, who wrote the introduction to the 2019 edition of *April Twilights*, not only kept Bernice's introduction but called it one of the most brilliant pieces of scholarship he'd ever read. With over sixty volumes by and about Cather in its catalog, including the *Cather Studies* journal, the University of Nebraska Press has more than realized Virginia and Bernice's vision.

Ed resigned as CEO of the Woodmen in 1984, but he continued to come to the office daily, still sat on the Republican party state committee and the board of Bryan Memorial Hospital, still took an interest in the annual Phi Psi fraternity rush. In 1986 his activities and record of accomplishments led the *Lincoln Journal Star* to name him one of the ten most influential people in Lincoln. Like Virginia and Bernice, his only hobby was his work. Retirement was out of the question.

But also like them, he was slowed by age and health. Jean died of a heart attack in 1991. Though the house on South Street stopped being a place where Ed could entertain and began to fall into disrepair, he stayed on. After decades of taking talented young men at the Woodmen under his wing, they began looking after him. Toward the end of the summer of 1992, he was persuaded to move to the Madonna home where he could get full-time care. He died there on October 9, 1992, at the age of eighty-one. In his will, he left $1.3 million to UNL, including an endowment for an annual professorship in actuarial science and development of a program in actuarial science. He also left money for the English department to add to Virginia's library. Though he'd destroyed the papers he found in Virginia's apartment, he left her literary estate to the university. If anyone ever reissues Virginia's work, it will benefit the university he loved and that enabled Virginia and Bernice to pursue the projects that gave shape and purpose to their two decades together. In the meantime, the foundation of research and recovery publishing they built continues to sustain successive generations of Cather scholars.

A Note on Sources

This book relies heavily on unpublished letters and papers from its principal players, starting with those held in the University of Nebraska Lincoln Library Special Collections: Virginia Faulkner, Bernice Slote, Edwin J. Faulkner Jr., Wright Morris, Erwin Krause, and Robert Knoll. The papers of *Prairie Schooner* and the University of Nebraska Press held by UNL Special Collections are also essential sources. Dana Suesse's letters and daybooks held in the Library of Congress provide details of her life and work with Virginia, and Ann Watkins's papers at Columbia University Archives cover Virginia's work on Polly Adler's autobiography, *A House Is Not a Home*. Virginia's surviving notebook and papers from *A House Is Not a Home* were made available by a private collector. Mildred Bennett's papers at the Willa Cather Foundation detail the complicated history of her work and relationship with Virginia. Mari Sandoz's papers at History Nebraska cover her work with Virginia and the University of Nebraska Press. Hazel Barnes's papers at the University of Colorado Boulder detail her personal and professional relationship with Virginia and include Virginia's soul-baring letter from September 1963.

Dozens of interviews were conducted between February 2020 and April 2024, including with Tyler Alpern, Debbie Applegate, Steve Cox, Woody Eno, Clarke Faulkner Jr., Richard Faulkner and Carol Knolle, Will Fellows, Richard Giannone, John Haessler, Tom Henning, Pauline Hester, Melissa Homestead, Ron Hull, Elizabeth Knoll, Virginia Knoll, David Madden, Mary Mignon, Peter Mintun, Margaretta Mitchell, John Murphy, Kathy Nelson, Douglas Nicoll, Laurie Obbink, Giovanna Bowsky Oettinger, Paul Olson, Susan Perry, Hilda Raz, Willis Regier, Fred Rickers, Ann Robinson

Gerike and Cathy and David Robinson, Timothy Schaffert, Samantha Shada, Betty Jean Steinshouer, David Stouck, Robert Thacker, James Wilson, and George Wolf. Debbie Applegate generously provided notes from interviews conducted for research on *Madam: The Biography of Polly Adler, Icon of the Jazz Age*. Peter Mintun graciously shared his unpublished biography of Dana Suesse and David Stouck shared his correspondence with Virginia on *Willa Cather's Imagination*. Tiffany Dziurman provided information from her research into the history of the Haven sanatorium. Timothy Schaffert shared notes from a talk on the "Anniversary" controversy. Will Fellows provided invaluable advice along with information from his biography in progress of Mildred Bennett. Jeannie Zier of Assurity Inc. provided a copy of a private memorial volume prepared by the Woodmen Accident and Life Company at the time of Ed Faulkner's death.

The Nebraska Newspapers digital archive provided by UNL and History Nebraska is a primary source for tracing the paths of the Faulkners, Meyers, and Slotes. I was fortunate to study the lives of these people at a time when their comings, goings, parties, births, deaths, and achievements were recorded in their local newspapers, particularly in the society pages, in extraordinary detail. Newspapers.com and the *Washington Post* archive supplemented this source with events in Virginia's life in New York City and Hollywood, her contributions to the *Post*, and reviews of her books and shows. Digital archives of *Liberty*, *The Saturday Evening Post*, *Town & Country*, and other magazines contain copies of most of Virginia's magazine stories. The Lincoln High School History and Archives document Virginia and Ed Faulkner's activities at Lincoln High. The Schlesinger Library's digital collection on the history of women in America provides records of Virginia's time at Radcliffe as well as her contributions to the Junior League magazine. The Internet Archive provides access to innumerable other sources ranging from *Michigan Psychologist* to *Variety*.

Virginia Faulkner's and Bernice Slote's own books, as well as the books they edited, are mentioned extensively in the text. A brochure written by Edwin Faulkner Jr. for the Newcomen Society, *Prairie Pioneer of Personal Insurance: Woodmen Accident and Life* provides the history of the Woodmen insurance companies. Gottfried Reinhardt's memoirs, *Der Apfel fiel vom Stamm* and *Gottfried Reinhardt: Hollywood, Hollywood*, provide details on the studio projects he worked on with Virginia, though neither book mentions her. Ruth Bernhard's autobiography, *Ruth Bernhard: Between Art and Life*, written with Margaretta Mitchell, includes her account of her relationship with Virginia in Hollywood. Joan Acocella's book *Willa Cather and the Politics of Criticism* recounts the evolution of Cather scholarship and criticism, including Bernice and Virginia's resistance to feminist and lesbian approaches. *Big House on the Prairie: 75 Years of the University of Nebraska Press* and Paul R. Stewart's *The* Prairie Schooner *Story: A Little Magazine's First 25 Years* provide overviews of the history of the press and the magazine.